subversive ***ceramics***

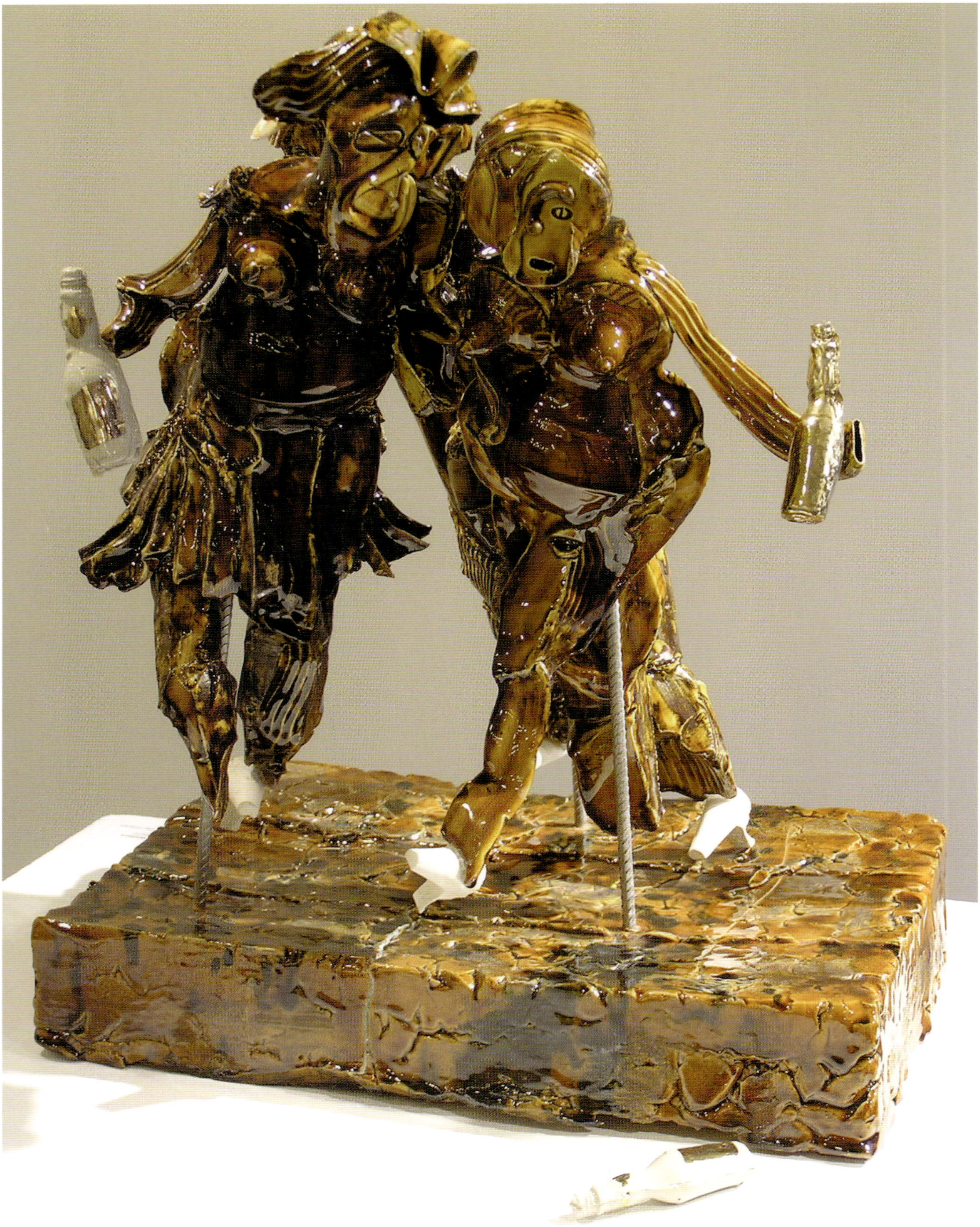

subversive ***ceramics***

claudia clare

HERBERT PRESS
LONDON • OXFORD • NEW YORK • NEW DELHI • SYDNEY

HERBERT PRESS
Bloomsbury Publishing Plc
50 Bedford Square, London, WC1B 3DP, UK

BLOOMSBURY, HERBERT PRESS and the Herbert Press logo are trademarks of Bloomsbury Publishing Plc

First published in Great Britain 2016

A catalogue record for this book is available from the British Library

Library of Congress Cataloguing-in-Publication data has been applied for

ISBN: HB: 978-1-4725-2854-4; eBook: 978-1-4742-5797-8;
ePDF: 978-1-4742-5796-1

2 4 6 8 10 9 7 5 3 1

Designed and typeset in Trade Gothic LT Std by Susan McIntyre
Printed and bound in India by Replika Press

MIX
Paper from responsible sources
FSC® C016779

Contents

Dedication 6

Epigraph 7

Acknowledgements 9

Introduction 11

PART ONE:

SUBVERSION AND SATIRE: Definitions and history 13

1 **Vice and Folly** 15

2 **Objection!** A history of protest 35

PART TWO:

BREAKING OUT: The influence of political and social movements on the studio potter and ceramicist 65

3 **The Peasants' Revolt:** Form and message 67

4 **Emancipation:** New methods of production 99

5 **The Campaigning Trail** 123

Conclusion: Observations and recommendations 151

Bibliography 154

Index 158

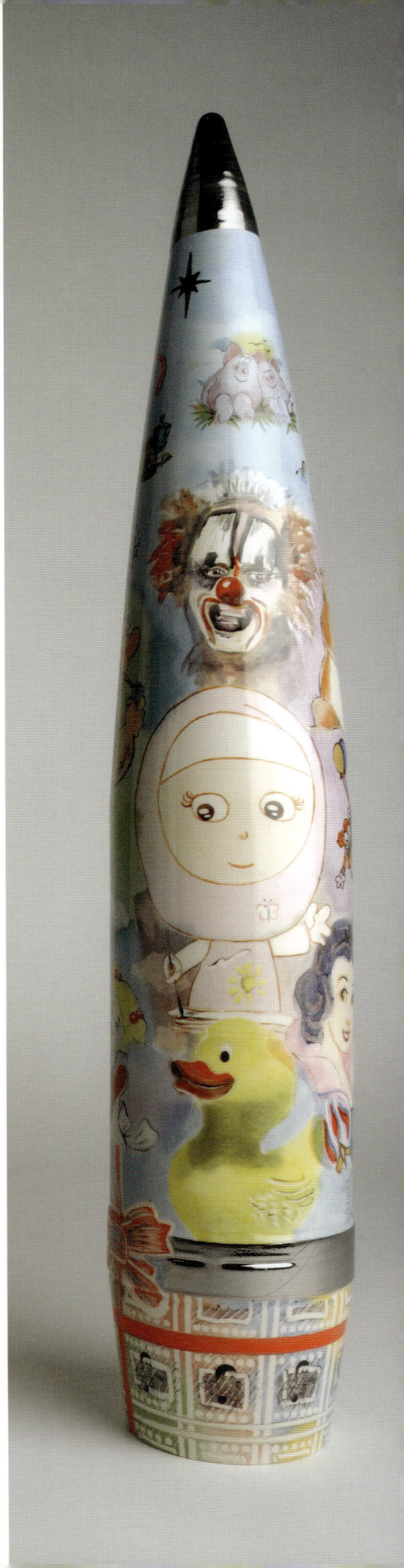

For Tina (1961–2001),

ex-Catholic lesbian and labour-movement feminist, who loved blasphemy, irreverence, satire and blue stockings.

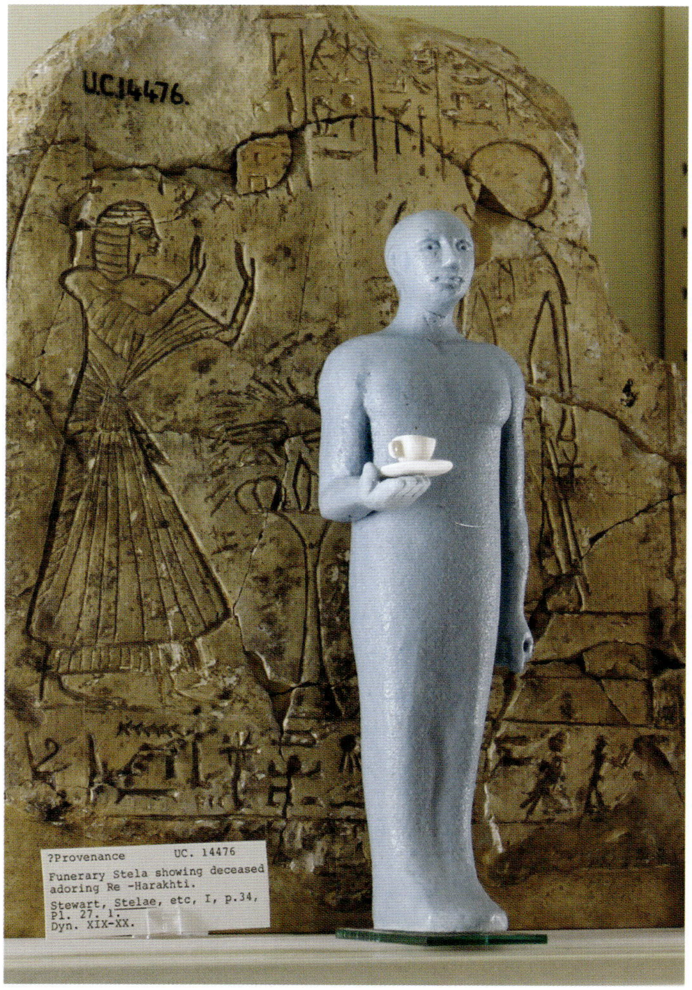

As a subversive, I strongly object to the idea that living in a family unit is in any way more natural or superior to less conventional arrangements such as friendship groups or living alone.

Julie Bindel

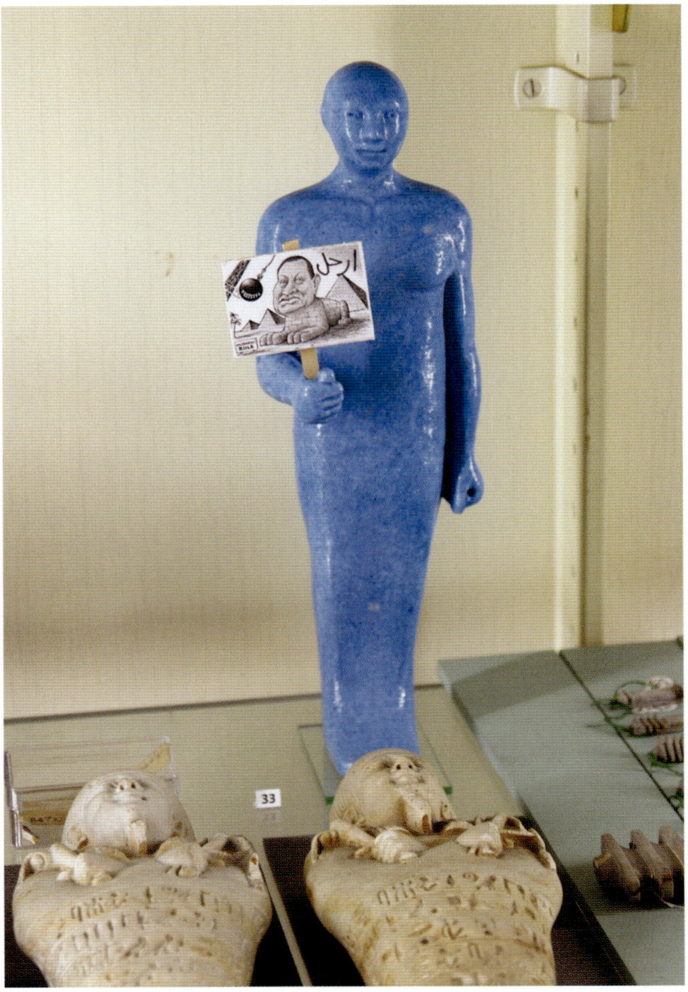

Frontispiece: *The Three Disgraces*, 2008, Rose Wallace, courtesy of the artist, see p. 86

Contents page: *155H*, (detail) 2010, Peter Lewis, courtesy of the artist, see p. 145

Page 6: *Nu-shabti on a tea-break*, 2014, Zahed Tajeddin, courtesy of the artist, see p. 96

Page 7: *Nu-shabti protester*, 2014, Zahed Tajeddin, courtesy of the artist, see p. 96

Acknowledgements

I owe thanks to many for help and support with this book and the first among them must be The Society of Authors. Without their generous and timely support the writing of this book would not have been possible. To Christina Bolt, whose efficiency and tenacity brought in all the pictures with the minimum of fuss – it is a tooth-grindingly arduous task and I am grateful beyond words. I am extremely grateful also to all the artists who agreed to let me use their pictures. They did so on trust, without checking or attempting in any way to control my words. Commitment to free expression is a rare thing these days and theirs should be robustly applauded. Thanks are due to those who went well beyond the call of duty to help secure images, find artists or help with other seemingly intractable problems, they are: Roger Surridge, for tracing the source of some of the French Revolutionary faience images and, latterly, discussing the satire and cartoons in *Charlie Hebdo*; Moira Vincentelli and Louise Chennell for securing images of works from the Aberystwyth University Ceramic Collection; Shlomit Bauman for sourcing Eytan Gross's images; the Northern Potters' Association – the entire committee and more besides – for tracing two of the artists whose work is represented in this book; and to Kent Boese for his excellent blog including a piece on Waylande Gregory's mural. Thanks are also due to the Bowes Museum, County Durham, for help with sourcing images for the French Revolutionary faience section.

I owe a considerable debt of gratitude to James Beighton and Dr Bonnie Kemske for sharing their thoughts on the matter of 'subversion' in art and craft, and to Tessa Peters for reading the manuscript and for many helpful comments and corrections.

I am also grateful to Nick Cohen for writing inspiring books, and for help with sourcing articles on the politics of the Middle East, and to Julie Bindel for sticking at it, publishing, being damned and carrying on anyway. The meeting of art and politics is never a simple matter and reading the work of both of these persistent campaigning writers has helped me to crystallize some of the ideas in this book. I am further indebted to those whose research, scholarship and writing forms the basis for my research: Leonard Todd, for his groundbreaking research on David Drake; Garth Clark and Judith Schwarz on satire in ceramics; Liz Kelly on feminism and research; Griselda Pollock, Lubaina Himid and Nina Edge on feminism and art; and also to my erstwhile PhD supervisors, Edmund de Waal and Christie Brown, who encouraged me to write as well as make pots. I would also like to acknowledge the contribution of my late father, Frank Stott (medical researcher), who understood the meeting of art and science, knew and understood pots better than most and who was and continues to be a source of inspiration.

Huge thanks to the rest of my ever tolerant and supportive family, especially to my sister, Frances Bates, who has come to every exhibition I have ever had; to my trusty studio assistant and 'perfect flatmate' Hussein Sahabi-Balakhkanlo, whose unfailing support keeps everything going; and to my oldest friend in the world, Serena Mackesy whose advice on writing is always inspiring and helpful. Finally, a big thank you to all you wonderful Facebookers – potters, writers, dancers and thinkers – for sharing your knowledge and experience, being generally helpful and, above all, for being entertaining.

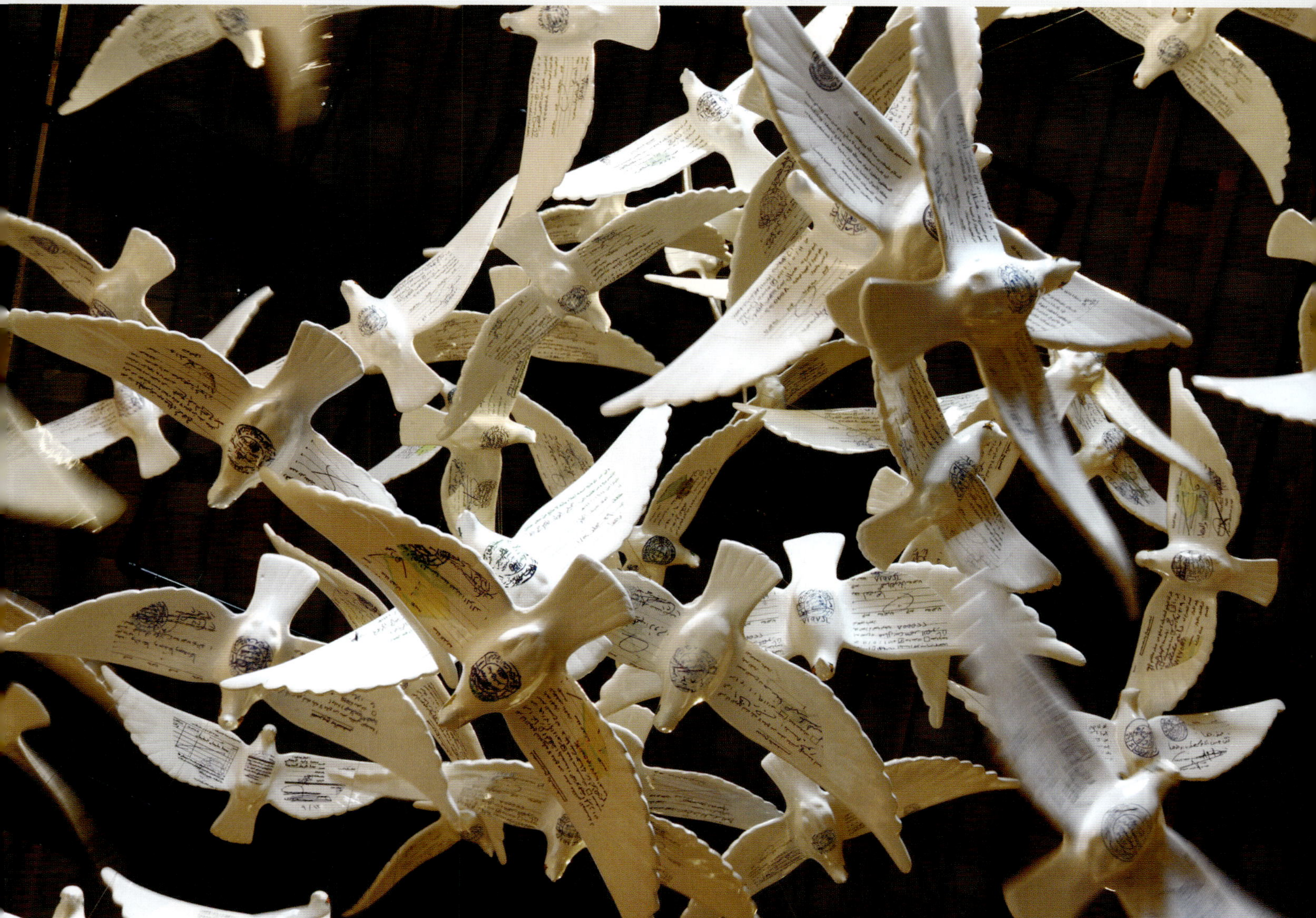

Introduction

In November 2012 I was asked to give a paper for a symposium at the Holburne Museum in Bath, entitled 'Subversive Ceramics'. I was delighted to be asked, but I was and still am a sceptic. When working on *The Pot Book* in 2011,[1] I was struck by the number of contemporary practitioners either declaring their work 'subversive', or having it described as such by others. I was similarly struck by the absence of any evidence to support the claim. In most cases, the artists concerned were doing what artists should do: experimenting with new ways of doing things. The conference, however, was oversubscribed; there was clearly a great deal of interest in the subject. The result is this book, which aims to provide a different and, I hope, more productive set of analytical criteria with which to understand and appraise the disparate work which has been marshalled under the 'subversive' umbrella.

Had I attempted a 'survey book', a study of all the contemporary ceramic work that is described as 'subversive', it would have run to ten volumes. Instead I have used a critical framework and selected specific works that best illustrate the arguments I am making. Some of the artists and individual ceramic works cited are very well known, others largely unknown, including some student work and work by artists no longer making ceramics. I define 'subversive' in political terms and discuss the works in their political context. I argue that much of the work featured in this book is satirical rather than subversive. The artist may not always intend it so but it can certainly be understood using satire as a critical framework. I have drawn on the literary tradition of satire and applied it to ceramics, building on Judith Schwarz's groundbreaking PhD thesis from 1983. I have also considered many of the featured works from a feminist position. This is because I am a feminist and feminism therefore shapes my political analysis. Although the contemporary artists whose works are featured in this book have connections with fifteen different countries, most are British, or resident in Britain, or show their work in Britain or in the 'West', so it has a British, European or American context. I have deliberately set these limits, partly in the interests of containment but mainly because I need to understand the context of the work in order to analyse it.

The book is divided into two parts: the first half discusses satirical and political work made towards the end of the twentieth century and, in the second chapter, discusses a selection of historical works. Part two, divided into three chapters,

Opposite: *Suspended Together*, 2012, Manal AlDowayan, see p. 127

[1] Edmund de Waal, *The Pot Book*, London: Phaidon, 2011.

discusses contemporary work made since the beginning of the twenty-first century. This is not an overly academic book. It is referenced but it is also opinionated and, at times, personal. A second aim of this book was to encourage debate, so I hope there is plenty to disagree with, and vehemently enough that readers are provoked into a written response. This would add to the existing writing and go some way towards building a substantial body of knowledge on the relationship between ceramics, politics and political movements, and the way we express these ideas through the form and also how we debate them.

PART ONE

SUBVERSION AND SATIRE: Definitions and history

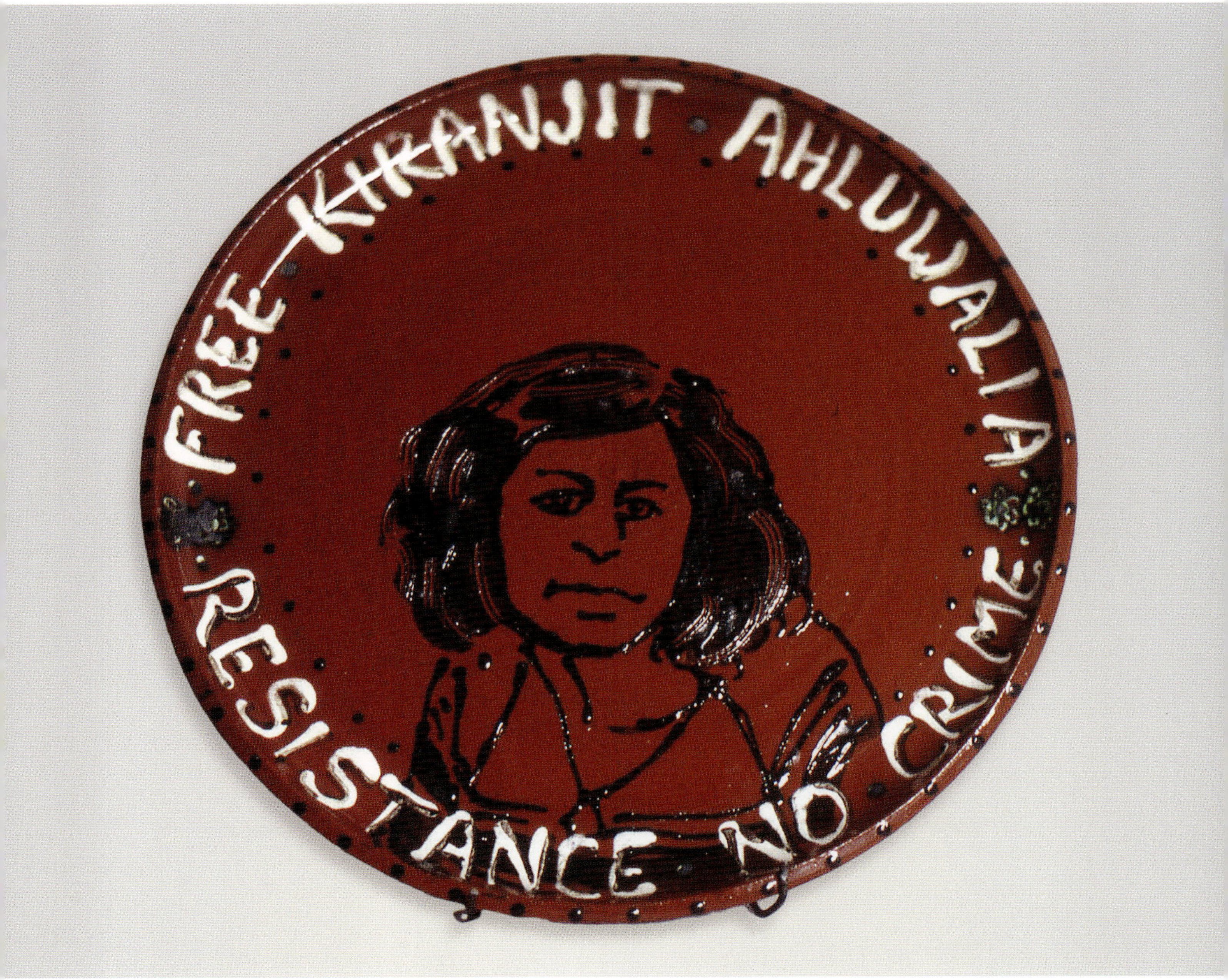

1.1 Previous page: *Free Kiranjit Ahluwalia!* plate, 1992, Claudia Clare, courtesy of the artist

1

Vice and Folly

Campaigning craft and covert histories

Free Kiranjit Ahluwalia! Resistance No Crime! (Figure 1.1) is one of a series of slipware plates I made in 1992, in support of the Justice for Women campaigns.[1] Ahluwalia had been sentenced to life imprisonment for killing her violent husband, but the conviction was overturned on appeal after a prolonged campaign by Southall Black Sisters with support from Justice for Women. Researching this book involved extensive reshuffling of papers, journals and catalogues of various exhibitions going back some twenty years. One, *The World Service* (1996, private collection), included a short essay by a journalist, Mary Hockaday, about some of my earliest ceramics including that slipware plate. She writes: 'She used the slipware tradition ... subverting it to use as a campaigning craft.'

Hockaday's expression, 'campaigning craft', was a precise and useful description. It is still useful now, sifting through the possibilities of what may or may not be considered subversive. In ceramic terms, my campaigning mugs and other tableware were consistent with a long tradition in British slipware: simple, black and white slip-trailing, on an earthenware, wheel-thrown plate. The subversion was in the message and in the campaign itself, which did present a significant challenge to the authority of law, to government and, above all, to patriarchal entitlement, particularly in the domestic realm, in the context of marriage and in the criminal justice system. Presenting such a message on a plate, an otherwise conventional item of domestic tableware, had a certain poetic subversion, perhaps, but more than that, it was a call for action in craft form.

The World Service itself was a covert political device, reflecting on the relationship between the Oxford Botanic Gardens, the history of plant-hunting and the development of trade in commodities: 'Into this most private and decorative artefact, a tea set, Claudia has smuggled ideas and material for a sort of politics of plants.'[2] It was a deceptively appealing way to present an aspect of colonial history. *The Huddersfield Daily Examiner* generously declared that it 'packs a political punch',[3] but I doubt that Tate & Lyle so much as flinched. It was less hard-hitting than the plate, and could be viewed as a luxuriantly floral, oversized tea service. Revisiting these two early works helps to set up at least two possible ways of thinking about what 'subversive ceramics' might be.

[1] Justice for Women, established 1990, is a feminist campaigning group that advocates on behalf of women who have fought back against or killed violent male partners. http://www.justiceforwomen.org.uk/kiranjit-ahluwalia/ accessed 1 November 2014.

[2] Mary Hockaday, *The World Service*, exhibition catalogue, 1996, 2.

[3] David Hammond, *The Huddersfield Daily Examiner*, 27 September 1996.

Defining subversion

To subvert something, or to be 'a subversive', implies a specifically political character and intention. It means 'to overthrow' or 'overturn', usually with reference to a regime, government, religious authority or dominant social norm. 'A subversive' is defined as a revolutionary. It is a strong word, or should be. Little, if any, of the ceramic work characterized as subversive in recent years is politically subversive, or presents any serious challenge to institutions or to a dominant social order. Even if we shift the meaning of the term to an art or craft context, it should still imply that an established tradition or an authoritative school of thought has been overturned, but these kinds of challenges are difficult to prove. Both art and craft are in a continuous state of flux – what is oppressively dominant to one group of artists may be wholly irrelevant to another.

In the last decade or so, the term 'subversive' has been applied to almost every kind of ceramic object that is not tableware, splashed about like a graffiti tag, a convenient holdall with multiple meanings, depending on context. From 2012 to 2014, it occurred in the title of an international conference, a museum symposium, a Crafts Council exhibition, a university event and in numerous reviews, previews and statements from artists and curators, as well as in magazines and journal articles.[4] One has to ask why so many ceramic artists, and their curators, wish to have their work characterized as subversive. What charge does this epithet carry that is apparently so desirable?

The term 'subversive' has acquired an additional meaning in the context of contemporary art and craft that it does not and should not possess. It has become a value judgement, one which implies that the work is exceptionally good, a bit 'edgy' and, above all, worthy of attention and status. James Beighton, in his paper at the Subversive Ceramics symposium 2012, suggests that this may have emerged from a desire, among some ceramicists, to be recognized as contemporary artists in the broader sense, and that contemporary art is often taken to be inherently subversive, particularly since the appearance in the 1990s of the Young British Artists (YBAs).[5] These artists acquired considerable status and some became international celebrities, whose work still commands huge prices on the art market where investments are fiercely protected. Beighton suggests that this is behind the faulty reasoning in the following triangulation: 'Contemporary art is both lucrative and high-status. Contemporary art is also subversive, so subversion must be lucrative and equate to status.' He believes many craftspeople – ceramicists in particular – are under the impression that all art – as opposed to craft – attracts high prices, resulting in a better living than that attained by most craftspeople: a belief for which there is no evidence whatsoever, but for which there is some evidence to the contrary.[6] If we add to this the success, in both in art market and celebrity terms, of Grayson Perry, whose work is routinely described as 'subversive', it is little wonder that subversion has become an attractive idea to potters. When one considers the real meaning of

[4] Subversive Clay, 2012, Australian Ceramics Triennale; Subversive Ceramics, Holburne Museum, Bath, 2012; 'Hidden Agenda and Material Subversion', The Naughton Gallery, Queen's University, Belfast, 2014; and 'On Subversive Ceramics: Keith Harrison in Conversation', at the University of Bath, 2014. In *Ceramic Review* in 2012 alone, four of the six editions (nos 253, 254, 256, 258), carried articles about 'subversive' ceramics.

[5] James Beighton, 'A Matter of Manners: Subversion in the Ceramics Field', Subversive Ceramics symposium, unpublished paper, 2012.

[6] Beighton 2012. Beighton is referring to the comparative valuation of a ceramics collection and a collection of modern British art from the same period.

'subversive', however, this is an extraordinary state of affairs. Nothing could be further from the truth. Artists in any medium who are genuinely politically subversive usually end up doing a spell in prison, as the next chapter shows, and as the Chinese artist, Ai Wei Wei, could attest.

Subversion in art and craft

The Australian Ceramics Triennale helpfully offered an explanation of sorts for its otherwise mystifying title, 'Subversive Clay'. The aim of the conference was to explore 'clay as a medium capable of challenging artistic, social and cultural issues through the investigation of past traditions and the exploration of new discoveries and directions'. The central thesis seemed to be that clay, and by implication, makers, should toughen up and start challenging, but there is little indication as to how or why they might wish to do so. The Naughton Gallery at Queen's University, Belfast, by contrast, had no problem whatever in committing to purpose. Where the Australian conference was vague, including all possible issues except political ones, in Belfast they were both proscriptive and precise. Visitors were required 'to consider [their] relationship with the political, economic and social environment through form, iconography, materials and technique', and, as if that were not enough, they were then prompted to 'question the role of material and its relationship to form'.

Perish the thought that the audience might just enjoy themselves! They were there to learn, to be challenged and to acquire appropriate moral and intellectual discourse models with which to analyse an exhibition of craft. I am exaggerating, but only up to a point. This is craft's didactic side, its salutary, reformist impulse: 'Think appropriately', it admonishes, 'that you may achieve rightness and appreciate these works in the artistically correct manner'. So the unthinkable has happened. Subversion itself has been subverted, by the venerable institution of craft, and rehabilitated as part of craft's moral project to improve the mind and soul, and reform any errant makers who might be leaning towards the fecklessness of art or, worse, pleasure.

Craft, in reality, is not good at challenging things directly: it lacks the urgency of response; but it does have staying power. What it does very well is to be part of the cultural apparatus of an ongoing protest campaign or growing social movement: the campaigning crockery in the kitchen, in all probability, represents the thoughts, the reality, the lives and the social positioning of its owners. Paul Scott's plates, *Cana Massacre* (1996) and *Carnage Produce of Israel* (2003),[7] protesting Israeli military intervention in southern Lebanon and calling for a boycott of Israeli goods, for example, are appropriate display ware for the *bien pensant* of the left. My feminist mugs and kissing lesbians are found, to this day, in the kitchens of feminists and lesbians. They are not adorning the tables of gay-hating, firebrand preachers. To this end, Jorunn Veiteberg's thesis on the 'affective' side of craft is entirely apposite.[8] Far

[7] Dinah Winch and Peter Lewis, *Fired Up: Ceramics and Meaning*, Gallery Oldham, 2010, 28–29.

[8] Jorunn Veiteberg, *Craft in Transition*, Bergen National Academy of the Arts, 2005, 60.

from being subversive, my mugs are precisely what a correspondent to the former editor of *Ceramic Review*, Bonnie Kemske, was calling for: 'simple pots',[9] or – whisper it – 'honest' pots in the Leach tradition. Scott's are partisan protest ware, similarly honest, but closer to the Wedgwood tradition of protest.

Craft also has an emancipatory element, particularly in relation to feminist work where, as a disparaged art form, associated with the domestic sphere and particularly with women, it is often mobilized as a call for action. This is also true of anti-racist and anti-imperialist work, often referred to in academic and art world language as 'postcolonial', but to a lesser extent. At its simplest, the term 'emancipatory' refers to a way of conducting social research in which those whose needs are being researched are also involved in the process.[10] In practice, in social research, it has been found wanting, but applied to craft, I suggest the term has some value and can be applied where the maker is part of the group affected by the change being demanded.

Of the ceramic work that has attracted the 'subversive' tag, most of it either seeks to disrupt an established convention related to form, use or process, or it uses the context – the gallery or museum – in an unconventional way. The subversive 'charge' of these projects depends on how long the supposed convention has persisted, whether or not it still does, and on the curator's understanding of the audience's expectations.[11] Politically motivated work is more often partisan or commemorative than genuinely subversive, and social comment is invariably just that: a wry, often satiric, comment rather than a serious challenge.

What constitutes a serious challenge to a social norm depends upon the political or social position, affiliation or opinion of the viewer: what is subversive to one person may be profoundly reactionary to the next – this is particularly noticeable where sexual politics are concerned. Subversion tends to be local, time-sensitive, politically situated and often highly subjective. In the context of the politics of government, of a theocratic or other totalitarian dictatorship, it ought to be possible to find a consensus, but in the context of social politics – social norms and mores – there is more disagreement. What appears subversive in one decade can proceed to being part of the norm in the next, and a lingering but related question, posed by the artist Conor Wilson at the Subversive Ceramics symposium, is 'Can an artist be subversive in a democracy?'

The various ways of trying to undermine ceramic or applied art conventions may not be subversive, but they still produce work of genuine artistic value and interest, of which there is much else that might be said. The persistence of the 'subversive' descriptor, particularly when it is clearly a misnomer, has become both limiting and self-defeating, often revealing what the work is not, rather than what it is. Much of the work that is characterized in this way is not so much subversive as satirical. This is a well understood and recognized form, very much alive in contemporary ceramics, and I would suggest, one of its defining features.

9 Bonnie Kemske, 'When Subversion Becomes the Norm', Subversive Ceramics symposium, Holburne Museum, Bath, unpublished paper, 2012.

10 Liz Kelly, Sheila Burton, Linda Regan, 'Researching Women's Lives or Studying Women's Oppression? Reflections on What Constitutes Feminist Research', in *Researching Women's Lives from a Feminist Perspective*, Mary Maynard and June Purvis, London: Taylor & Francis, 1994, 27–48.

11 Grayson Perry, *Midweek*, BBC Radio 4, 9 February 2005.

Introducing satire

Satire is an established field of scholarship with a vast literature of its own. It is considered primarily a literary tradition, but transfers well to film and broadcast media. It is also a significant strand in British and French visual arts, particularly in the form of prints and, in eighteenth-century England, in paintings by Hogarth. In nineteenth-century France, Daumier was pre-eminent. On a basic definition of satire there is little disagreement: it aims to attack, or, at the very least, expose and ridicule the 'vice and folly' of others, in particular those in positions of power or authority. There is some dispute over its intended impact. Gilbert Highet, in *The Anatomy of Satire* (1962), asserts a reformist moral purpose as the principle aim of the satirist. The satirist, he writes, 'believes that most people are purblind, insensitive, perhaps anaesthetised by custom and dulness [sic] and resignation. He writes to make them see the truth – at least that part of the truth which they habitually ignore.'[12] Dustin Griffin, in *Satire: A Critical Reintroduction* (1994), is fiercely critical of this position. He rejects any attempt 'to domesticate the shaggy, obscene, and transgressive satyr ... and make it into the model of a moral citizen', and further, disputes the notion of serious reformist intention. On the contrary, he emphasizes its meandering formlessness. 'Satire', he writes, 'is problematic, open-ended, essayistic, ambiguous in its relationship to history, uncertain in its political effect, resistant to formal closure, more inclined to ask questions than to provide answers, and ambivalent about the pleasures it offers'.[13]

How does a literary and verbal form, associated with attack and mockery, connect to a visual and tactile form, known for its 'stillness', its concern with harmony and satisfaction, where, often, the greatest compliment is to declare the work, 'pleasing'? Satire aims to create noise, disharmony and discomfort – to be anything but pleasing. Caricature and cartoon, the grotesque, obscenity, invective, morbid sarcasm, irony, pathos, pastiche, parody, nostalgia and allegory are all devices in the armoury of satire. It is, of course, that very inversion, what Johanna Dahn has called, 'playing against convention',[14] that is the point. Satire in ceramic form aims to confound expectations and overturn a conventional form or process – imagery or inscription might be added to generate a more specific social comment. I have selected a number of works produced by eight different artists in the last decades of the twentieth century to consider, in detail, how they use satire in their work and whether its impact is subversive, emancipatory or something else entirely.

The vagina goes public: Judy Chicago and Hannah Wilke

It is impossible to discuss subversive art, in ceramics or any other material, without mentioning Judy Chicago's *The Dinner Party* (1975–1979, Brooklyn Museum). Completed in 1979, it has become one of the most significant and resonant works of twentieth-century feminist art. Dating from the heyday of second wave feminism, it

[12] Gilbert Highet, *The Anatomy of Satire*, Princeton University Press, 1962, 19.

[13] Dustin Griffin, *Satire: A Critical Reintroduction*, University Press of Kentucky, 1994, 3.

[14] Johanna Dahn, introductory address to Subversive Ceramics symposium, 2012.

is a classic example of an emancipatory work: a loud, confrontational statement that aims to reclaim and liberate a hidden history, and in doing so, bring about change. The thirty-nine place settings for *The Dinner Party* each represent a woman whose contribution to history has been ignored. The 'plates' are ceramic vaginas, beautifully constructed, mostly three-dimensional and highly decorated. Part of Chicago's strategy was to use painted ceramics – a low-status craft form, practiced by many women as a hobby – as an act of art world rebellion. Her use of the vagina image was intended to assert a feminist presence in an otherwise intensely patriarchal context.

The Dinner Party caused a furore when it was first exhibited in the United States. It was greeted with huge excitement and fierce criticism in equal measure – the latter came not only from the religious right, or, indeed, peevish male art critics squawking about 'vulgarity'.[15] Feminists criticized Chicago for using the skills of women china painters but neither paying them nor naming them, which threatened to undermine the very story she was trying to tell. She was further criticized for reducing the image of the women she represented to an elaborate vagina form, and surrounding them with cutlery in preparation for a banquet. It remains a controversial but important work, argued over to this day. It now has the quality of a heroic but flawed work: heroic in intention but undermined by its somewhat reductive imagery. While it may be problematic as a feminist work, it is a triumph of American art, showing the risky, innovative, devil-may-care attitude of American culture at its best. In its use of traditional craft forms it is pure Americana. Coupled with its loud and celebratory feminism, it could not have been made anywhere else in the world, and certainly not at that time.

Hannah Wilke, Chicago's predecessor, blazed the trail linking second wave feminist thinking to ceramics. Wilke was a celebrated exponent of a strand of feminist thinking which sought to find a new visual and material language to express concerns with picturing woman, self and the feminine without resorting to the dominant 'phallocentric' vision in art and image-making in the 1960s and 1970s. *Untitled, 103 terracotta sculptures* (Figure 1.2) is a ceramic floor piece that makes these concerns material as well as visual. The vaginal imagery, commonly referred to as 'cunt art', was as revolutionary and controversial then as it is commonplace now. Regarded by some as essentialist and reductive, by others as subversive, satirical parody, and yet by others as a serious quest into a tender feminine vision, it generated explosive debate, not least among feminists, and placed feminist art discourse at the centre of art debates, with enduring consequences. Wilke's ceramic works are part of her wider investigation into an intensely physical, visceral, sometimes painful portrayal of herself as a woman – as an embodiment of the feminine. She does not concern herself with the prettiness of being female except to dangle it in front of the viewer and then disrupt it. The pretty painted pink exterior of the one-fold sculptures maintains an appearance of softness, in spite of being fired and unyielding to the touch. There is a gutsy materiality to these ceramic works. They are immensely tactile – there is a strong desire to touch, to test the hardness or softness of the material. They were groundbreaking and hugely confrontational at the time, and continue to resonate in changed – and changing – social circumstances.

[15] Hilton Kramer, 'Judy Chicago's *The Dinner Party* Comes to Brooklyn Museum', *The New York Times*, 17 October 1980.

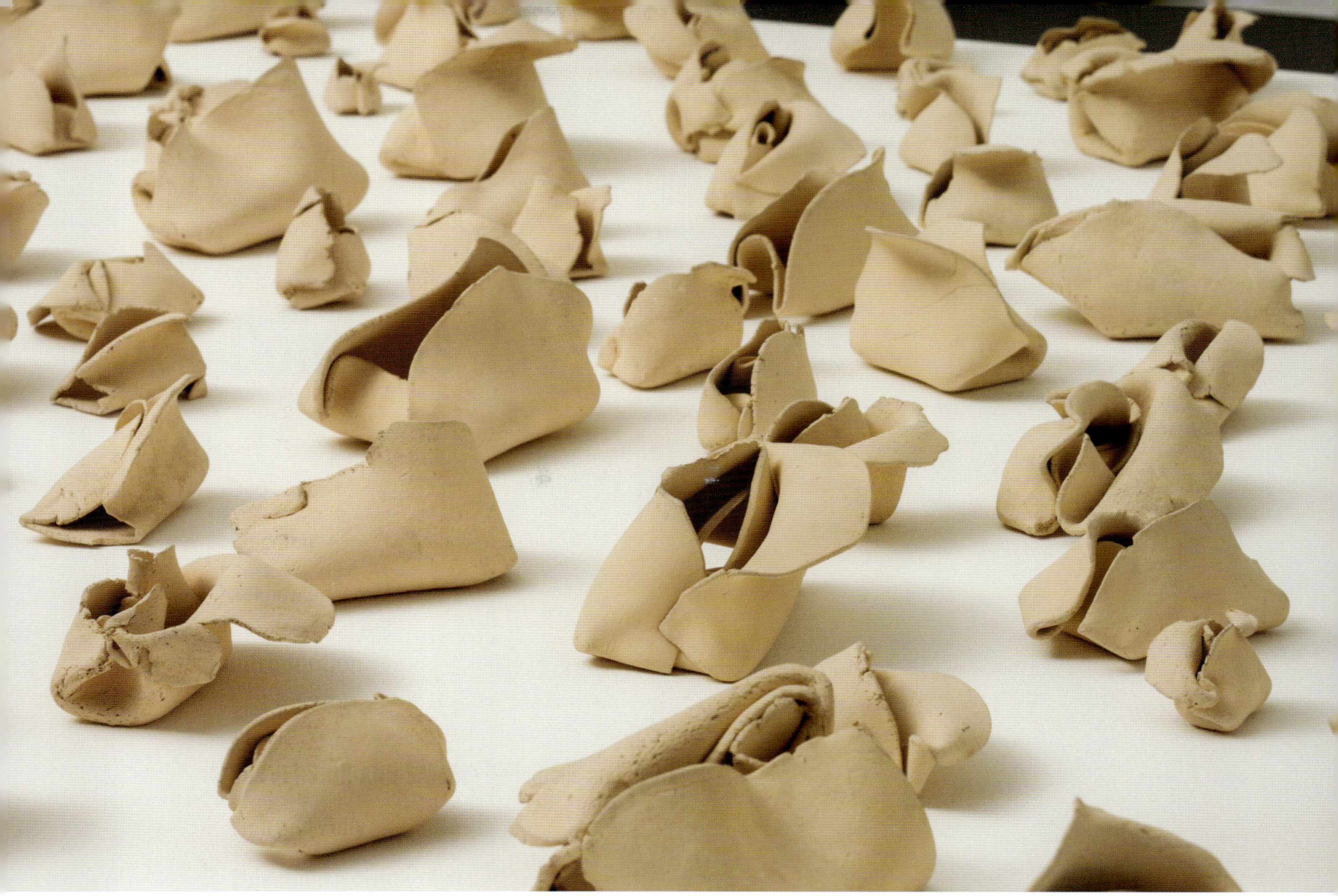

1.2 *Untitled, 103 terracotta sculptures* (detail), various sizes, 1974–1977, Hannah Wilke, courtesy Alison Jacques Gallery, London, photo: Michael Brzezinski, © Marsie, Emanuelle, Damon and Andrew Scharlatt/VAGA, NY/DACS, London 2014

Biting the hand that feeds: Marisa Rueda

Similarly visceral in her use of material, but with a different set of concerns and priorities, Marisa Rueda introduced her work at her 1978 exhibition, 'Realism to the Rescue', at Battersea Arts Centre in London, thus:

> Everything is an attempt to talk about what has happened, about what is happening now, about those things we do not want to forget: ultimately an attempt to produce a reaction against hate, poverty and impotence.
>
> I am more interested in what the works can say than in aesthetic considerations, more interested in them being rejected than accepted, and overall I am concerned that they are not considered beautiful objects.[16]

She, too, rejects beauty as a strategy to engage the attention of the audience. The slumped, mutilated ceramic body parts, torn and hanging over wooden struts, are powerful, unyielding images (Figure 1.3). There is no seduction, no attempt to create a comfortable route to the meaning of the work; it is relentless, horrible and unforgiving. These are angry memorials to the dead, the tortured and the anonymous 'disappeared', visually reminiscent of images of lynchings in the southern United

[16] Marisa Rueda, *Artist's Statement*, Battersea Arts Centre, 1978, archived in the Women's Art Library, Goldsmiths, University of London.

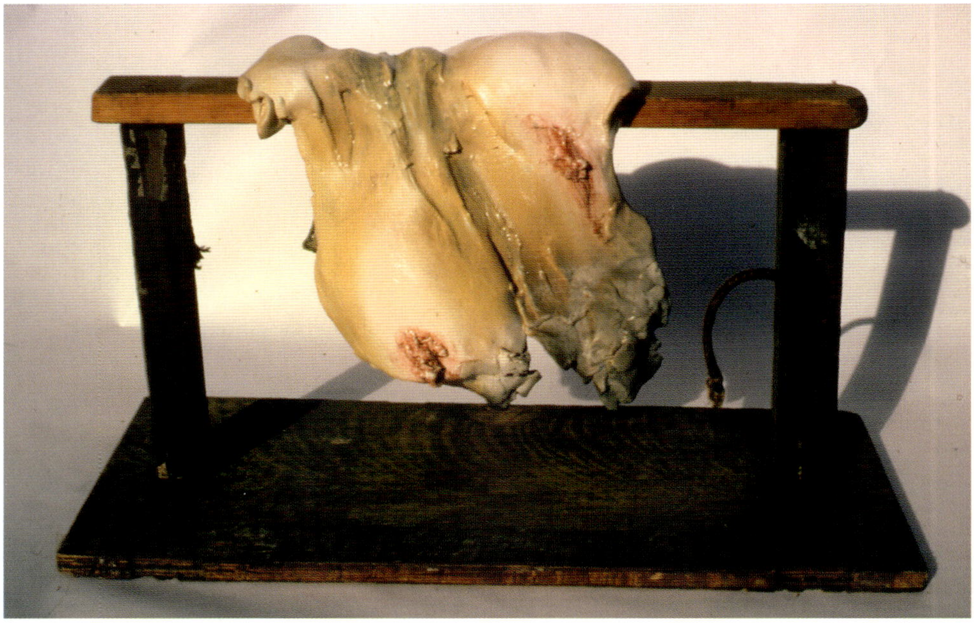

1.3 *From Latin America with Hate*, 1975, Marisa Rueda, courtesy of the artist

States. She uses the inherent qualities of the ceramic material. A body shape or form made in soft clay can be allowed to slump in this way. There is a searing sense of corporeality present in this work, which the artist has been able to express through the language of the material. She does not mobilize any of the complicating tropes of satire to make her case, she just uses the clay to articulate the question posed in the title of another work in this group, direct and unflinching: *And as for our dead, how will they be heard?* (1977)[17]

These are the works Rueda exhibited two years after she arrived in London after the 1976 coup in her native Argentina. Fiercely political, hers is the art of protest; her anger, in the early years, was directed at the Argentinian military junta which prompted her flight to Britain. After the 1978 exhibition, Rueda went on to make a series of ceramic figures portraying Argentinian generals, whose grotesque appearances, sustained the rejection of beautiful objects.[18] The method she used to make the figures, beating the clay with wood to establish the form as roughly as possible, is clearly evident in the finished pieces; they have an urgent, uncompromising energy. Raw and unembellished, but executed with consummate skill, they are both memorable and compelling. These pieces mix the material sensibilities of the earlier works with a recognizably satirical approach. Rueda draws on the familiar sculptural bust form, reserved for authority figures and civic dignitaries, and ridicules it, mercilessly.

Rueda introduced the grotesque comedy of murderous generals joyfully crunching on tiny raw chicken bones, to emphasize the viciousness and might of the military junta against the absolute powerlessness of its victims. These were impoverished men, women and children, terrified, marginal and insignificant, caught in the path of the all-powerful military machine. She condemns the savage cruelty of the generals

[17] Women's Art Library/Make, Goldsmiths, University of London.

[18] Pamela Johnson, 'Subversive Ceramics', in *Crafts* magazine no. 95, 1988, 35–37.

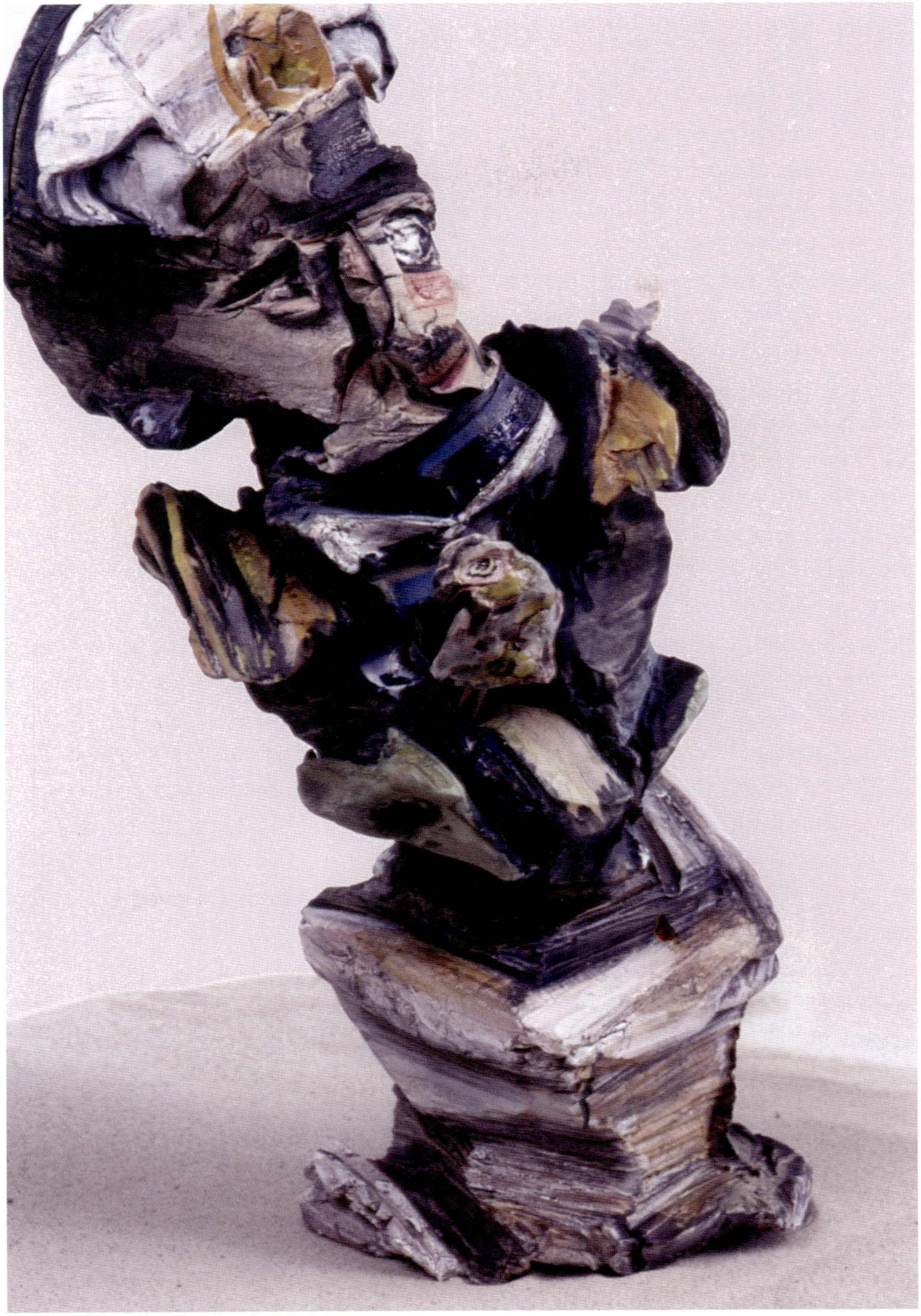

1.4 *Falling General*, 1988, Marisa Rueda, courtesy of the artist

at the same time as subjecting them to ridicule and contempt. Whereas her earlier works were memorials to acknowledge the suffering of the powerless and to honour their resistance, the generals mark a shift in focus, her target now is the site of power: 'given the circumstances, I work for the bourgeoisie and because of it, I try for my work to be aggressive'.

Magic and allegory: Nina Edge and Bita Fayyazi

'Let's hear it for the Indian rope trick!' The crowd cheers wildly. The magician, splendidly costumed, strides into the circle, picks up the wicker basket, shows it to the expectant crowd. They peer in, just to check there's no jiggery-pokery. The magician picks up an elegantly twisted jute rope, holds one end and waves it up and down to introduce ripples. Yes, we are convinced the rope is just a normal, limp length of rope. Another stride around the circle, for theatrical effect, and now ... drum roll ... let the magic begin! The magician puts the rope in the basket, reaches for his pipes and plays sweet music. Out of the basket comes the rope, stiff and straight, standing some three or four metres high at full stretch. This is an outdoor trick so no wires hang from the ceiling and no floor conceals a place from which a rope-clad pole might protrude. This is pure magic.

The story changes after that, depending on which account you read and from what era. Some include a little boy who shins up the rope and disappears into a cloud and all manner of wonder ensues. It is a magnificent tale, rich in 'exoticism of the East', mysterious and utterly captivating. Even as I read the accounts now available on the internet, the will to believe is overwhelming at times. I peer into the sepia photographs and wish it could be true. Then a new process begins. There are YouTube videos with banal and wholly unconvincing explanations. There are scholarly papers, tracing the trajectory of the story and how it came to the West. Then there is an article in *The Independent* in 2009 that seems believable.[19] I read about Ishmahuddin Khan, a magician in New Delhi, who, also captivated by the tale, decided to replicate it as closely as he could, and in 1995 succeeded. He repeated his trick a second time in Udupi, southern India, but this time to an audience of thirty thousand. The video made of the performance was seen worldwide.

Professors of magic around the world believe it and say they have no idea how he has done it. He performs a simple version but, by all accounts, it is utterly convincing. There is no little boy running up the rope or clouds into which characters disappear and reappear, just the rising rope, which stands proud, a few metres high without the aid of props. And here is what really convinces: this lowly magician, who has found a way to replicate the dreamworld convincingly, earns no additional money at all. He still lives in poverty in the Kathputli, the performers' district, in West Delhi. He still performs the trick. The Western professors are fascinated, but the Indian ruling class, new middle class and intelligentsia care not one jot. Either he is simply too old fashioned, or perhaps he killed the dream. Either way there is no reward.

Snakes and Ladders (1988) (Figure 1.5) is the title of a mixed media work by Nina Edge that was exhibited three times in England between 1989 and 1991.[20] A large, floor-to-ceiling image, made using batik on paper, portrays a woman performing the rope trick while balanced on a narrow ledge, holding a clay pot, out of which two snakes are unwinding. In front of the performing woman are two pots, one on each side, on plinths. Written on the plinths, which are painted and part of

[19] Andrew Buncombe, 'Rise and Fall of the Indian Rope Trick', *The Independent*, 19 November 2009.

[20] Sutapa Biswas, Sarah Edge, Clare Slattery, *Along the Lines of Resistance: An Exhibition of Contemporary Feminist Art*, Cooper Gallery, Barnsley, 1988.

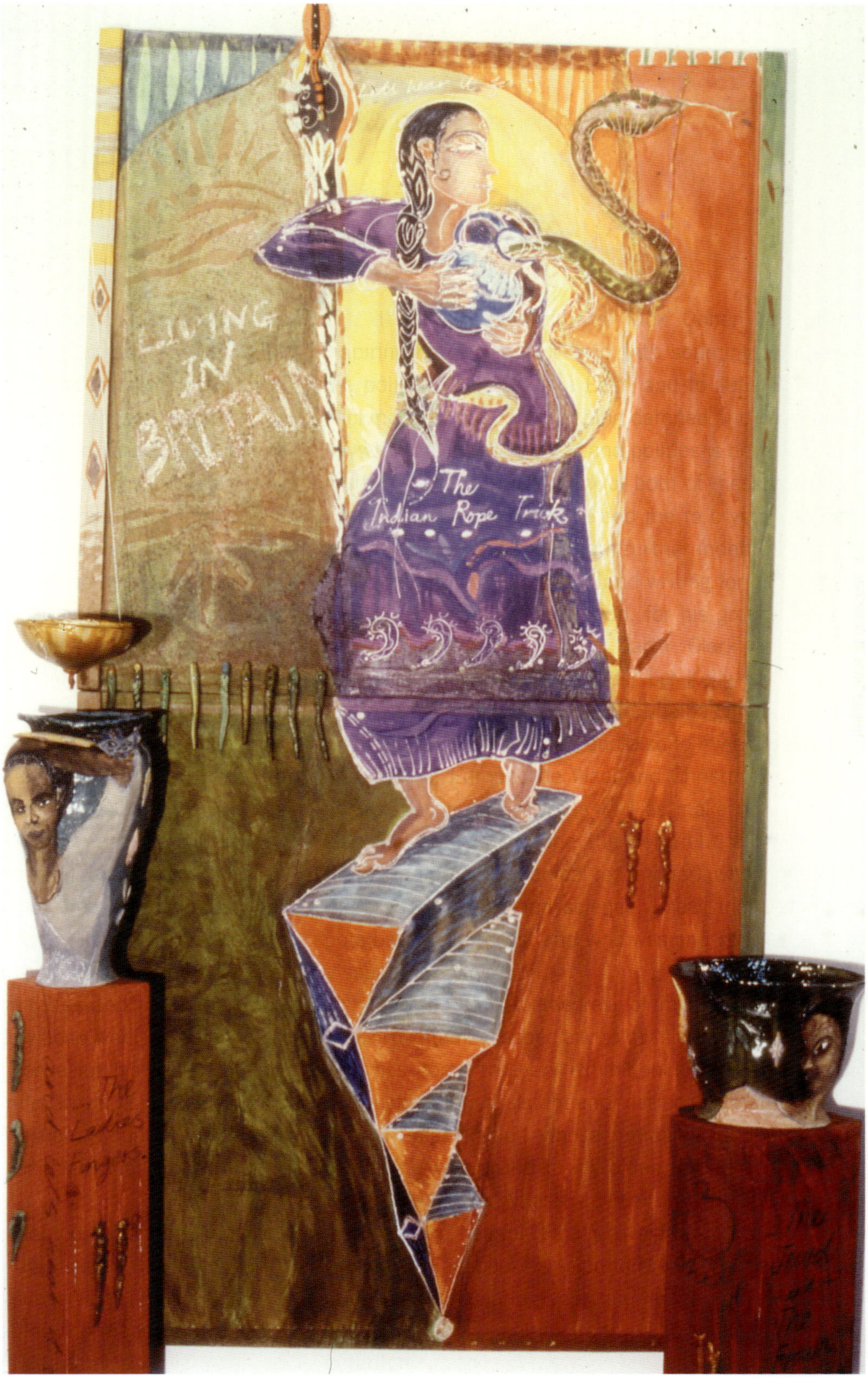

1.5 *Snakes and Ladders*, installation with pots: *The Jewel and the Frown*, 1988, Nina Edge, shown at the Pavilion, Leeds, 1989, Chapter Arts Cardiff, 1988, courtesy of the artist

the whole, are two exhortations: 'Let's hear it for ... The Ladies' Fingers', says one; '3 cheers for the ... The Jewel and the Frown', says the other. The pots, handbuilt using the coil method, portray more women, curved around the surfaces of the pots, one with a snake coming out of her hair. 'Let's hear it for the Indian Rope Trick', is written across the woman in the batik image, along with 'Living in Britain'. It is sharp, satiric and laced with mordant humour and, for those fortunate enough to have seen it, was an immensely impressive work, energetic and urgent. Its sparkle and originality communicated its messages forcefully, with striking wit and just a hint of venom.

Completed in 1988 for the touring exhibition 'Along the Lines of Resistance', it brought social politics into craft and images of black women into mainstream art galleries and museums. It was a large, defiant and witty allegory, a critique of British racism as well as a compelling comment on migration.[21] The precariously balanced Indian woman is negotiating the consequences of a shattered dream, the Indian Rope Trick, the dream of migrating to England for a better life, where poverty and impotence were supposed to vanish into a cloud. The snakes and ladders are the constant dangers, life balanced on a knife-edge, perilous, challenging and frustrating. Edge's work is peppered with jokes, visual and verbal. 'I like to see who gets the joke. I like to see who takes offence. Occasionally I place the viewer in the position in which white culture places me. Then I watch and wait.'[22] These are not the narratives of pathos, nostalgia or even just anger. Edge's woman magician – and it is, often, women who bear the brunt of the pressures of migration – is laughing in the face of danger. She is deriving energy from her precariousness but she is not going to keep quiet about it. She's training those snakes to perform as she needs them to.

British Indians still experience racism, but their country of origin has changed out of all recognition. India is now far wealthier than fifty years ago and, although the majority are untouched by its new-found wealth, it means that expectations have changed considerably and dreams are different. Ishmahuddin Khan must also contend with a shattered dream. Not only does his resolute dedication to his craft go unrewarded, but his entire community of performers now face forced eviction. Their traditional quarter of West Delhi is too valuable as real estate for developers. As the headline writer to Andrew Buncombe's most recent update on the trials of Mr Khan, put it: 'It will take a magic trick to protect Delhi's unique colony of performers.'[23]

Bita Fayyazi

Allegory is also central to Bita Fayyazi's critique of social and religious norms. *Road Kill* (1997) (Figure 1.6) is a collection of road-killed dogs made from terracotta clay and fired. I interviewed the artist about this work last time I was in Iran, in 2008. The number of dead dogs equates to the number of cars and the corresponding carelessness of their drivers. This she connects to a general disregard for both

[21] The batik work on paper, in particular, proved immensely popular and, in Edge's words, 'went on to visit more British towns than I have, winding up as the cover image for Maud Sulter's *Passion* [*sic*]', from 'Nina Edge' in *Artists' Stories*, Anna Douglas and Nicholas Wegner, AN Publications, 1996.

[22] Nina Edge, contribution to article 'Along the Lines of Resistance', in *Feminist Art News*, vol. 2, no. 9, 8–15.

[23] Andrew Buncombe, 'Letter from Asia', *The Independent*, 18 February 2014.

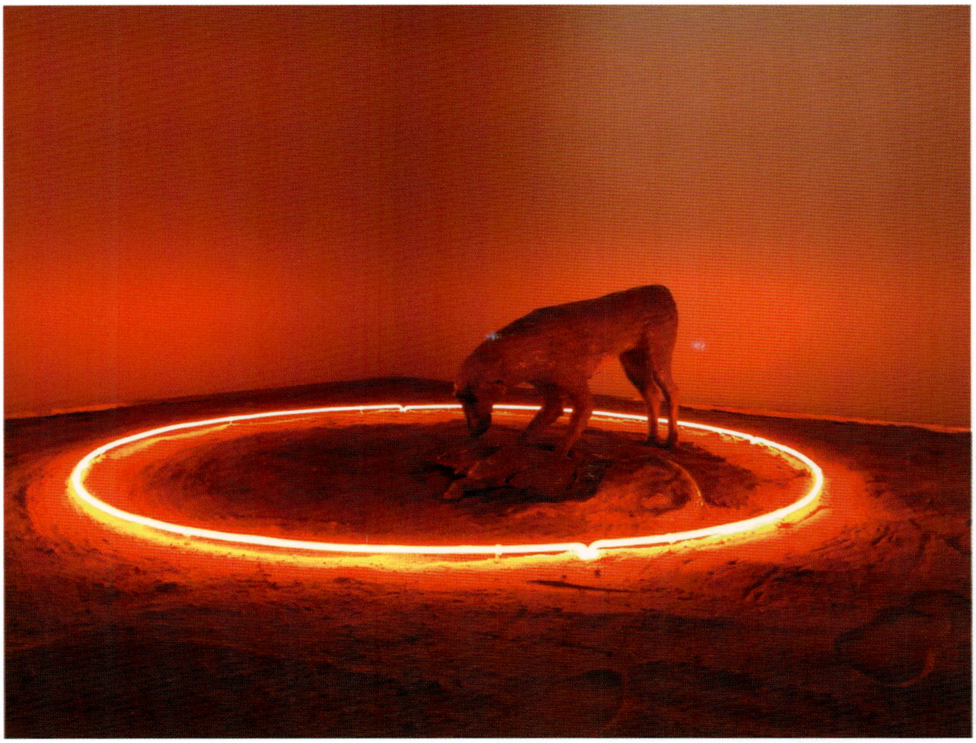

1.6 *Road Kill*, 1997/2013, Bita Fayyazi, photographer: Ramin Haerizadeh

life and nature in Iranian society. Moreover, dogs in Shia Islam are *nejes*, which translates approximately as unclean, defiled or untouchable. They are widely regarded with fear and disgust. Fayyazi collected the dead dogs, kept their corpses at home and made clay sculptures of them. She showed the ceramic corpses in numerous locations around Tehran and photographed them. She eventually buried both the real corpses and the sculptures, in a ceremony which she filmed. She now shows the photographs and some of the dogs, most recently she showed them in Dubai, in 2014 (Figure 1.6).[24] The entire process challenges Iran's social mores and norms very profoundly. It is also an act of opposition to religious doctrine. In a theocratic dictatorship, this can have serious consequences. At the time she made the work, in 1997, the very conservative, orthodox nature of the Iranian regime was beginning to open up, so it is no coincidence that Fayyazi began to do public and performance work at that point.

Since 2009 the Iranian regime has become much harsher and this kind of act now would certainly mark her out as *mohareb*, or enemy of god. *Mohareb* is an accusation that can attract the death penalty, in some cases, and always results in imprisonment. By anybody's definition then, this is a highly subversive work. It is also an extraordinarily moving piece of work. It does constitute a challenge to what counts as important and moral, and what is considered unimportant and defiled. While Western European sensibilities might identify the use of pathos and the allegorical mode of storytelling in this work as mildly eccentric, in Iran, now, the work would be seen in numerous different ways. Owning a pet dog has, in the last few years, become

[24] Bita Fayyazi, *Rearranged*, Isabelle Van Den Eynde, Dubai, 2014.

very fashionable among the dissident upper classes and cool among dissidents of all classes, so it might now generate sympathy and interest. That said, there is still a substantial group of people who would find the notion of giving a dead dog a ceremonial burial disgusting, offensive, grotesque and, of course, blasphemous. The *basiji* routinely arrest people with dogs.

Fayyazi is compelled to exercise caution in the way she phrases any critique of the Iranian political or social establishment. Hasan Javadi, in *Satire in Persian Literature* (1998), notes that satire emerges in Iran during 'brief moments of democracy' and press freedom.[25] Referring to the period of the Islamic Republic since 1982, he states that Iranian satirical critique tends to be 'either shrouded in obscure symbolism, or told in the form of a timeless parable'.[26] Certainly direct expressions of dissent are not tolerated, and any critique Fayyazi wishes to mount must be articulated through a system of metaphor, symbols and allegory. The subversive nature of this work has, in the last three or four years, become much more pronounced, as has the sympathy it might also arouse. At the time of writing, the leadership in Iran is changing. Although there is some reshuffling in foreign policy, there is little or no sign, as yet, of any let-up on dissidents within Iran.

Histories and ornament: Lubna Chowdhary

Lubna Chowdhary's *Acknowledged Sources* (2001) (Figure 1.7), commissioned by Hastings Museum in 2000, is a response to the building, and a rewriting, in ceramic form, of the version of history implied by the museum's architecture. Identified by Chowdhary as 'a cultural and architectural impossibility anywhere outside Britain',[27] it is a concoction of Islamic, Hindu and Buddhist references: a monument to the imperial and orientalist preoccupations of the period. Chowdhary painstakingly collected groups of tableware from flea markets and charity shops, recording the history of each piece in the same way that a museum would. These were examples of English industrial heritage, mass-produced tableware, depicting iconic and idealized images of colonial history, or idealized British scenes. She then overprinted them, adding a new layer of imagery, partially obscuring and complicating the original. Queen Victoria, Empress of India, is superimposed with the Indian and Pakistani leaders Ghandi or Jinnah; hunting scenes and familiar floral decoration are overprinted with the 'Paisley' pattern; and the colonizers are depicted being carried in a litter or pulled manually in a rickshaw by Indian men, the colonized people. Her purpose was 'to confuse one history and tell another'.[28] The success of this work is predicated as much on the care taken in selecting the original pieces, as it is on the imagery selected for the overprinting. *Acknowledged Sources* is a rich, satiric mix of pastiche, parody and irony, wry, as well as thoughtful and reflective.

[25] Hassan Javadi, *Satire in Persian Literature*, Fairleigh Dickinson University Press, London: Associated University Presses, 1998, 198. Since 2009, religious, social and political satire have become immensely popular in Iran, though remain as risky as ever, both on satellite television, produced in the US and Europe, and as cartoons, published by diaspora Iranians on the internet.

[26] Javadi, 1998, 198.

[27] Conversation with the author.

[28] Claudia Clare, 'Constructive Dialogue', *Ceramic Review*, 208, 24.

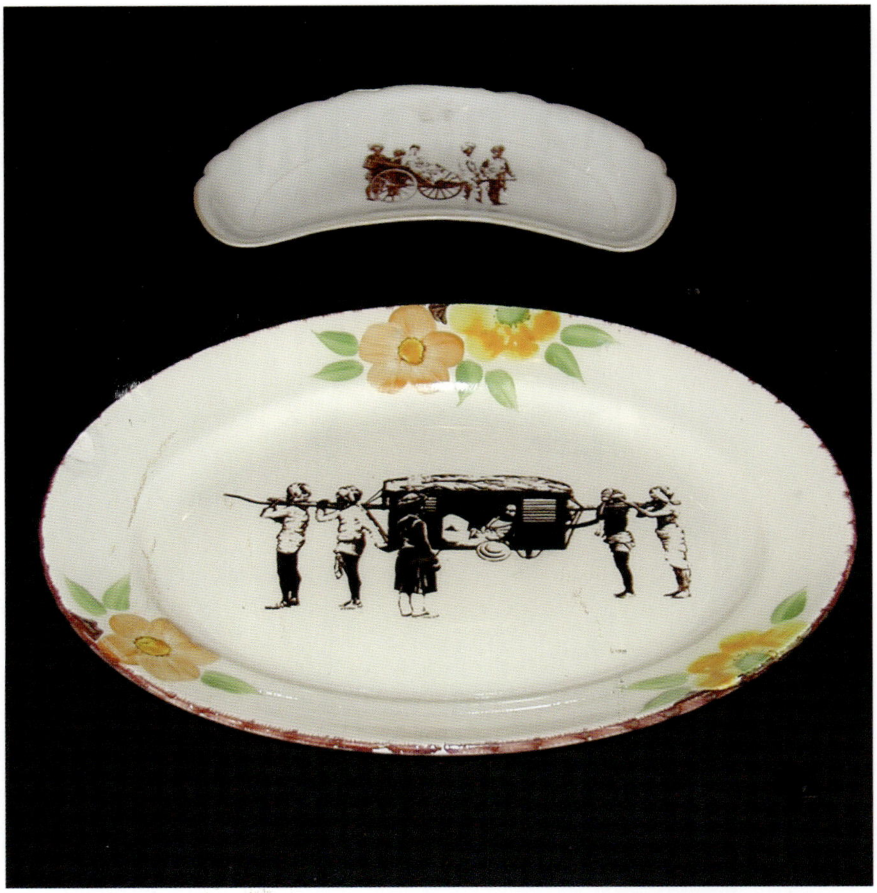

1.7 *Acknowledged Sources*, 2001, Lubna Chowdhary, photographer: Nick Higgins

The vexed question of women and nakedness: Justin Novak and Justine Cawsey

Justin Novak

Justin Novak used a combination of parody and the grotesque to create a series of *Disfigurines* (1998–2001) (Figure 1.8), that critiques the idealism inherent in the perfectly formed ceramic figurine, and articulates the damage done by trying to live up to such ideals in real life, in particular with regard to body image. His is a confrontational vision, sometimes intensely painful, even cruel. One *Disfigurine*, a very thin young woman, who might be beautiful but for her excruciating vulnerability, takes a vast, brutish-looking pair of scissors, and extending one arm in front of her, carefully, and with a look of intense concentration, snips into the skin on the wrist of the extended arm. It is a devastatingly painful work to see, the more so because of the care she is taking to commit this act of extraordinary violence against herself, carrying it out with such precision. It is an image of horror, but it is still a small, beautifully made ceramic figurine. It is the disjuncture between the violence of the act and the

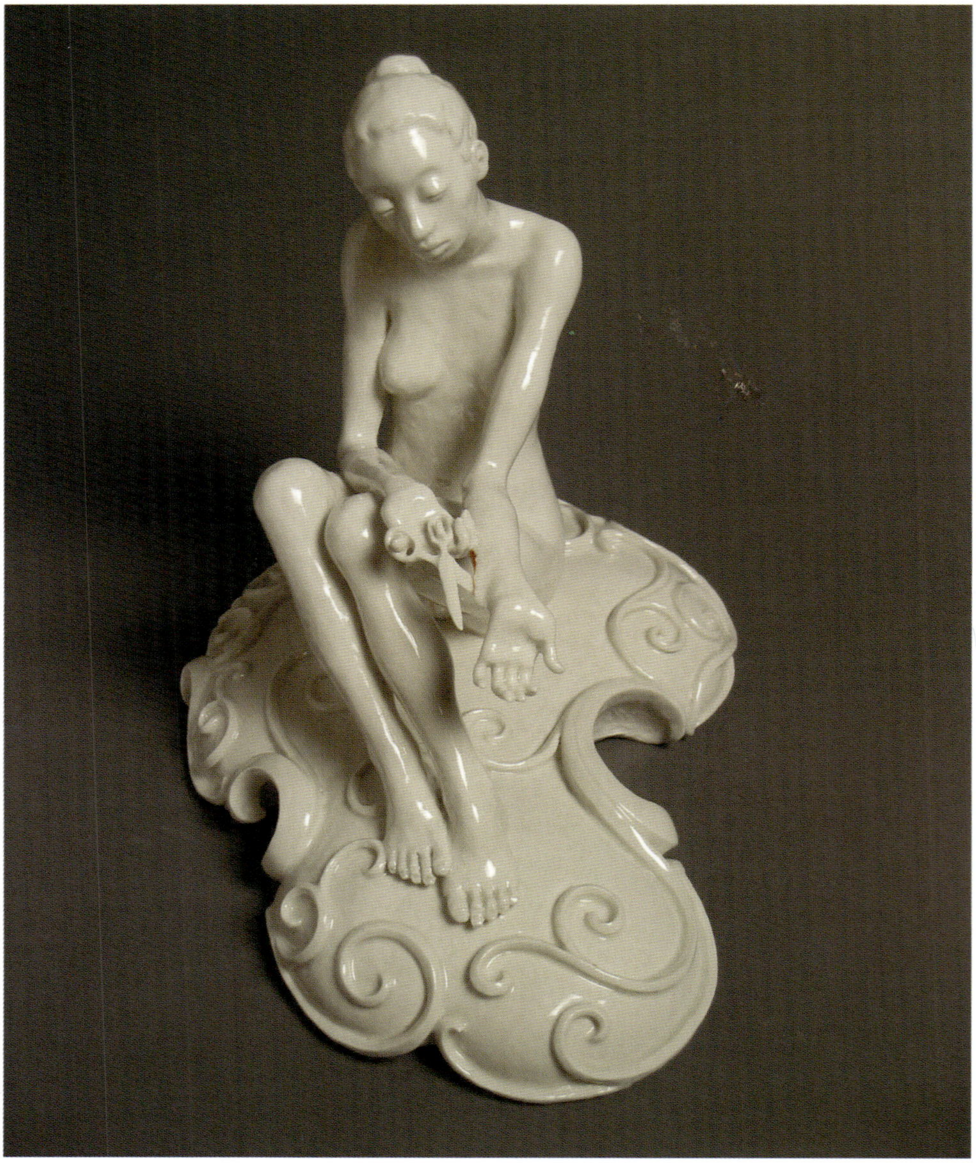

1.8 *Disfigurines*, 1998–2001, Justin Novak, courtesy of the artist

innocence of the figurine that generates the shock, but it is also the visceral self-hatred the fictionalized young woman is expressing.

'Ornamentation', says Novak, 'is the meeting of beauty and order, but often it is an employment of beauty in the service of order, and specifically, of social order'.[29] Novak provides his disfigures with ornamental plinths, which sharpen the contrast between the violence and what he calls the 'dreamworld' of the figurine. In the same series, the young woman is sewing herself up with a needle and thread. It is an intimation of healing but of a peculiarly grotesque and brutal sort. Both works linger on the sensation of wounding. The second work is more masochistic than it is healing. As a political indictment of a social culture, they are unforgiving, and in their exposure of what Novak calls the 'sentimental affectations' of the ceramic figurine, merciless.

[29] Justin Novak, 'Freeze Frame: A Moment in Narrative', Storytelling & Poetry seminar, Guldagergaard, International Ceramic Research Centre, Denmark, 2005.

Geoffrey Galt Harpham, in his *Introduction to the Grotesque* (1982) states that 'the grotesque places an enormous strain on the marriage of form and content by foregrounding them both, so they appear not as a partnership, but as a warfare, a struggle'.[30] This 'enormous strain' perfectly characterizes Novak's work. The cuteness of the figurine combined with its polar opposite in the case of the self-harming *Disfigurines* is precisely what creates the tension that is so compelling in these works. Figurines indulging in violent, potentially suicidal or, as in some of his other works, criminal practices, is a truly bizarre concept, and handled differently has comic potential. However laughter is not what we get from Novak's extreme expressions of incongruity. It is the visceral nature of the work combined with the fineness of the making, 'the sense that things which should be kept apart are fused together', that generates the 'distinct feeling of repulsion'.[31]

The problem with this work, politically, is the deeply masochistic strand, to the extent that the social critique is hijacked entirely by the pale, fragile prettiness of the work – paradoxically, also part of its power to shock. It holds up an ironic mirror to reflect a social ill but, in doing so, reproduces and fetishizes the social violence it seeks to critique – there is a hefty dose of pop star romanticism in it. This work certainly conforms to every definition of satire, not the least of which would be Dustin Griffin's point about satire's resistance to closing down an argument. The ceramic prototype is subverted, certainly, but politically it has a baleful quality consistent with the masochistic values of the beauty industry it attacks. As a feminist critique which, in principle, at least, it should be, it is an attack that is repelled by the power of the imagery. The imagery, however, for all its problems, is unforgettable. Even if not strictly subversive, it is still immensely thought provoking.

Justine Cawsey

The polar opposite of the *Disfigurines* are Justine Cawsey's figures. They walk towards you, a face-to-face confrontation. A fully naked adult woman, small-breasted with full hips, rounded belly and a full complement of pubic hair presents a no-nonsense figure of a woman, *State of Grace* (1998) (Figure 1.9). We might imagine that she has just got out of the bath and realized she's forgotten her towel, or, if she's wandered into the art gallery, then she has decided, for no discernible reason, that it would be pleasant to walk around naked for the day. She is deliciously ordinary, fascinatingly so. Cawsey noticed the way that pornographic images artificially enlarge and reduce different parts of the female body to define which parts are sexual and desirable, and which are not.[32] After a time, one notices slight distortions in Cawsey's figures – in the length of the arms, for example, but nothing which appears extreme. The surprise is in the frank, full-frontal nakedness as though one had encountered her in the pet-food aisle at the supermarket. The more you look at these very human-looking figures, the more alive they seem to be. They are not headless torsos like most art figures. Child size, but taller on their plinths, they have faces with expressions,

[30] Geoffrey Galt Harpham, *Introduction to the Grotesque*, Princeton University Press, 1982, 7.

[31] Harpham, 1982, 11.

[32] Claudia Clare, 'Woman, Mysterious and Eternal', *Ceramic Review*, 214, 2005, 38–39.

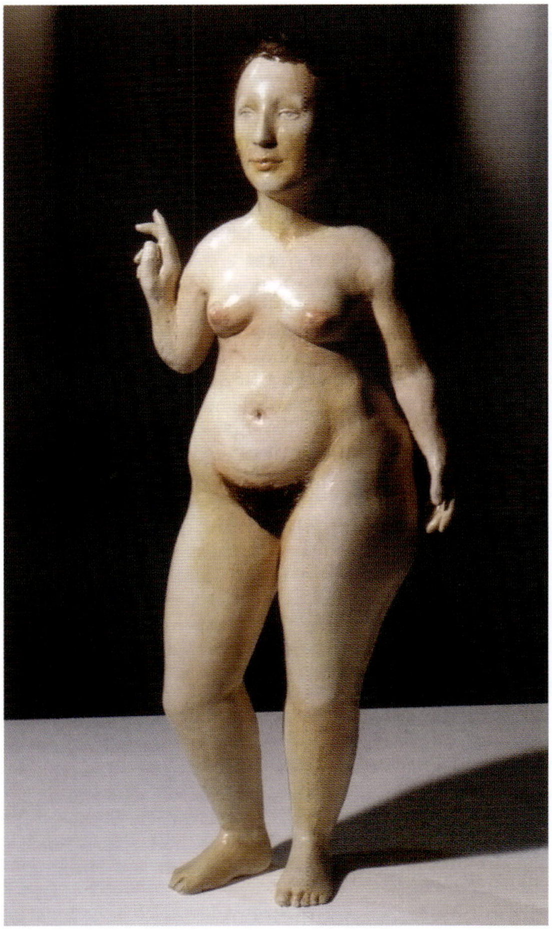

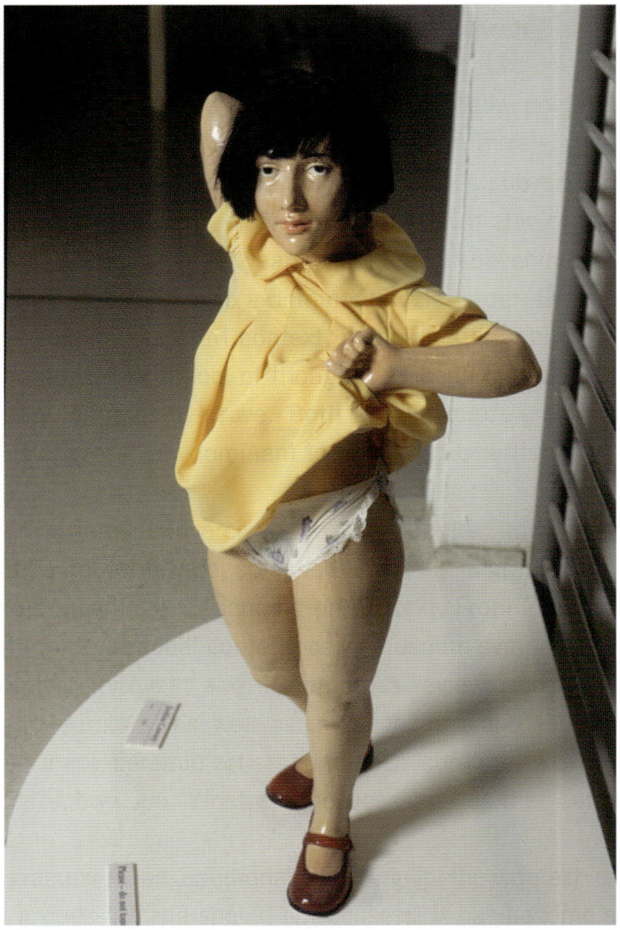

1.9 Left: *State of Grace*, 1998, Justine Cawsey, courtesy of the artist

1.10 Right: *Love and Other Options*, 1999, Justine Cawsey, Royal College of Art, photo: Dominic Tschudin

eyebrows and lashes, and real head, pubic and body hair. They are almost hyper-real, particularly in terms of their detail, but not to the point of being creepy. To an extent they parody the ceramic doll, but there is also an edge of irony here. The figures reflect the distortion inherent in the constructed feminine ideal, particularly one which is fostered by pornographic imagery. The distortions are slight, the realness of the figures seems to fight back. Anything further from art figures would be difficult to imagine, and yet they are pure artifice.

Cawsey also made clothed figures, one of which is undressing. In *Love and Other Options* (1999), the fabric and hair seem to emphasize the nakedness of the figure. They bear no resemblance to the familiar figures in life drawings or 'nudes'. Cawsey's figures are either naked – as opposed to nude – dressed, or undressing. The figure is an adult woman but the clothes suggest an adolescent girlish quality too – a parallel to sexualized or pornographic images, which present women as similar to little girls but with adult sexual parts. The critique is levelled at a society that infantilizes adult women – not least in its insistence on the removal of body hair, and the reduction of body mass – with the intention of making them look more like children. This is the same society that professes to deplore child rape.

The extreme artifice of the smooth, pinkish glazed ceramic body, combined with the hair and the clothes, corresponds with the constructed artifice of the fetishized, feminine ideal. It is in the distortions and the artifice that the critique is located. In recent years these distortions in the imaging of women have become increasingly exaggerated and extreme. It is now even more surprising to see a representation of a woman with pubic hair, especially 'unstyled' pubic hair. For some it is nothing short of obscene or unhygienic. Social norms, always in a state of flux, have regressed considerably in the last decade. The new generation of feminists in their early twenties must contend with far more aggressive and damaging distortions in the portrayal of the perfect female body than any of the second wave activists did. Made sixteen years ago, these works have not only stood the test of time, but they have become more relevant and more meaningful than they were when they were made. If they were subversive then, they are even more so now.

Redressing men: Grayson Perry

One cannot talk about satire in ceramics without discussing the work of Grayson Perry. Since 2012, Perry has been making anthropological, documentary-style television programmes with Channel 4. His artwork is derived from time spent with his subjects, television has become part of his process. *The Vanity of Small Differences* (2012) was a study of British class and taste, and his latest venture, *Who do you think you are*, is a study of British identity based on interviewing a random selection of people, one of whom is the former Liberal Party MP and minister in the 2010–2015 coalition government, Chris Huhne. Huhne was prosecuted for perverting the course of justice and served a short prison sentence. Perry's pot *The Chris Huhne Vase* (2014), based on Huhne's 'rise and fall', is a critical presentation of his theory of 'Default Man', in Perry's words, 'A white, middle-class, middle-aged, heterosexual man, an identity group that hides in plain sight.'[33] The pot itself is duller than ditchwater, small and grey, with unremarkable repeated patterns. Perry broke it using a hammer, which produces an instantly recognizable pattern in the lines of breakage, and restored it using the kintsugi method which, in principle, makes the pot more interesting as gold veins display the marks of a venerable life of service. Nothing, however, could make this pot interesting; it is a conceit. Like its eponymous subject, it has not performed valuable service, it just acquired the gold. In a museum collection it would vanish from view; in other words, it is hiding 'in plain sight'. Deliberately making a boring pot, placing it in the National Portrait Gallery and broadcasting it on national television is an audacious strategy, but it works. As an attack on male privilege it works brilliantly, brought to life by television in a way the pot alone could not achieve.

Perry has a history of mocking the construction of contemporary masculinity. *Hot Afternoon in 75* (2000, private collection)[34] depicts the teenage Perry in his sister's clothes in rural Essex. He captures the heat and glare of that memorable

[33] Louise Jury, 'Huhne's A Smashing Subject for Grayson', *Evening Standard*, 21 October 2014.

[34] Grayson Perry, 'Guerrilla Tactics', Stedelijk Museum, Amsterdam, 2000, 39.

summer perfectly, it hums with frustration and anticipation. Where teenage boys are concerned, transvestism is still, potentially, a subversive social story. He does not present himself as a sad social freak, or pervert, or as a shocking or comic burlesque; it is a simple and highly effective coming-of-age story and still one of his most significant pieces. Perry's work is a highly effective exposure of the limitations and restrictions that masculinity imposes on men and boys, and the unmerited privilege of the dominant male is now also in his target range. Thus far, this has not included any discernible attack on male oppression of women, but there is still time. In common with many satirists he plays safe, and, to his credit, he fully acknowledges this.[35] His great gift is in human observation combined with insightful and entertaining critique. He has never expressed a desire for revolutionary change: he is reformist at most, and makes great pots.

Conclusion

Subversion has become a desirable commodity, used at least as much as a marketing strategy as an analysis. Conversely, it has also become part of craft's moral project, a wholesome and necessary adjunct to 'proper' ceramics. Beyond the confusion there is a meaningful word, and some ceramic works are genuinely subversive. Most of the artists discussed in this chapter bring a satiric voice to their work, and all the works featured have a subversive edge to some degree. Only Bita Fayyazi's work still presents a serious challenge to government, but all the works I have selected stand the test of time and continue to resonate meaningfully in their changed social contexts. The next chapter introduces the historical context of this book. From outrageous lampooning to covert allegory, from frighteningly subversive 'underground' messaging, to political protest and social movements, it is all there, fired into the ceramic historical record.

[35] Nick Cohen, *You Can't Read This Book*, Fourth Estate, 2012, 53.

2

Objection! A history of protest

Most historic examples of political and social comment in ceramics underscore the dominant political narrative of the time and place they were made. From the glazed-brick and tiled mosques of Persia to the royal commemorative ware of the European monarchies to the blue and white delftware celebrating the growth of colonial trade, ceramics have been used to normalize dominant political ideologies by means of ordinary, everyday things. It is not surprising then that revolutionary and oppositionist movements have sought to overturn the process by using commonplace ceramic objects to project their visions, articulate their ideologies and agitate among the masses.

Attic red ware: Satire in ancient Athens

Ancient Athens is often cited as the birthplace of satire, and the playwright, Aristophanes, as one of its major exponents. The potters of ancient Athens were as much given to lampooning and parody – to say nothing of obscenity and the grotesque – as the playwrights were. Produced in vast quantities, Athenians considered pottery a debased and, according to some theories, disposable product, but this appears to be contradicted by the discovery in the eighteenth century of perfectly preserved examples in Etruscan tombs.[1] Attic red figure ware, at its height, depicts and visually describes in some detail a great many aspects of Athenian life, and with it can be discerned a good deal about social life, norms, transgressions and attitudes.

Attic vase painters used the relationship between the interior and exterior planes of the pot to articulate their narratives visually. The imagery extended from the outer walls of the vase, including the shoulder and foot, to the internal walls and *tondo*, the latter usually an image painted into an inscribed circle at the bottom of a cup. Red figure ware depicted a huge range of subjects in considerable detail, including domestic genre scenes, religious ceremony, public, social, sporting and political life, preparations for war, the glories and cruelties of war, and post-conflict. Kitchen activities show what was in the pantry, what the lady of a big house and her servant both wore, their attitudes to each other and who came to visit. There are workshop scenes, showing carpentry, metal-smithing, ship-building and pottery.

There are wild parties, symposia, depicting learned and arty Athenian men arguing, reciting poetry, playing musical instruments and cavorting with younger men and with the *hetaerai*, educated women who were hired to provide entertainment and,

1 Nigel Spivey, 'Greek Vases in Etruria', in *Looking at Greek Vases*, Tom Rasmussen and Nigel Spivey (eds), Cambridge University Press, 1991, 131–150.

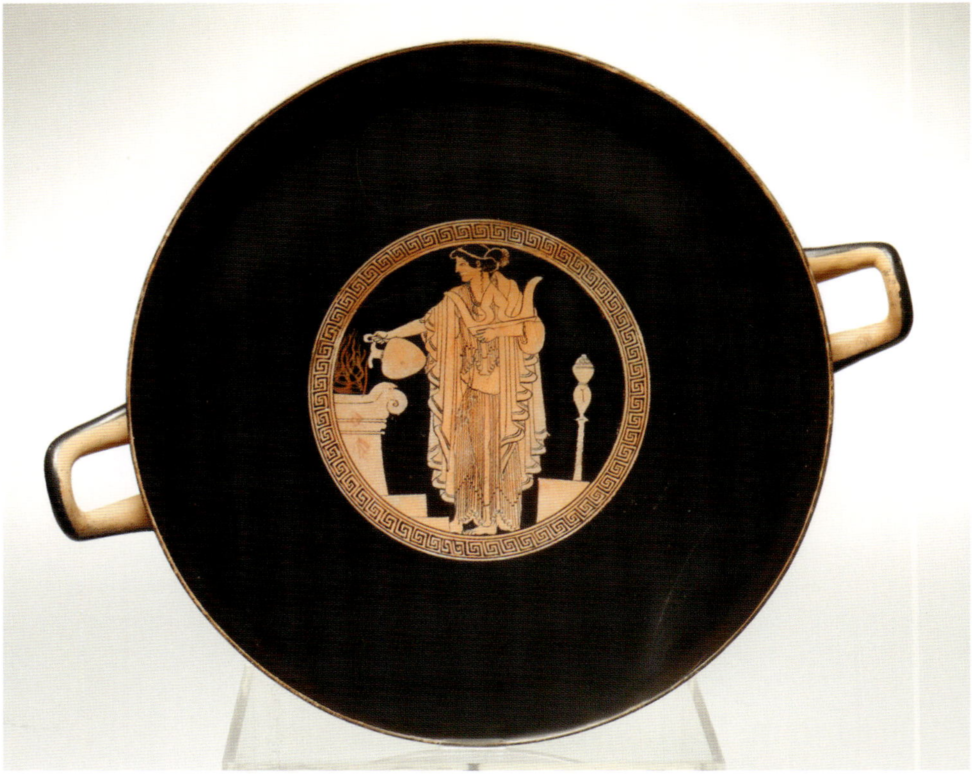

2.1 Attributed to Makron Painter (Greek, Attic), *kylix* with woman sacrificing (*tondo*), about 490–480 BC, wheel-thrown, slip-decorated earthenware, height 11 cm, diameter at lip 28.9 cm, diameter with handles 36 cm, Toledo Museum of Art, purchased with funds from the Libbey Endowment, Gift of Edward Drummond Libbey, 1972.55

as often as not, sexual services too. The potters lost no opportunity to expose their probably richer and socially superior fellow citizens in undignified and compromising situations.[2] A family of red figure ware made specifically for the symposium – the *kylikes*, or drinking cups – show sexual activity and general debauchery in such eye-poppingly graphic detail that contemporary attempts at the same pale by comparison. Red figure ware also illustrates the myths and stories of Athenian theatre along with musical and literary events. It is a detailed document of life high and low, public and private, real and imagined, much of it indicative of the social values of the period.

Attic red figure ware is rich in satirical imagery, social comment, humorous asides, critique, protest and caricature. Satire, particularly caricature, also features on black figure ware but red figure ware is regarded as the introduction of properly satirical visual narrative in Western art, and it is with this body of ceramics that caricature and commentary really developed.[3] There is a series of vases dating from the fifth century BC, by members of the Pioneer group, where the artists name check themselves, compete with one another, and subject each other to merciless satirical ridicule. A well known and endlessly discussed belly amphora by the painter Euthymides, c. 510 BC (Munich 2307), in the State Collection of Antiquities in Munich, is a good example of the competitive boast in vase painting. On one side, three naked male revellers are drinking and disporting themselves. One is painted with impressive anatomical accuracy, twisted away from the viewer, fully three dimensional except for the head, which is still in silhouette. 'As never Euphronius' is thought to be

2 Eva C. Keuls, *The Painter and Poet in Ancient Greece: Iconography and the Literary Arts*, Stuttgart: Teubner, 1997, 283–301.

3 Keuls, 292.

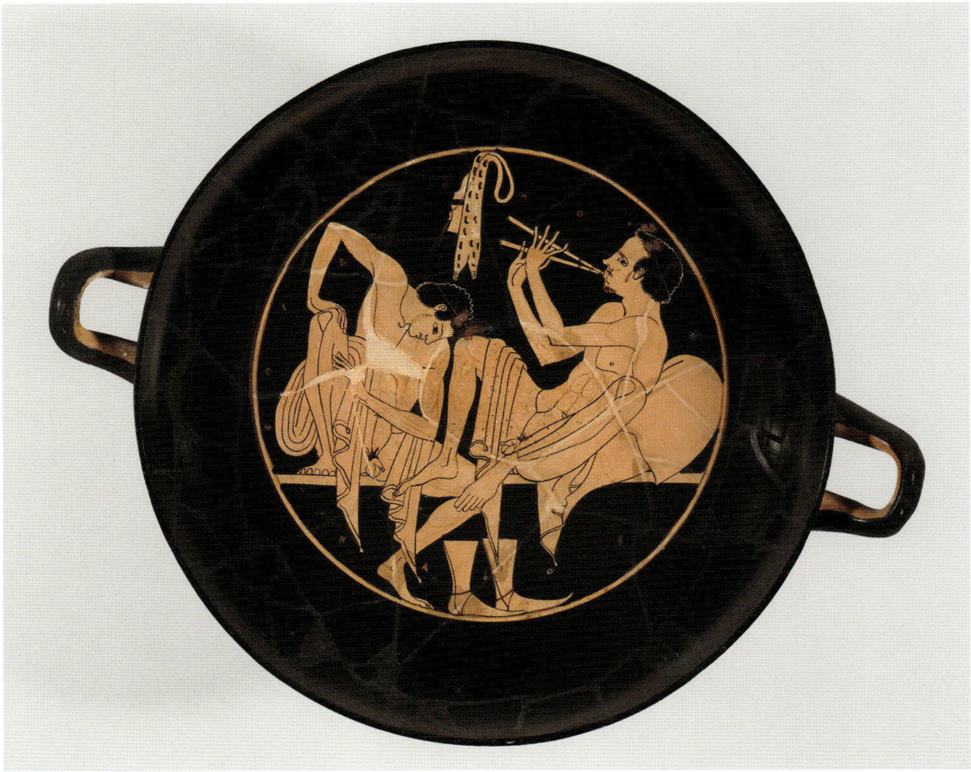

2.2 The Proto-Panaitian Group, drinking cup (*kylix*), Greek, Late Archaic Period, c. 510–500 BC. Ceramic, red figure, height 9 cm, Museum of Fine Arts, Boston, Henry Lillie Pierce Fund, 01.8018, © 2015, Museum of Fine Arts, Boston

a challenge to his rival painter, who, he asserts, cannot paint the human figure as well as he can. There are many more in this vein, mostly *kylikes*, where the painter-potters depict each other in compromising or embarrassing social and sexual situations.

Fragments of painted pots with very pronounced, energetically drawn, expressive caricature, found embedded in the ground around the Acropolis, suggest that satirical work of this sort was mostly very local, the shards suggesting the pots were considered disposable party ware rather than valued for export. There are a number of extant *kylikes*, however, some fully restored, some only fragments, depicting and, perhaps, commenting satirically on the social conduct of the Athenian male, particularly when attending the symposium. In one we see the men haggling with the *hetaerai*, presumably over the price of their services, while the *tondo* shows a woman, representing a high-class Athenian wife, making libation at home (Figure 2.1). It exposes numerous double standards, both between men and women and among women, who are cast in specifically defined and limited roles. Many more *kylikes* show the predilection of Athenian men for 'binge drinking', The exterior of the cups show cavorting symposiasts, in various degrees of sexual gratification and alcoholic indulgence, while the *tondo* shows the same man vomiting generously, sometimes supported by obliging *hetaerai*, sometimes by a more youthful male companion (Figure 2.2). These bear comparison to some contemporary examples commenting on the same social phenomenon in Britain. The Athenian versions look more robustly decadent, however, suggesting there were not the same anxieties about indulgent drinking as there are now.

Italian Renaissance maiolica: Status, power, wealth and consumerism

Writing about the Italian Renaissance, Lisa Jardine argues that the extraordinary developments in the arts across Europe were connected not only to the growth of humanism and the value accorded to knowledge, but also to the growth in a robust and proud consumerism. Jardine contends that trade, economic growth and a culture of rampant acquisitiveness were the engines driving the flowering of knowledge.[4] Literature was popularized through print and the printed book. Science, including medical, anatomical, biological and botanical research expanded, as did overseas exploration and astronomy, and every area of the arts and crafts flourished. The development of painting, sculpture and textiles, of furniture design and carpet manufacture, of architecture and ceramics, all, she argues, were driven by a colossal and hitherto unmatched desire to hunt, discover, buy, possess and display an orgy of desirable objects.[5] The aim, aside from displaying one's immense wealth and vastly superior knowledge, was to be admired by awestruck guests, whether they were courtiers, visiting dignitaries, or the hoi polloi.[6] Anyone willing to be amazed and to spread word of the splendid acquisitions they had just beheld was encouraged to do just that.

Maiolica from Spain was prized for its glittering lustre, its beauty and style, and its exquisite manufacture, and conferred considerable status on the owner. As Italian maiolica became increasingly proficient, so it became correspondingly desirable to noble and entitled Italian families, and by the end of the fifteenth century it had supplanted Spanish lustreware at the top end of the market. The whiteness of the tin-glazed ground mattered: it proved quality in the material and manufacture and trumpeted its cost. Tin was imported and pricey, as was the cobalt that produced a clear and regal blue. The beauty and detail of the painted imagery indicated the quality of craftsmanship and technical expertise. Knowledge and exotic innovations from abroad – whether material or technical – all came with a price in this flourishing consumer market where everything was commoditized, including the use of certain colours and particularly lustre.[7]

Ruling families started to commission potters to produce ware carrying their heraldic insignia. These families had considerable power over the lives of their subject population, and decorated maiolica, though expensive by pottery standards and certainly ware destined for display, had considerable propagandist value – so owning it was a good way to declare political support and curry favour. For the potters, making and selling this ware was also an indicator of toeing the line politically. According to Elisa Sani, contemporaneous reports tell of potters having their work smashed in 1508, after the fall of the Medici in Florence, and also some thirty years later, in Bologna, after the fall of the Bentivoglio family, when work bearing that family's insignia was smashed and the potters punished by the new rulers.[8]

4 Lisa Jardine, *Worldly Goods*, Macmillan, 1997, 9–10.

5 Jardine, 12.

6 Jardine, 19.

7 Timothy Wilson, 'Le Maioliche', in *Il Rinascimento Itlaiano e l'Europa, IV, Commercio e Culture Mercantile*, F. Franceschi, R. Goldthwaite and R. Mueller (eds), 217–245.

8 Elisa P. Sani, *Italian Renaissance Maiolica*, V&A publishing, 2012, 50.

Narrative painting on pottery, *istoriato*, was a unique and startlingly new innovation, derived from engravings and woodcuts illustrating popular texts and the Bible. The maiolica painters used the illustrations of Ovid's *Metamorphoses* to devise allegorical and mythological designs but, for compositions expressing a moral purpose, they looked to Aesop's *Fables*. In Tim Wilson's words, 'Such ceramics had a cultural value of their own, such "cosa di villa," constituted a conversation piece and sign of taste and humanist culture.'[9] Craftsmen from the most celebrated workshops and the finest and best known pottery painters were of central importance to the commissioning process. They, according to Lisa Jardine, could guarantee that the luxury objects acquired would 'make an impact'.[10] However, since the patron and commissioner were understood to be the 'creator' of the work, they acquired the status, not the artist. Fine pieces of maiolica not only conferred status in the lifetime of the owner but were an investment in future reputation.

A dish from Gubbio, dated 1510, illustrates the fable of the shepherd and the wolf. The tale Aesop tells is of a shepherd who grows to trust a wolf who daily comes to look at the sheep without making any aggressive advance towards them.

[9] Wilson, 220.

[10] Jardine, 19.

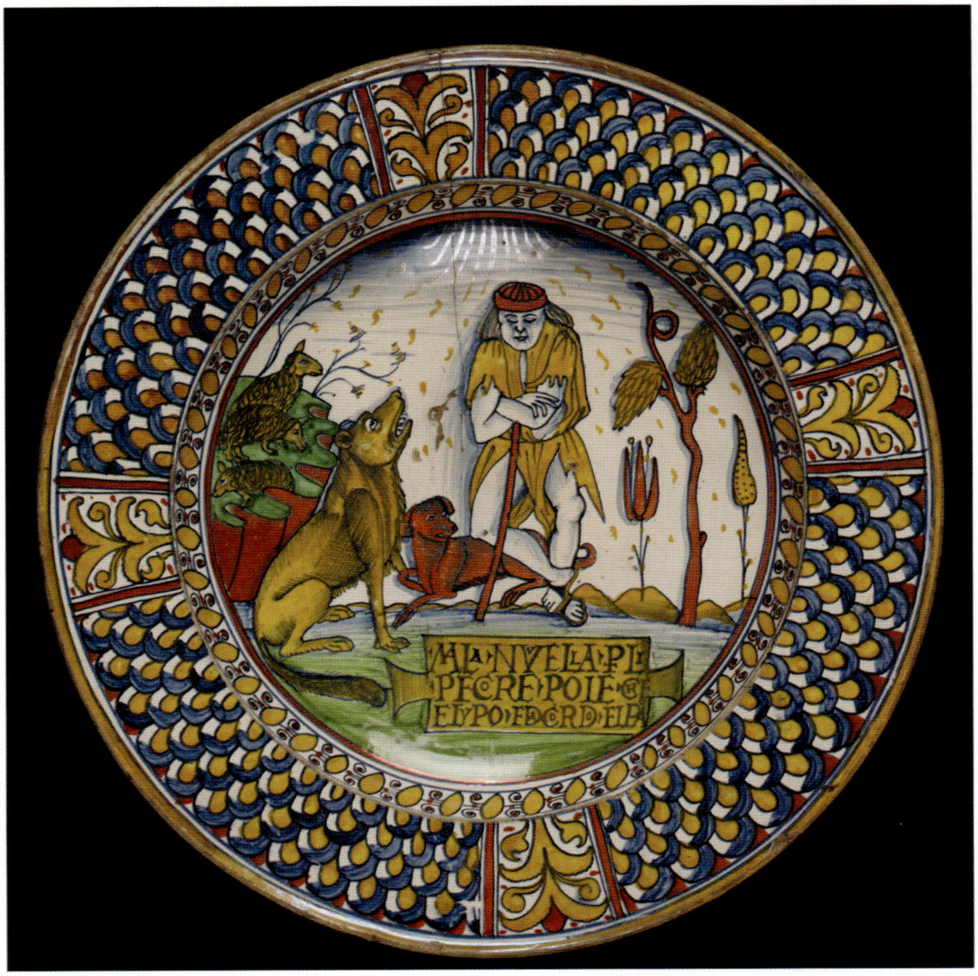

2.3 Dish, c. 1510, artist unknown, Gubbio, Italy © Victoria and Albert Museum, London

The shepherd, lulled into a false sense of security, goes on an errand leaving his sheep in the 'care' of the wolf, resulting in inevitable carnage. The dish is inscribed: 'Bad luck for the sheep when the shepherd is in league with the wolf', a tantalizing commentary in almost any historical or political context. Adapted from a version of the *Fables* published in 1485, it is a simple social or moral truism but, to a twenty-first-century audience, it is tempting to imagine that the makers were thinking of a local political scandal, however minor. In London 2014, with European economies still reeling from the impact of the banking crises which began six years earlier, it is difficult not to imagine the wolf as a voracious 'casino' bank, the shepherd as a government placing too much trust in the markets, and the sheep meeting a sticky end as a result.

Another dish from Gubbio, made at about the same time, depicts an everyday religious scene. In the centre is an organ, in front of which sits a Franciscan friar with a younger monk who holds the sheet music. To the right a man operates the bellows of the organ, while to the left is a howling dog. The text reads: *'Adi cello el mio lamento'*, 'Hear, oh Heaven, my lament!' Dogs are not exalted beasts in religious

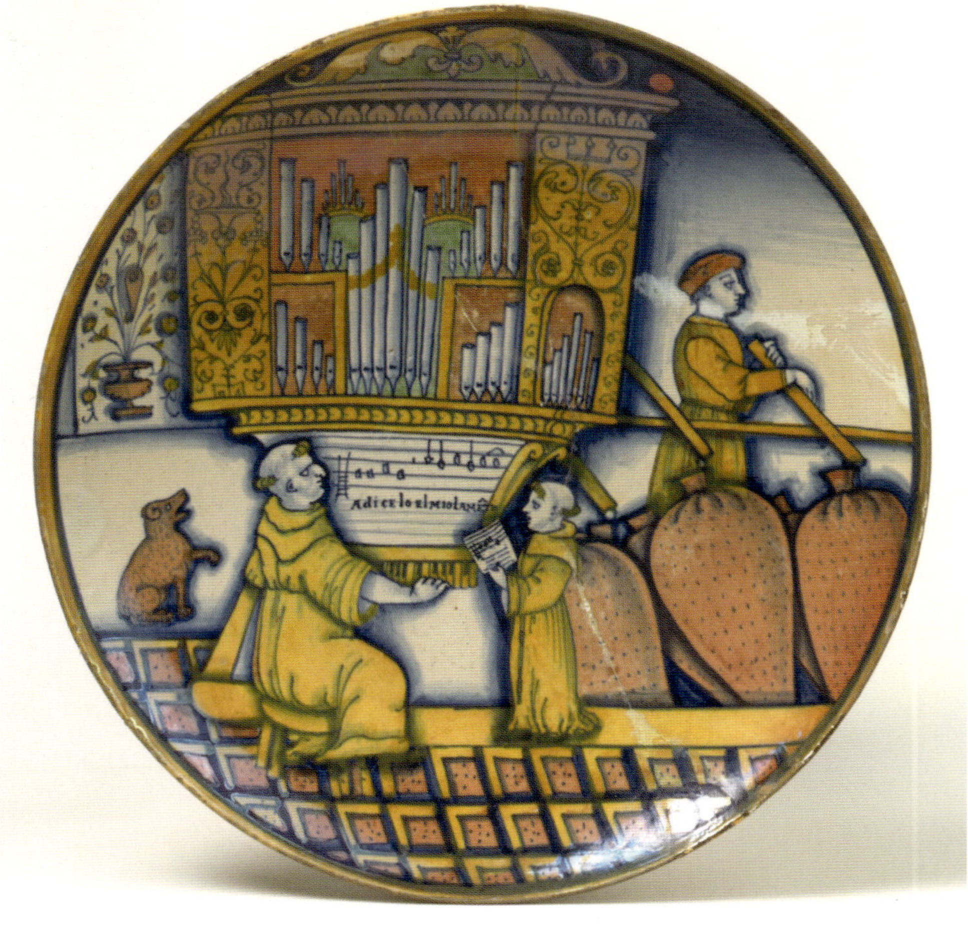

2.4 Fruit Dish, c. 1520, Georgio Andreoli, Gubbio, Italy © Victoria and Albert Museum, London

terms, so it is tempting to read this dish in the spirit of satire commenting on the less than glorious sound of the local monks at evensong or matins. Another dish depicts a donkey having its head lovingly washed by a man who, according to the inscription is merely 'wasting soap'. Also regarded as low beasts, depraved and graceless, this one is making a fool of the man – wasting time on worthless celebrities, perhaps? The last depicts Cupid astride a unicorn, a symbol of virginity and purity, but one that also has sexual connotations. Cupid, son of Venus, is anything but pure. He is a mischievous character and indicates sexual love and caper. Riding a unicorn suggests, at its mildest, the deflowering of virginity, but has connotations of something much more knowing and bawdy. It has been suggested that the dish originally had a ewer, in which case the image would have been hidden, which makes it seem even less innocent. It was probably intended for the bedroom, so it may have been a gift for a mistress, or possibly a new wife.

These four works appear loaded with meaning but are frustratingly obscure. We do know, however, that the Italian city states of the Renaissance period were highly politicized environments. Protestantism was a growing force and a great many of the

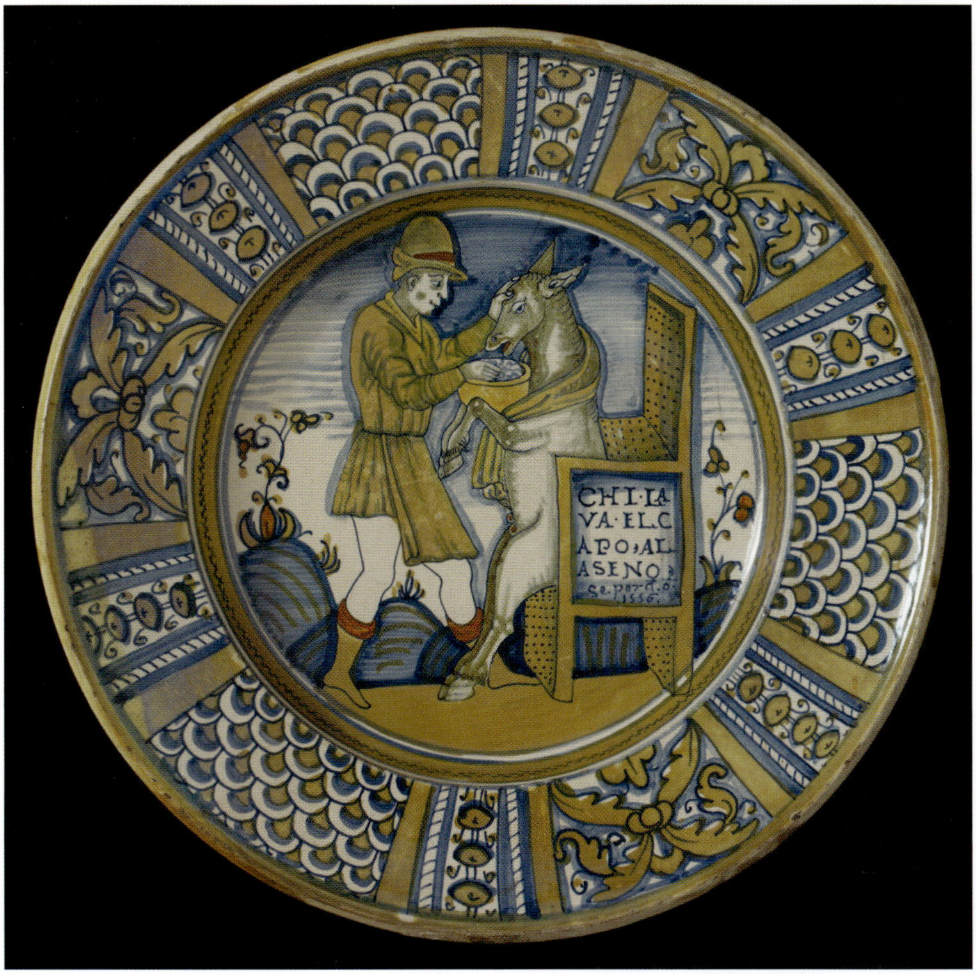

2.5 Dish, 1556, artist unknown, Deruta, Italy © Victoria and Albert Museum, London

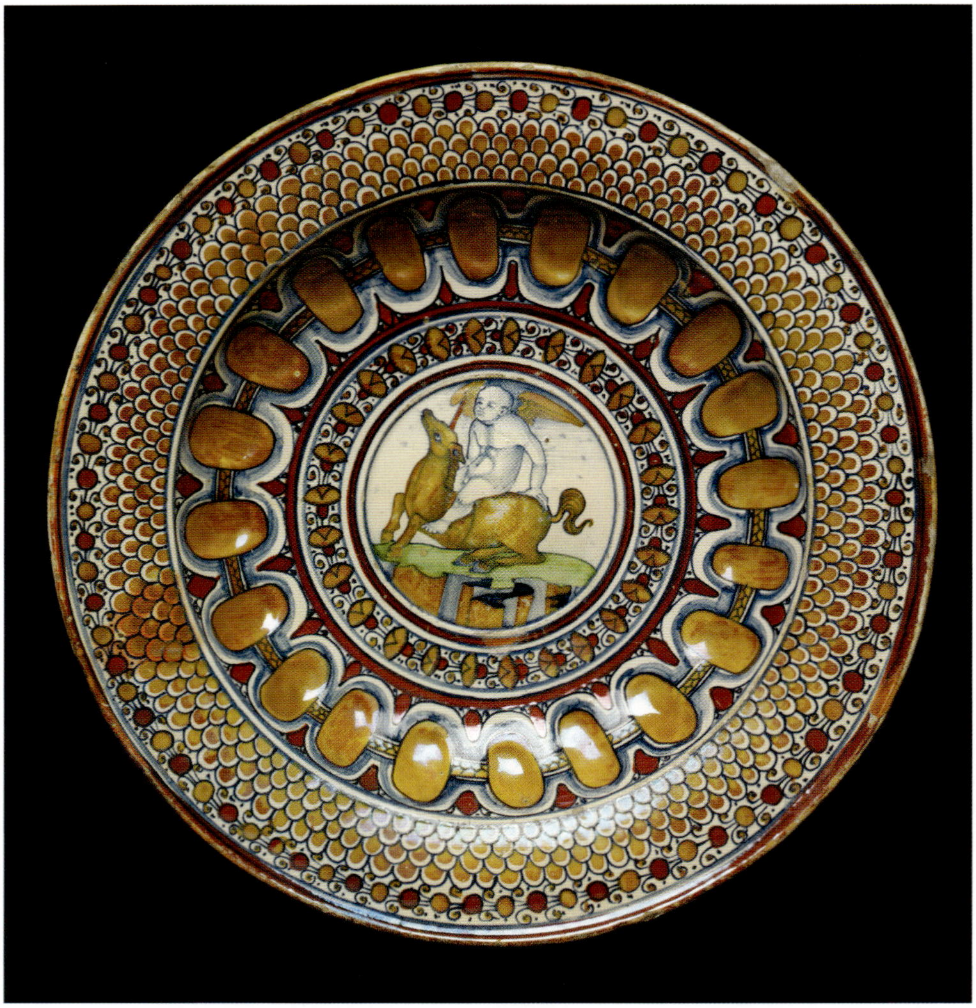

2.6 Dish, c. 1510, artist unknown, Gubbio, Italy © Victoria and Albert Museum, London

Faenza potters, who were Protestants, were executed for following the religion in 1569.[11] Potters and painters went on strike for improved wages and conditions,[12] and potters who made work supporting an opposition family risked damage to themselves and their work. It is inconceivable, given the political organizing of some potters and the oppositionist religious affiliations of others, that political commentary, however obscure, did not appear, from time to time.

French Revolutionary faience

The French Revolution, like most, was an extended period of turmoil. From a string of new constitutions with additional decrees and oaths to the declaration of the Republic, the Terror, and the Thermidorean reaction, its impact reverberated across Europe. Within France, it affected everything from civic architecture to kitchen crockery, from bank notes to biscuit tins. The French Revolutionary faience, a tin-glazed earthenware

[11] Wilson, 226.

[12] Sani, 26.

for use and display, is perhaps unique in that it provides an incidental record of the process of revolution in one country, from start to finish. Unlike Soviet porcelain it met the needs of its local market. It was commissioned, manufactured and sold, bought, used and displayed by the new class of relatively prosperous peasants and rural clergy. In its design and what might be called its sociology, it provides an exceptional, if oblique, record of the revolutionary period.

Even with access to workshop records, it would be difficult to assess to what extent the makers were expressing their own opinions through the designs they devised, but we do know certain things that can enable an informed guess. During the revolutionary period, potters were either self-employed or employed in small workshops; either way, the living was hard and matters of wages and conditions, taxation and social attitudes would likely have been a matter of concern. Potters, historically, have tended to be politically engaged. The French potter, Bernard Pallisy (c. 1510 – c.1590), a committed and outspoken Protestant reformist, was imprisoned twice and finally sentenced to death for refusing to conform, and the Italian Protestant potters also paid the ultimate price for their resistance to Catholic tyranny. Working successfully with ceramics is difficult: neither the materials nor the process tolerate fools gladly. Potters were and still are, necessarily, committed to understanding and developing the alignment of art and science, intuition, knowledge and reason; they embody the emancipated and exploratory spirit of the Enlightenment. They could not have escaped the political environment, so they must, at the very least, have had opinions.

The revolutionary designs emerged gradually, their political character growing alongside the changing political context. Popular faience, according to Edith Mannoni, had always responded to political context, and to some extent popular culture.[13] Religious imagery and references to the monarchy were commonplace, as were designs responding to momentous cultural or national occasions. A celebrated French military victory in 1745 resulted in a new and immensely popular decorative device known as the 'Fanfare', which produced the template onto which the revolutionary motifs were grafted in the 1790s. In the central medallion, where there might previously have been a flower, there was now the Fanfare, comprised of a shield, behind which were crossed four flags and sometimes musical instruments or weapons. Below the shield were a collection of wind instruments, a drum and drumsticks. There are numerous variations, but the underlying design structure is largely consistent.

The Fanfare design gradually mutated into the 'Flags', a design in praise of the king but still including military and musical references. The first of the designs properly associated with the revolutionary period was the *Trois Ordres*, or Three Estates, which, itself, mutated into numerous other versions reflecting the progress of the Revolution. The *Trois Ordres* design comprised two essential elements: the symbols of the Three Estates and a central binding motif. The Three Estates were symbolized by the sword representing nobility, the crosier representing the clergy and a spade to represent the peasants (Figure 2.7). The central motif was either a shield

[13] Edith Mannoni, *Les Faiences Revolutionnaires*, Massin, 1989, 3–6.

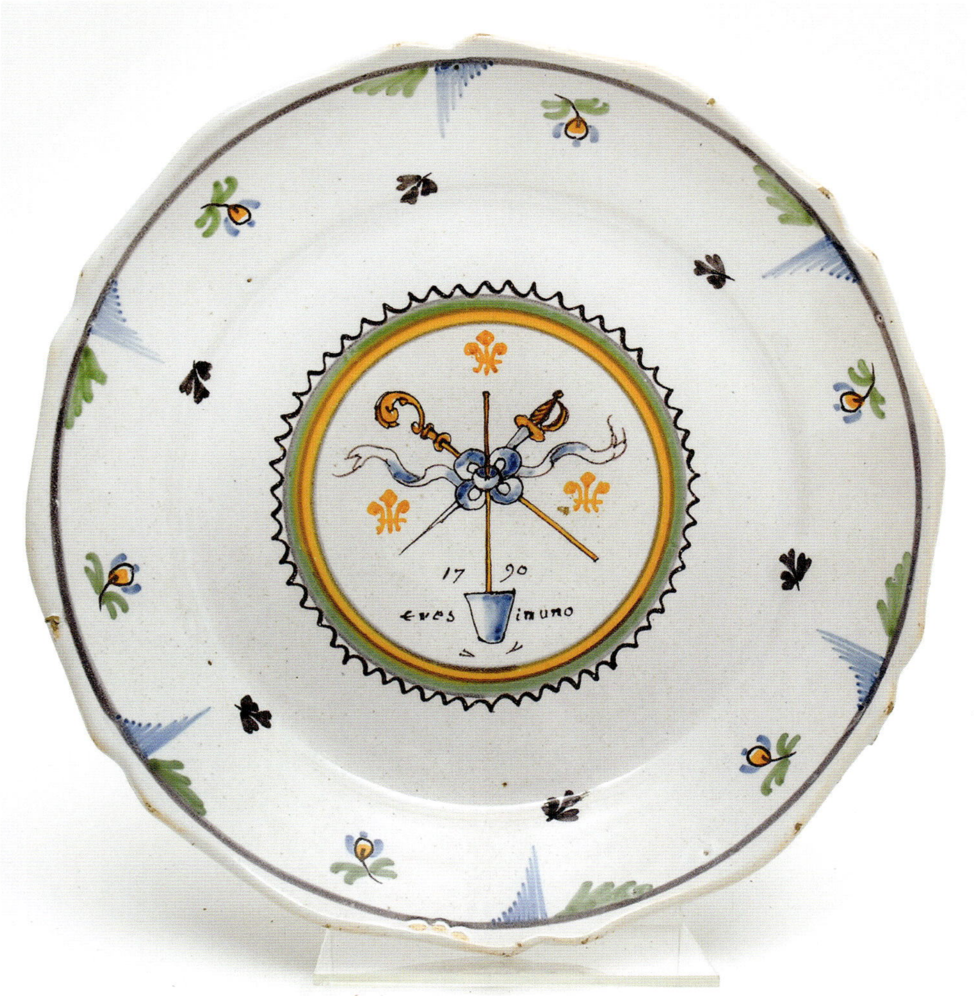

2.7 Plate, 'Tres in Uno', c. 1790, Nevers, France, KHJ Coutts, Bowes Museum

or badge, or, not infrequently, a sheaf of corn, a blue bow or even the Bastille. These were contained either in a circle at the centre of the plate or in a wreath of leaves, palms or flowers. The design celebrating the 1792 Constitution uses the book of law itself as the motif containing the unified three symbols. During the time that the new constitution proscribed the limits of the monarch's power, the spade, almost always central and supporting the crosier and sword, was topped with a crown or *fleur de lys.* Later, during the republican period, the Phrygian cap appeared, and during the Terror all symbols associated with monarchy were eradicated.

The Phrygian cap, originally worn in ancient Greece by freed slaves, was adopted by the *sans culottes*, the urban working class who were considered the most radical group of revolutionaries, as a symbol of their emancipation and their loyalty to the Republic. The later revolutionary faience features the Phrygian cap, with classical-style garlands and the Tricolour, which replaced the blue ribbon. The symbols of the *Trois Ordres* were still there, but the central motif changed again. The *fasces lictoriae* – the bundle of rods, one bearing an axe head, symbolizing the absolute authority of

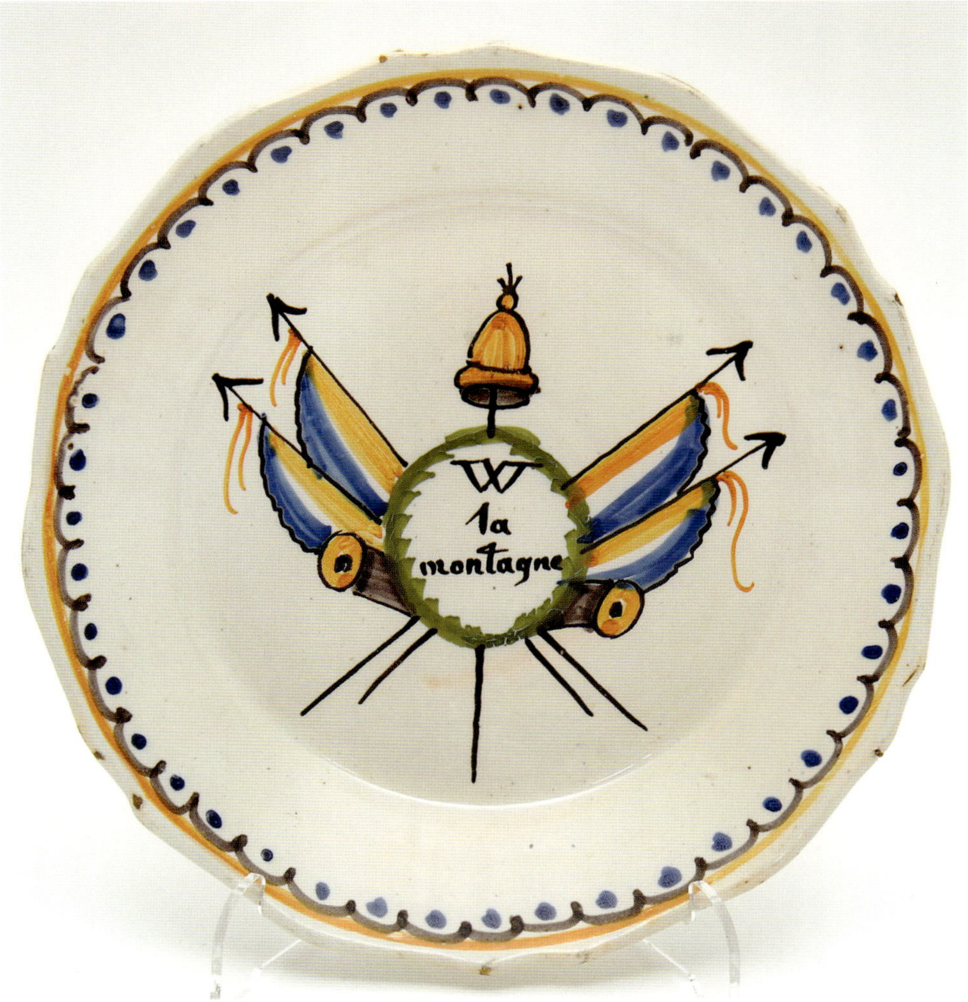

2.8 Plate, 'Vive La Montagne', c. 1792–1793, Nevers, France, KHJ Coutts, Bowes Museum

law – was used during the Republic, or alternatively, a written slogan: *'La Nation'*, *'La Loi'*, or *'Vive La République'*, added beneath the central symbol. In some there are the words of the *Carmagnole*, a revolutionary song that calls for the execution of the king and the aristocracy. *'Vive la Montagne'* ('Long live the Mountain') is a reference to the revolutionary faction, headed by Maximilien Robespierre, which agreed the execution of the king, and in 1794 ushered in the Reign of Terror.

Edith Mannoni argues that the majority of the rural poor held the king in high regard and trusted the monarchy more than any other authority, certainly more than the nobility – which was almost universally despised – or the urban intellectuals directing the course of the Revolution in Paris.[14] She points to the preponderance of designs displaying covert support for the monarch, where the spade is supporting a *fleur de lys* or is close to a burning heart, for example. The intended message, she suggests, is that the peasants mostly supported the king and were not always supportive of the revolutionary aims. Norman Davies in his history of Europe also asserts that the rural poor, and women in particular, resented the atheistic aims of

[14] Mannoni, 6.

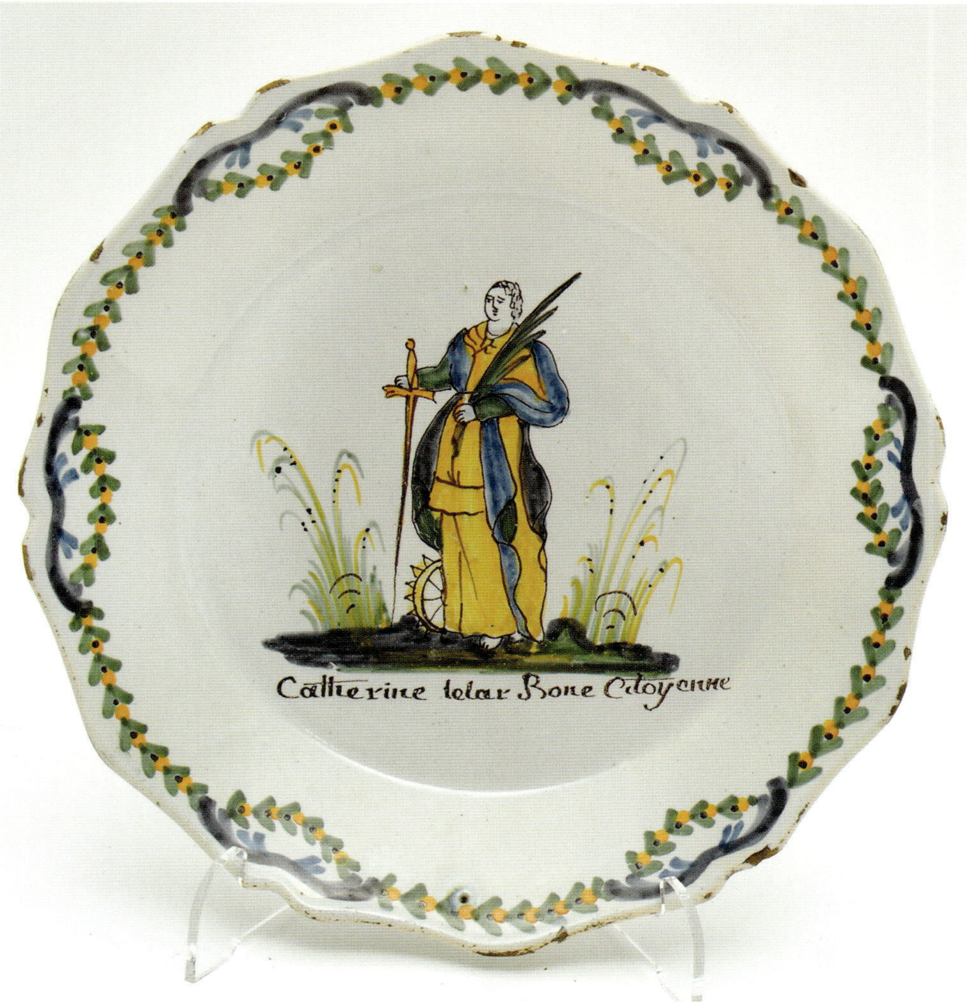

2.9 Plate, 'Catherine Lelar Bone, Citoyenne', c. 1793, Nevers, France, Coutts, Bowes Museum

the Revolution and the decree that required priests to take the oath of loyalty to the constitution or be ejected from the priesthood.[15] They trusted their own local clergy more than any newfangled constitution, to which they felt little allegiance and even less ownership. In spite of the restraining of clerical power and the growing atheism of the revolutionaries, the faience makers continued to produce ware depicting religious figures and scenes. Images of saints were surrounded by well known symbols of their story, but with the epithet *'citoyen'* ('citizen') placed after their name.

Rolf Reichardt and Hubertus Kohle point to visual evidence of the continuing influence of the Catholic Church throughout the revolutionary period: 'There are numerous instances of statues of the Virgin Mary that were provided with Phrygian caps and thereby transformed to an allegory of liberty.'[16] They cite examples of plates bearing the *Trois Ordres* design, suggesting that they also represent the Holy Trinity, what they call 'the charisma of Christianity', which they argue 'was transferred to the imagery and value system of the Revolution'.[17] The slogan *'tres in uno'* (Figure 2.7) could certainly be interpreted in both ways.

[15] Norman Davies, *Europe: A History*, Oxford University Press, 1996, 703.

[16] Rolf Reichardt and Hubertus Kohle, *Visualising the Revolution: Politics and the Pictorial Arts in Late Eighteenth-Century France*, Reaktion Books, 2008, 122.

[17] Reichardt and Kohle, 122.

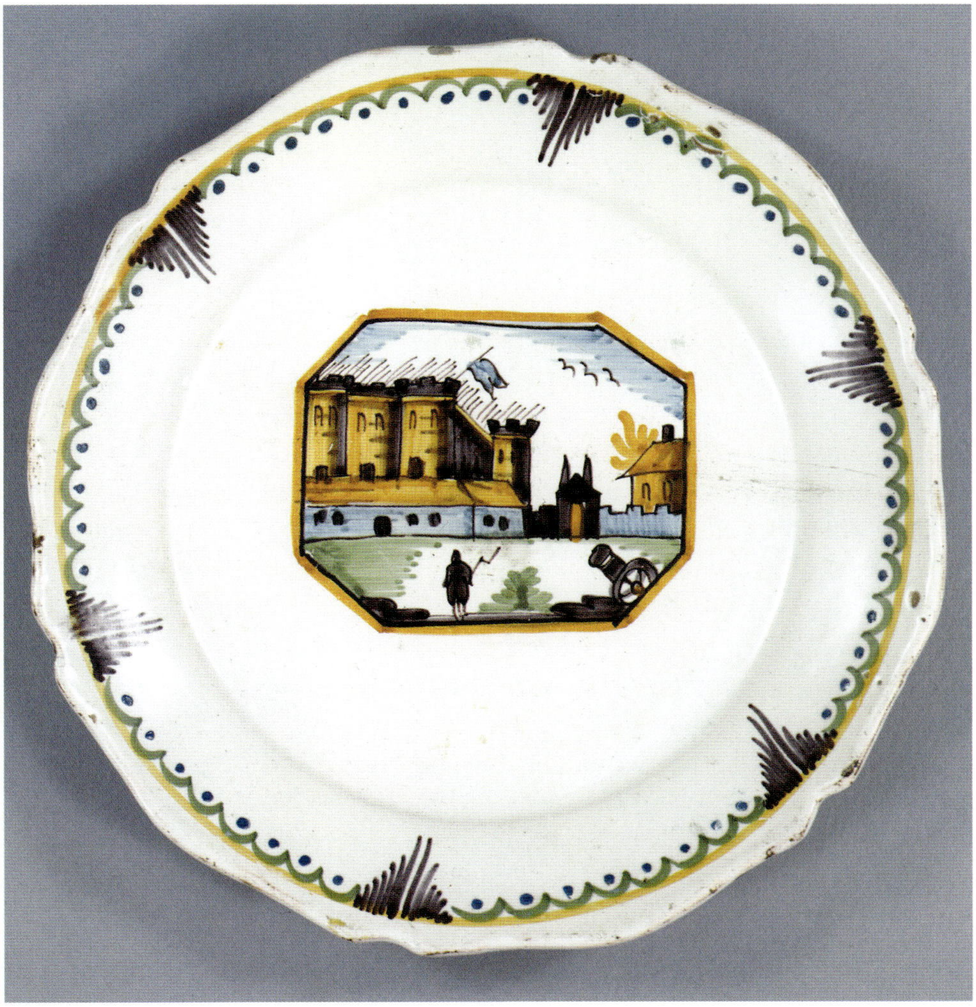

2.10 Bastille Plate, c. 1789, Nevers, France, Roger Viollet/Topfoto

Revolutionary faience includes a large number of pictorial plates depicting important moments of the Revolution. The storming of the Bastille appears in numerous forms, but almost always contained in a lozenge shape in the centre of the plate. The oath of loyalty to the Revolution by the clergy is depicted with and without additional slogans. There are rural scenes where the peasant farmer is carrying the symbols of the nobility and clergy while he works with his spade, saying, 'I'm tired of carrying them.' At a time of revolutionary turmoil, with a collapse of political structures and fragmentation of political groupings, potters were producing pictorial designs that could not escape expressing one kind of politics or another. During periods of political tension, 'no politics' equates to 'status quo', usually interpreted as opposition to the revolutionary spirit. There is always more thought going into the design of an image on a ceramic surface than the simple acquiescence of the artisan peasant. It is reasonable to assume that at least some of the revolutionary faience is an expression of genuine political opinion and, on occasion, resistance or protest.

Daumier: 'Celebrities of the Juste Milieu'

Daumier was a ferocious satirist. His targets included political institutions, politicians themselves and public officials. He also targeted the art world, notably the salon, and public attitudes to art. Born at the beginning of the nineteenth century, Daumier's working life spanned a tumultuous period of France's political history. He was a committed republican, mostly working in the context of a constitutional monarchy, and was a fierce critic of the king and his cronies.

Coming from a poor, if well-educated family, Daumier did not receive any formal training as an artist. He worked in an art bookshop, attended life classes and did an apprenticeship in lithography. He submitted his first drawing for publication at the age of fourteen and worked throughout his life as a caricaturist, much of the time for *Le Charivari*, the satirical journals of Charles Philipon. Daumier's satire arises from his own political affiliations, his somewhat impoverished position within the social and political context in which he lived, and from his opposition to the dominant concerns of the Paris art world in which he worked and was obliged to compete for recognition.

Daumier's use of clay was central to his working method and creative process. If drawing is central to painting, lithography and sculpture, then for Daumier, sculpting or, more accurately, modelling clay figures, was even more central. His drawings for the lithographs and paintings were based on the figures he modelled in clay. Marble sculpture, based on classical casts, was the propaganda art of choice for lionizing the heroes of the political classes, and it represented everything Daumier loathed. Lampooning the pomposity of those same heroes, their lackeys and henchmen, by modelling a cartoon likeness in clay, was an act of outrageous impudence.

Charles Philipon, proprietor editor of *Le Charivari*, the satirical journal for which Daumier worked, commissioned him in the 1830s to make *The Celebrities of the Juste Milieu.* They represented the politicians and officials who were members of Louis Philippe's government, those who represented the 'middle of the road'. King Louis Philippe gave a speech in 1831 in which he announced his aim of creating a society that would avoid the polarized political extremes that he characterized as 'anarchy', by which he meant popular power, and 'despotism', the overwhelming power of the monarch and nobility. This speech and the phrase, 'middle of the road', were the inspiration for the busts.[18]

They are exaggerated, caricatured portrait heads of the men they represent, roughly modelled in unfired clay and coloured with oil paint. Félix Barthe was a minister of education who had opposed the monarchy but relented in the face of a constitutional version that promised him power and favours. Daumier's interest in phrenology – the relationship between the characteristics of a person and the shape of their skull – is evident in the way he modelled the heads. Barthe has a noticeably reduced forehead and puffed out chest, indicating that he was thought vain and untrustworthy. Humour and the grotesque mix with pathos in these works, which look oddly human, in spite of the caricatured approach.

2.11 Opposite: *Celebrities of the Juste Milieu: Charles Philipon*, 1832, Honoré Daumier, Roger Viollet/Topfoto

[18] Edouard Papet, *Daumier: Sculpture and Lithography, Return Journeys*, Royal Academy of Arts, London, 2014, 212, ref 1.

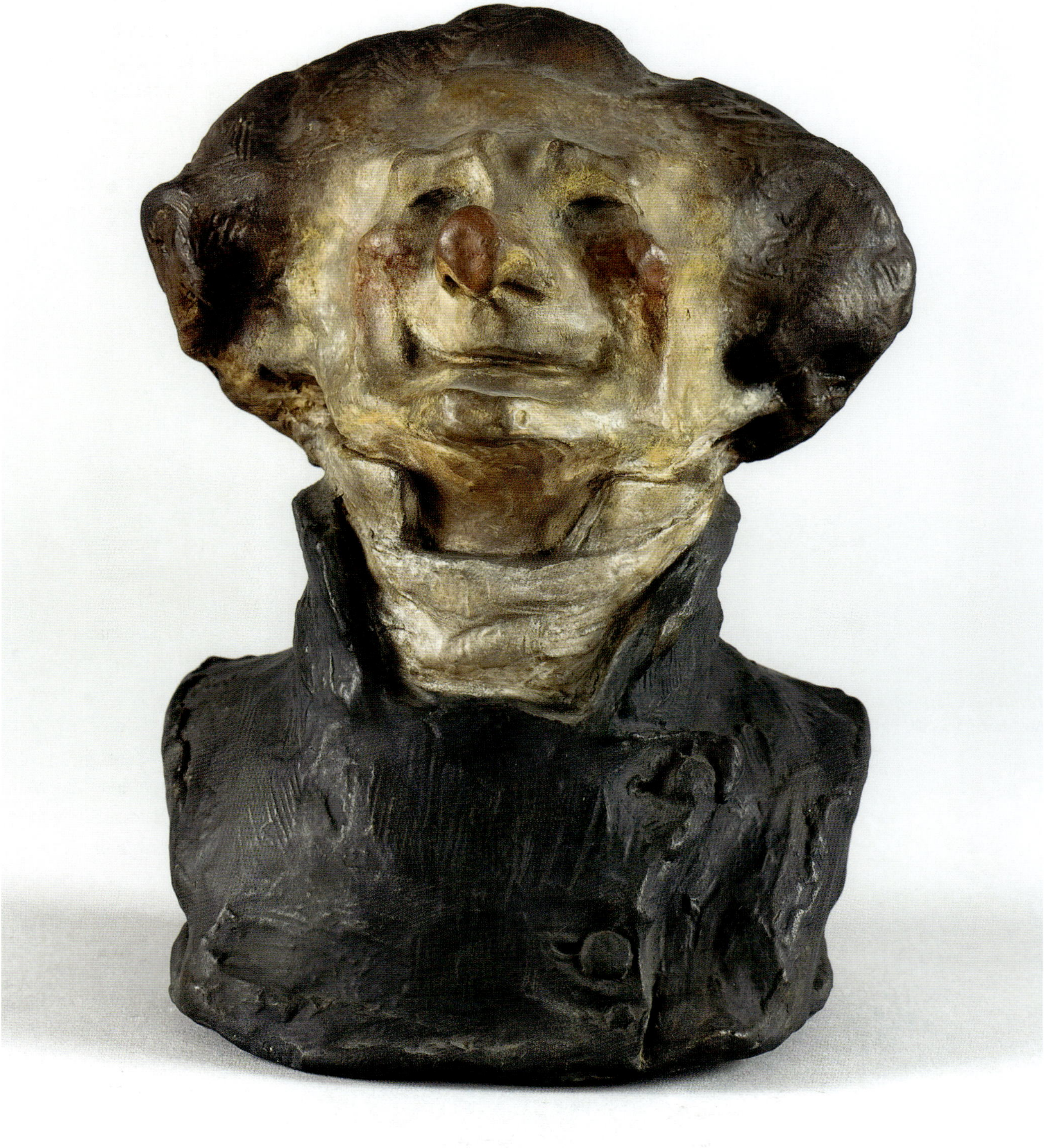

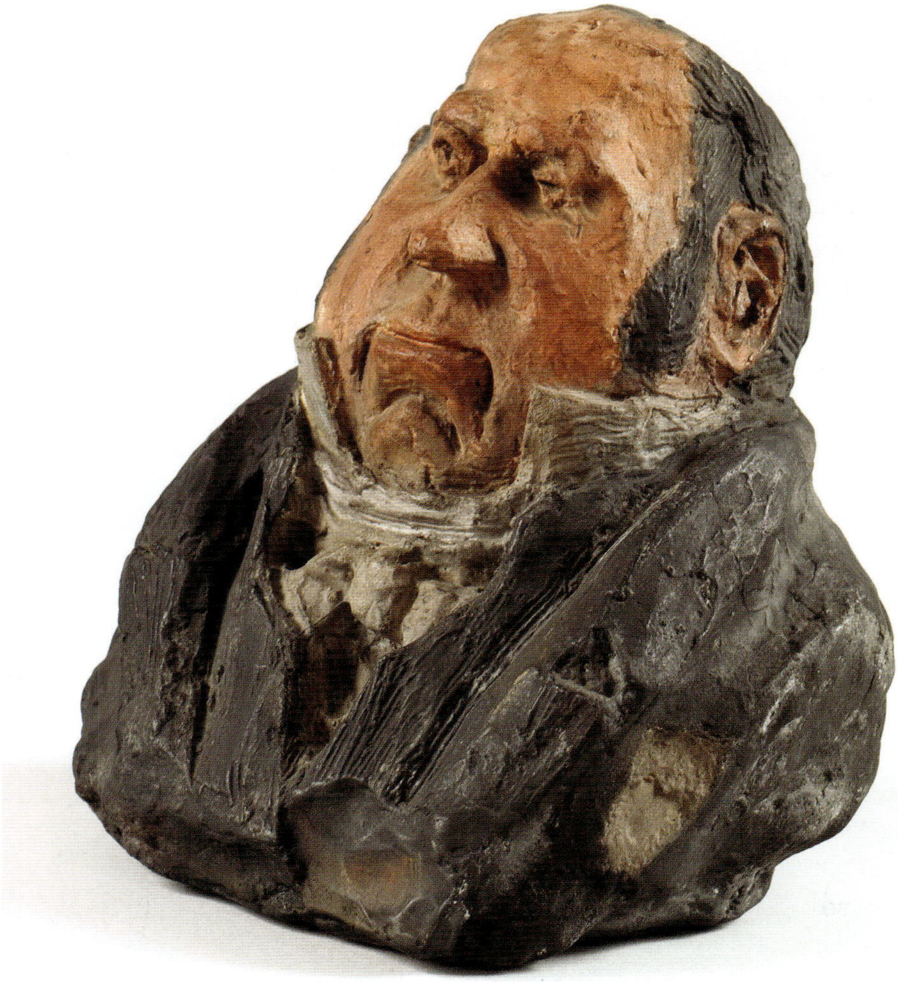

2.12 *Celebrities of the Juste Milieu: Félix Barthe*, 1832, Honoré Daumier, Roger Viollet/Topfoto

Though primarily intended to be studio maquettes, *The Celebrities of the Juste Milieu* were exhibited in the window of Philipon's print shop in Paris for a short time, much to the amusement of passers-by. Both Daumier and Philipon were arrested for breaches of censorship laws and imprisoned, Philipon on numerous occasions. Daumier's political sensibilities and concerns also led him to sculpt the *Fugitifs* (Fugitives) in the 1850s. These are bas-reliefs that focus on the sculpted form of the fugitives themselves and their relationship to each other, rather than to any wider visual context. They are profoundly human works that protest the suffering of the victims of political repression rather than exposing the viciousness of the perpetrators. Here too, however, he references classical antiquity and seeks to sear the conscience of the Parisian bourgeois audiences and art world by using the 'divine art', the one regarded as correct for the monarch and ruling class, to express the desperation of displaced and persecuted people.

Anti-slavery ware

A porcelain medallion depicting an enslaved black man, kneeling and shackled, is surrounded by the words, 'Am I not a man and a brother?' (1987, British Museum, 1.683). It was a rhetorical question, a statement, by the Society for the Abolition of the Slave Trade, who proposed that black men and women were human and therefore equal to white people. It represented the beginnings of the movement against slavery in Britain. Among Britain's white population, in the late eighteenth century, it was nothing short of a revolutionary concept. Issued by Josiah Wedgwood in 1787, the anti-slavery medallion, based on the seal designed by William Hackwood for the anti-slavery movement, was incorporated into a wide range of household items common to the wealthier classes, including brooches, hairpins, snuff boxes, tea caddies and tableware, for use and display. It became a fashion item, part of the ephemera of popular culture, an example of ceramic everyday objects as a form of mass communication.

Clare Midgley observes that women were particularly active in the anti-slavery movement for a number of reasons. According to the prevailing ideology of 'separate spheres', women presided over the household and private, family space, and men over the affairs of nation, the 'public', political sphere. As such, it was considered right that men organized through parliament and women, who did not have the vote at this time, could influence the domestic sphere.[19] Women who chose to support the anti-slavery movement wore the brooches and hair ornaments as a way of declaring, publicly, their allegiance with the movement. They also became keen supporters and were hugely instrumental in the success of the sugar and rum boycott. They decided on the household purchases and were therefore in a position to reject the use of slave-produced sugar in tea, in particular. Tea was still an expensive drink and associated with the wealthy classes, so although not a mass boycott, it was significant precisely because it was adopted by the ruling and influential classes.

Ceramic teaware supporting the boycott was produced to declare allegiance to the anti-slavery movement and to encourage abstinence from sugar produced by slaves. Simultaneously, there were those ready to support in a way that benefited their own interests. Ceramics companies produced the goods and made money while the East India Company promoted their own sugar as morally superior to the West Indies product, cheerfully pocketing the proceeds of what was, for them, a highly advantageous boycott. There were fairs in America dedicated entirely to the sale of anti-slavery ware in support of the abolition movement. For some it was a thriving business as well as a political cause. Though the aim was entirely laudable there was no suggestion that the conditions of East India Company workers improved in any way. While growing public support for the movement, aided by the visible fashionable apparel, was probably crucial to the ultimate success of its aims, its associated commercial concerns may have been rather more cynical at times.

[19] Clare Midgley, *Women Against Slavery: The British Campaigns 1780–1870*, Taylor & Francis, 1995, 37, 91–101.

A sugar bowl uses the image of the enslaved man featured on the medallion on one side, while the text on the other side extols the virtues of East Indies sugar. The message on the bowl reads: 'East India Sugar not made by Slaves. By Six Families using East India, instead of West India Sugar, one Slave less is required.' It is far sweeter than the version in William Fox's 1791 pamphlet[20] from which it was adapted. Fox's pamphlet states: 'A family that uses 5 lb. of sugar per week ... will, by abstaining from the consumption 21 months, prevent the slavery or murder of one fellow creature.' He goes on to provide the much harder-hitting analogy, 'that in every pound of sugar used ... we may be considered as consuming two ounces of human flesh'.

While ceramics bore the message of protest, print, notably by the Cruikshanks, became the purveyor of satire and was an important counterpoint to any inflated notions of moral superiority among the abolitionists. John Oldfield argues that although the satirists attacked the anti-slavery movement and, in particular, the rum and sugar boycotts, their critical attention and the satiric wit of their widely published cartoons helped to popularize the movement and, most importantly, expand the debate beyond the drawing rooms of the ruling classes, prompting a far wider demographic to engage politically: 'They helped to popularise abolition and give it a political voice. They helped to familarise the public with scenes of the most appalling cruelty. And, finally, they helped to make people think about the slave trade, its meaning, its relevance, and its significance, even as they smiled and laughed nervously out loud.'[21]

As the movement progressed, the imagery used on pro-abolition ceramics became more diverse. The increasing interest in humanism, as part of the Enlightenment,

[20] Sam Margolin, '"And Freedom to the Slave": Antislavery Ceramics 1787–1865' in *Ceramics in America*, Chipstone Foundation, Milwaukee, 2002, 81–109.

[21] John Oldfield, *Popular Politics and British Anti-slavery: The Mobilisation of Public Opinion against the Slave Trade 1787–1807*, Psychology Press, 1998, 177–179.

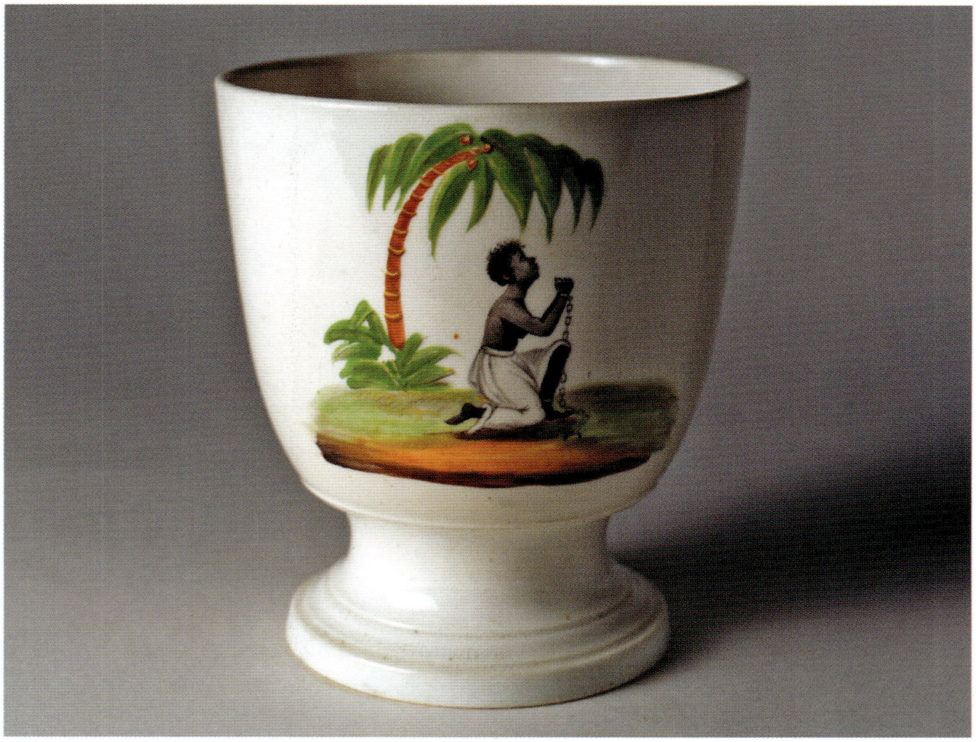

2.13 Creamware Sugar Bowl, 1825, artist unknown, courtesy of The Museum of London

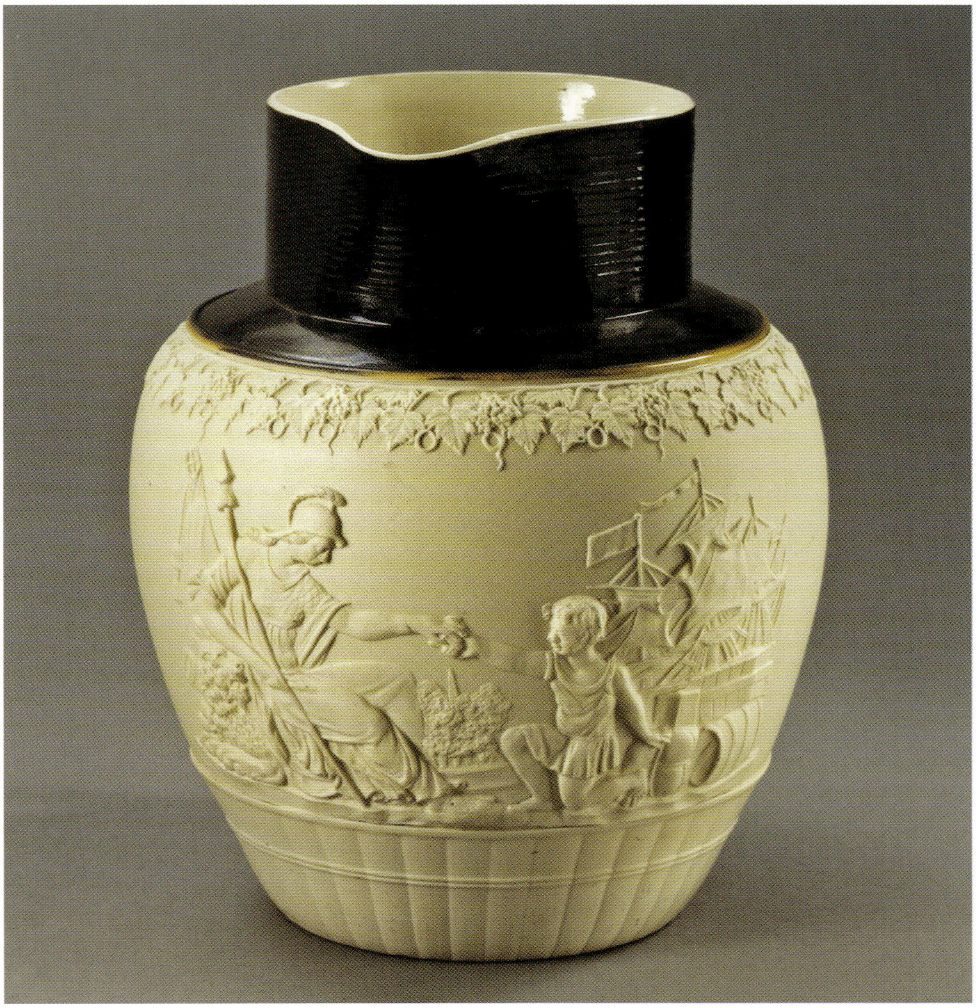

2.14 Creamware Jug, c. 1800, John Turner, Lane End England © Victoria and Albert Museum, London

focused attention on the ill treatment of slaves. Mugs with images of slaves being captured and separated from home and family were produced. Conversely, there were still many parts of Britain where the abolition movement was unpopular, notably the port cities of Liverpool and Bristol, where fortunes were made in the trade. A Staffordshire stoneware beer jug shows a still dominant Britannia protecting a young and supplicant slave. It has been suggested that it may have been commissioned by a prosperous client from one of those cities, unwilling to excite the wrath of his fellow citizens by possessing anything too overtly abolitionist.

The mid-nineteenth century introduced the first of the anti-slavery ceramics that were specifically American. Although trading in slaves had been abolished, slavery itself was still legal and proving stubbornly resistant to abolition in the southern United States. American slave owners, in a famous confrontation with Elija P. Lovejoy, an ordained Presbyterian minister who was also a printer, tried to outlaw public speaking, writing and campaigning by abolitionists on the grounds that it was a disruptive social influence and threatened the social order. Lovejoy objected and

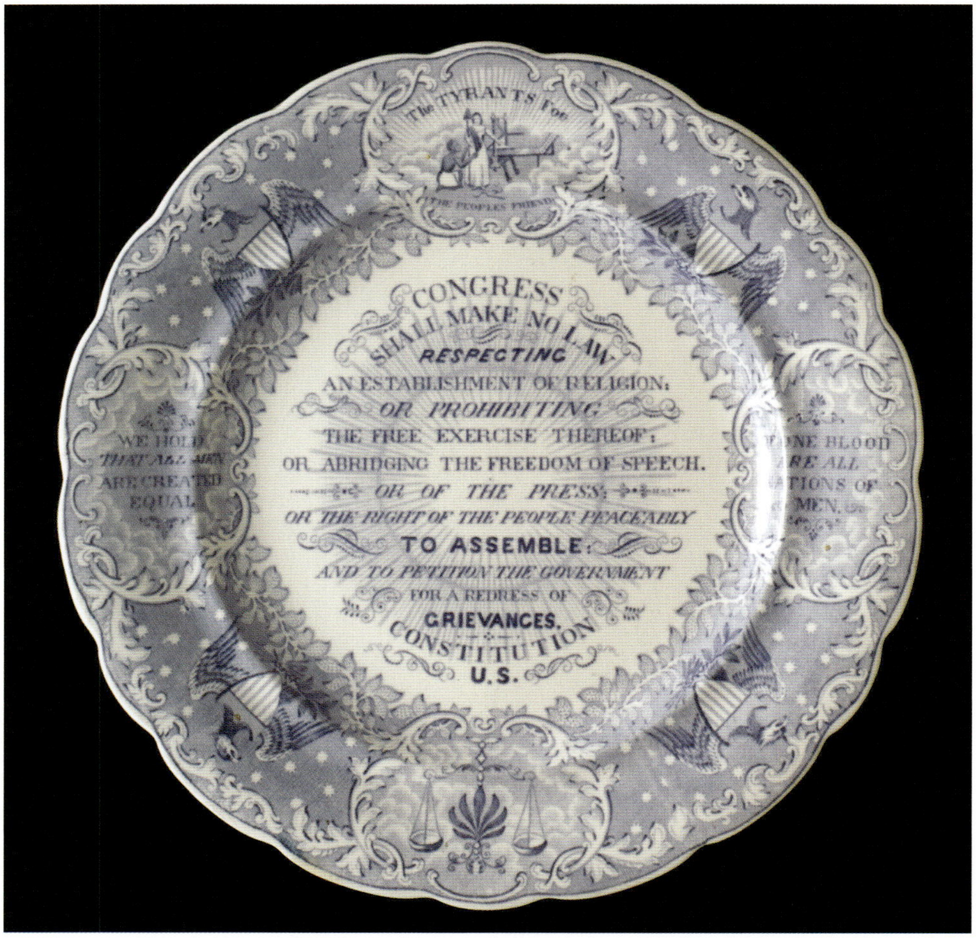

2.15 Plate, 'The Tyrant's Foe, The People's Friend', c. 1840, Staffordshire, England, Courtesy of LACMA

published a tract declaring his allegiance to the Fifth Amendment and the rights of the anti-slavery movement to campaign as they wished. He had his press destroyed four times and was eventually shot – a martyr for the cause.[22] Staffordshire potters produced a plate commemorating this event and Lovejoy's bravery in defending both abolition and free speech in 1837 and a second version in 1840.

The last word on anti-slavery ceramics must surely go to David Drake, born into slavery in America in 1801. He was a master potter and known to have worked in the potteries of Edgefield District, South Carolina, where he made an estimated forty thousand pots during his long career. The Edgefield potteries were run by enslaved workers, producing utilitarian stoneware to supply the plantations. Drake adopted his surname after he was freed, possibly in recognition of one of his first owner-employers, Harvey Drake, who taught him to read and write. Plantation owners and officials of South Carolina took a dim view of literacy among their enslaved population, fearing 'civil unrest' would result, and in 1834 criminalized it, imposing harsh penalties on offenders. Drake's simple act of signing and dating his work was a colossal act of defiance. He signed his pots in a large, cursive, practised and fluent hand. He wrote poems, two-line rhyming couplets, variously

[22] Margolin, 2002.

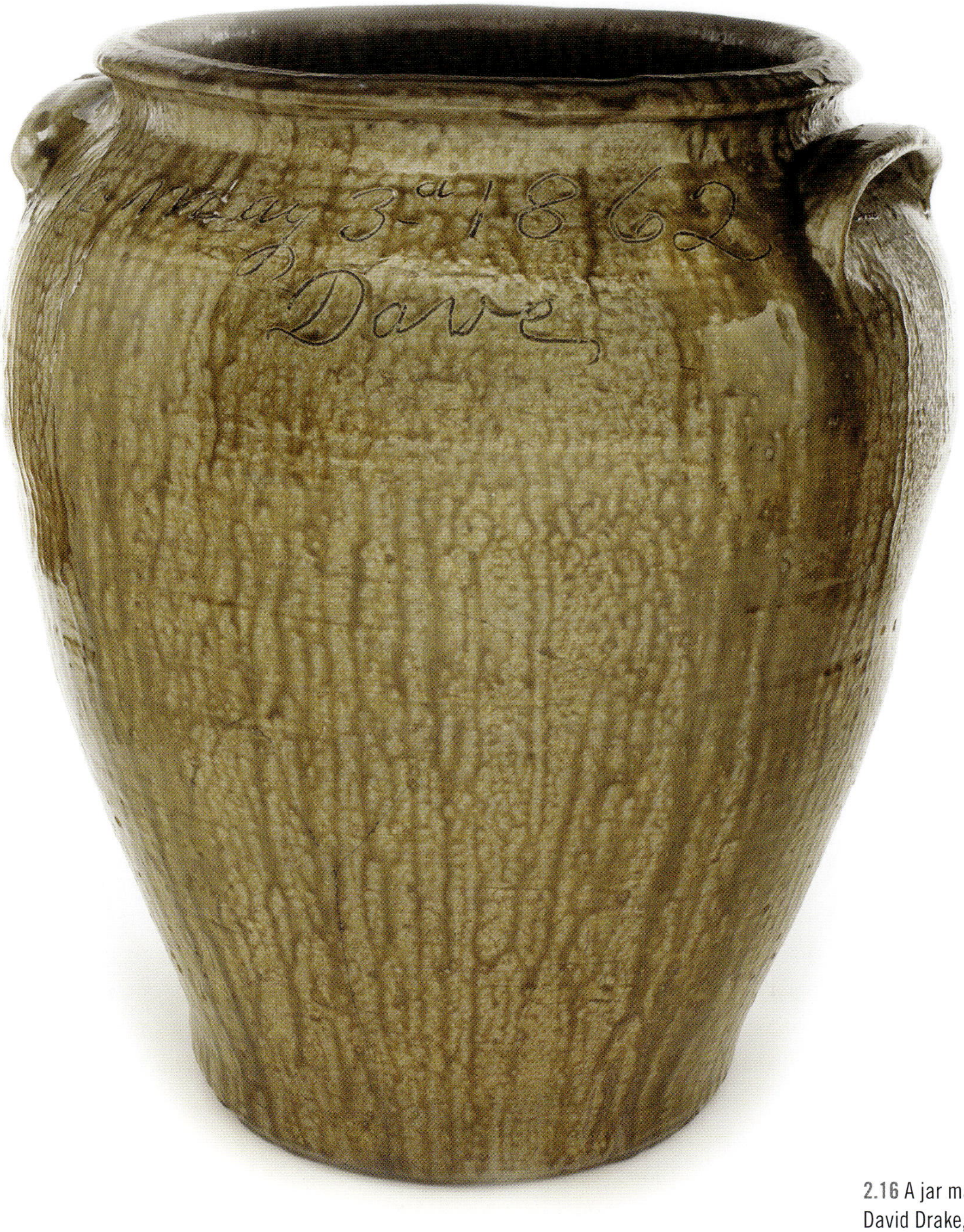

2.16 A jar made by 'Dave', 1862, David Drake, alkaline-glazed stoneware poem jar, 1862, David Drake, © Smithsonian Institution

cryptic, comic, romantic, satiric or religious. This went well beyond protest: it was seditious. He was displaying not just simple, functional literacy but the fact that enslaved workers had souls and that he could do much more than just write his name. He could think and reason independently. His forty or so surviving epigraphic stoneware jars are a monument to his courage and his commitment to justice and liberty as well as being a major contribution to American ceramics. Drake seems to have specialized in making large, stoneware jars and bottles, holding up to forty gallons.[23] They are graceful, well thrown, with good stout handles. 'Lm says this handle will crack', he wrote on one of them. One suspects he knew 'Lm' was wrong; it is still in perfect condition.

Soviet porcelain

Porcelain has always been a propaganda material. The 'white gold', as it was called, is still among China's most successful exports, and certainly its longest lasting ambassador. After decades of secret experimentation, plotting and conspiracy, a successful product was developed in Europe which came to represent the wealth, status, cultural and scientific superiority of nations. Frequently deployed in the service of diplomacy, it embodied the importance of the nation state on the international scene. Gifts of porcelain were used to honour the brave, pacify the predatory and paranoid, confer status on the powerful, inflate the egos of the already grandiose and flatter the affectations of the pompous.

When the Bolshevik party took over the reins of power after the October Revolution, 1917, their position was precarious. There was an urgent need to convince the Russian people to support and accept the new government. To this end Lenin called for a propaganda effort so ambitious and pervasive it would reach every town, large and small, and every village, no matter how distant. Monuments and memorials would be installed so that, in his words, 'what had happened might be fired into the people's imagination, and leave the deepest possible furrow in the popular memory'.[24] Trotsky toured the provinces in propaganda trains, decorated with revolutionary messages and decked out with classrooms, libraries, bookshops and a few short films on health care and farming methods. Engaging the proletariat, particularly the illiterate masses of the rural peasantry and winning their support, was vital to the survival of the new government and the involvement of artists was central to the new propaganda effort: it was the visual and material component of the new politics. The Imperial Porcelain Factory that had produced exquisitely painted work extolling royalty, aristocracy, the generals and the Orthodox Church, became the Soviet Porcelain Factory and lionized the foot soldiers, workers and government officials and, above all, the virtues of communism. The result, in the short term at least, was an extraordinarily dynamic, original and vibrant chapter in the long history of art and the political message.

[23] Leonard Todd, *Carolina Clay: The Life and Legend of the Slave Potter, Dave*, Norton, 2008, 115–130.

[24] Nina Lobanov-Rostovsky, *Revolutionary Ceramics: Soviet Porcelain 1917–1927*, New York: Rizzoli, 1990, 12.

Natalya Danko's chess set, *The Reds and the Whites* (1922–1932, Smithsonian Design Museum, New York), is arguably one of the best-known artefacts of Soviet Russia. Danko's figures, which reproduced the porcelain figurine as a revolutionary, were often awarded to families of fallen soldiers in honour of their service.[25] She made images of factory women speechifying, workers labouring for the greater cause – a woman sewing a banner is a good example – sailors and partisans, heroic workers singing and brandishing their rifles.[26] Danko, however, made little attempt to subvert either gender or race relations in the context of the new Russia, nor did she significantly rethink her imagery of class. Her revolutionary, politicized, urban workers – appropriately apparelled – are proud, if stereotypical, figures, but gypsy women are always beggars and the rural poor are crouching, supplicant and pitiable. Perhaps the most pronounced distinction however, is that between the fair-skinned, modern, urban Russians, who appear wholesome, whether workers or intelligentsia – their class affiliation is instantly discernible – and the Central Asians, portrayed as dark-skinned, 'exotic', undisciplined, backward and often violent. Figurines deal in stereotypes. They are cartoon characters. That is the genre, so the maker to some extent will always be working within that, but Danko does not appear to interrogate these stereotypes. The work of both Danko sisters, Natalya and Elena, suggest that they had an unassailable sense of the Uzbek woman as their 'other', a figure from whom clear separation must be maintained. Two outstanding examples are: *The Awakening East*,[27] sometimes called *Turkic Girl Reading*, by Elena Danko, and *The Fountain of Bakhchiserai*, by Natalya Danko.

The Awakening East shows a veiled Uzbek woman being enlightened by a Russian newspaper while, bizarrely, baring her breasts in classic exotic, erotic fantasy for the delectation of the Russian male master-audience exemplified by Zinoviev, whose silhouette fills the centre of the newspaper. She fingers her veil thoughtfully, as though about to strip if off, leaving her semi-naked. Not something White Russian women were encouraged to do, or not in public, anyway. While the question of whether or not it is legitimate to protest bare-breasted is the subject of many a heated argument for twenty-first century feminists, the Danko sisters appear unequivocal in their division of who does what. Proper Russian revolutionary (modern) women are modestly buttoned up; the naked or partially-revealed breast and sparkly clothing is reserved for the backward Uzbeks, the counter revolutionary bourgeois whore and the gypsy beggar. If Alexandra Kollontai's writing is anything to go by, attitudes to free love for women in Soviet Russia were as damning then as they are now. Women's emancipation was chiefly aimed at getting work hours out of them to improve the economy, not at achieving sexual equality.

Natalya Danko's *The Fountain of Bakhchiserai* is a group of three figurines representing a scene from Pushkin's poem of the same name. The poem tells the story of Maria, a virtuous Polish girl, who was abducted by the evil Khan Girei, and who was then stabbed by the violently jealous Zerema (Figure 2.17), a Georgian woman who was a rival for Girei's affections. This popular tale, according to Karen

[25] Lobanov-Rostovsky, 24.

[26] Lobanov-Rostovsky, 92–99.

[27] Lobanov-Rostovsky, 100.

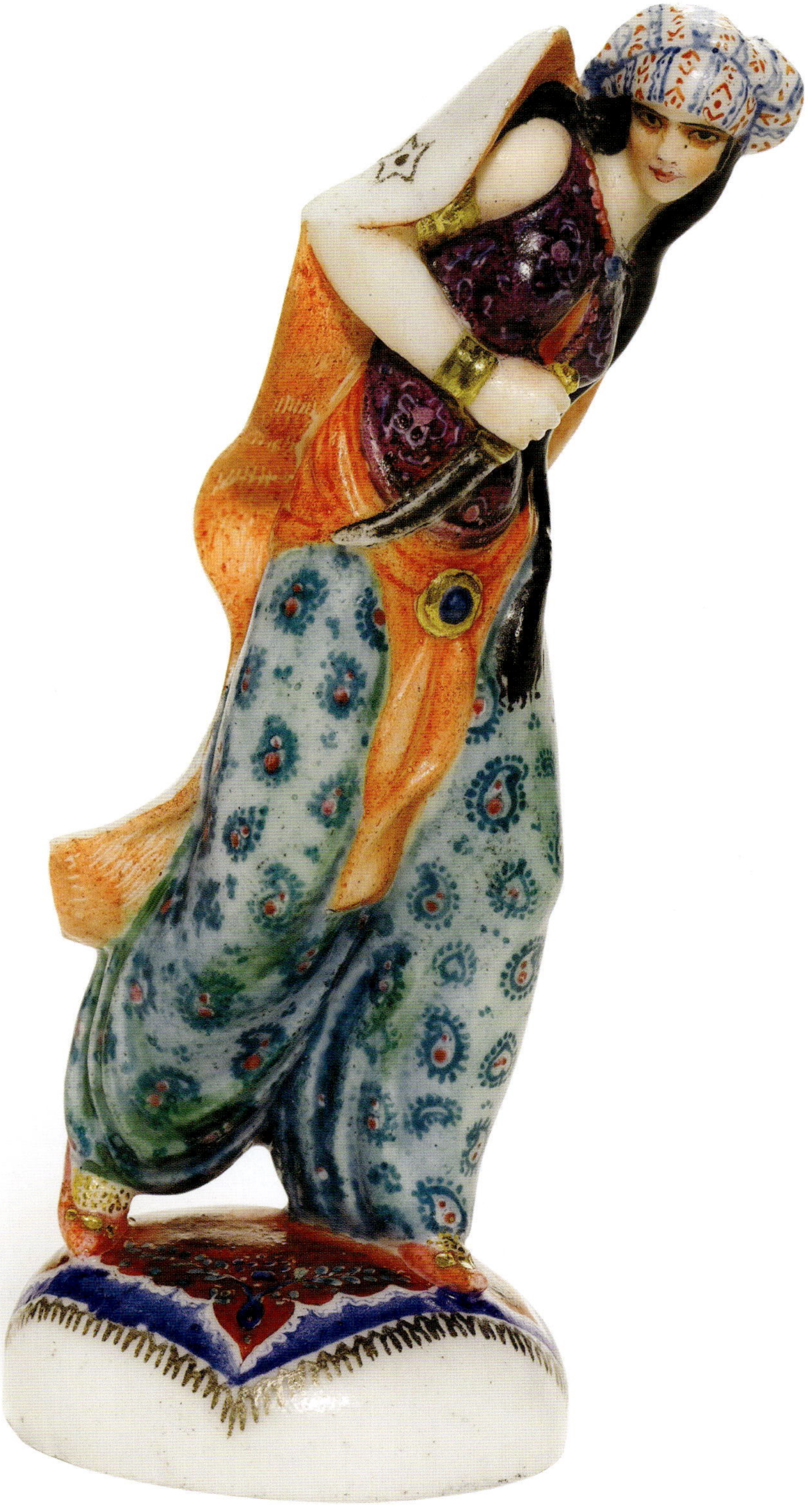

2.17 Zerema from *The Fountain of Bakhchiserai*, c. 1933 after 1923 design, Natalya Danko, Sotherby's

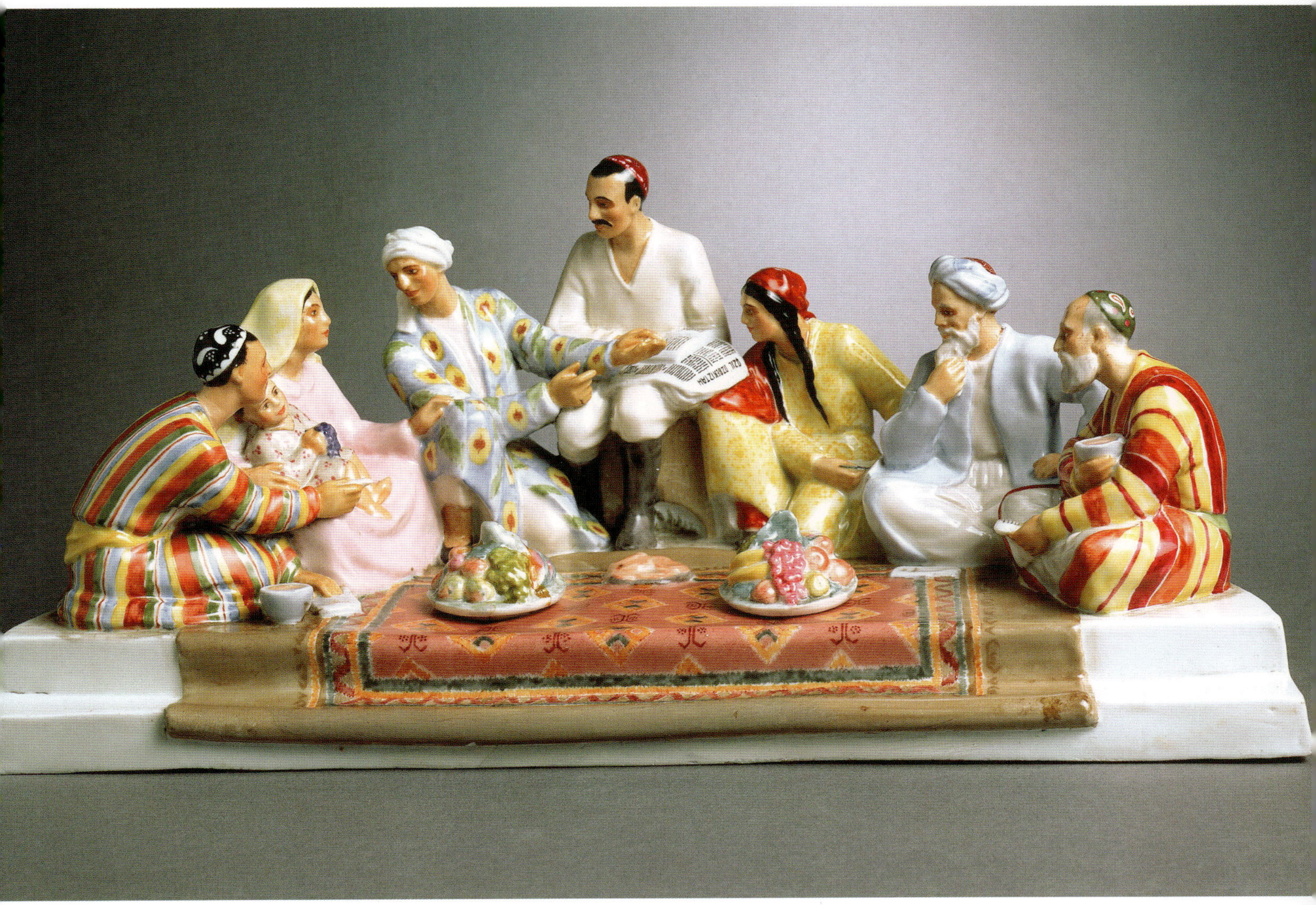

2.18 *Uzbeks Discussing the Stalin Constitution*, 1936, Natalya Danko. John Parnell © 2014. Cooper-Hewitt, National Design Museum, Smithsonian Institution/Art Resource, NY/Scala, Florence

Kettering, was widely believed to be true at the time.[28] The story Danko has chosen to depict is an exceptionally lurid example of the narrative of divide and rule, hardly consistent, one would think, with the aims of an egalitarian revolution. In one version, a blonde, weeping Maria, collapsed and close to death, is whispering her rosary for the last time as her life ebbs away and she gazes up to heaven. Opposite her is the dark, statuesque, menacing Zerema, clasping her dagger as her wild black hair streams about her. Between them stands Girei, too late to pacify the warring women with his manly intervention. It is difficult to imagine a scene that could speak less convincingly of the emancipation of women, which the Soviet state was supposed to have fostered, or that could suggest more vehemently either the 'natural' order of male rule or the wild unruly savagery of the Eastern 'other'. Zerema is eternally divided from her blonde sister by the racial and sexual divisions fostered by the Soviet state.

[28] Karen Kettering, 'Domesticating the Uzbeks: Central Asians in Soviet Decorative Art of the Twenties and Thirties', in *Colonialism and the Object: Empire, Material Culture and the Museum*, Tim Barringer and Tom Flynn (eds), Routledge, 1998, 95–110.

The Danko sisters were not exceptional among artists at the time. Their work, and the imagery it presents, is indicative of the values of the Soviet Revolution. Many Uzbeks were involved in the Revolution and supported the aims of the Bolsheviks, but were forbidden to take public office once the Soviet government was established. *Uzbeks Discussing the Stalin Constitution* (1936), an inkwell, also by Danko, shows an Uzbek family debating politics over a Russian newspaper. The two in the middle are the pro-Soviet comrades, while the rest of the family is resistant to 'Russification'. The revolutionary woman has her flowing hair only slightly covered; the only other woman in the piece has her hair fully covered. The comrades are in recognizably partisan clothing and are literate in Russian. There is a simple racialized political binary being played out within the body politic of the Muslim family: the modern Russian West 'civilizes' the backward Uzbek East. Even so, the differences alluded to in the family may well have been true at least among some Muslim families. There have always been Muslim women who have rebelled against their social and religious conventions and traditions, just as many Russian women did and still do. The confusion of sexual, racial and religious politics evident in all three of these works is as alive now, a hundred years later, as it was then.

American twentieth century

Waylande Gregory (1905–1971)

Democracy in Action (1941) is a gigantic mural, eighty-one feet long, made of low relief terracotta tiles, depicting the Metropolitan Police Department and District of Columbia Fire Department, Washington DC. It shows both departments in action, doing their civic duty, except in the central panel. This panel shows two police in violent confrontation with two black American men or, put more simply, beating them up. The artist, Waylande Gregory, one of the leading ceramicists in the United States in the early to mid-twentieth century, was commissioned to produce the work under the Welfare Art Programme, introduced to support artists during the Depression years. Sited on the Police Department Headquarters building, it scores as direct a hit as a critical, political artwork ever could. It caused uproar when it was first installed and the city's mayor supported the Police Department's demands to remove it. Eleanor Roosevelt intervened in support of the mural and it is there to this day. It is not immediately accessible to the public but it is available to view. Gregory was known for producing monumental ceramic sculptures, mainly figures, and was strongly influenced by art deco. There is no evidence of other politically motivated works by him, but some of his earlier sculptures, *Factory Farm Worker* (1939), one of a series celebrating American labour, for example – hint at socialist-inspired social realism.

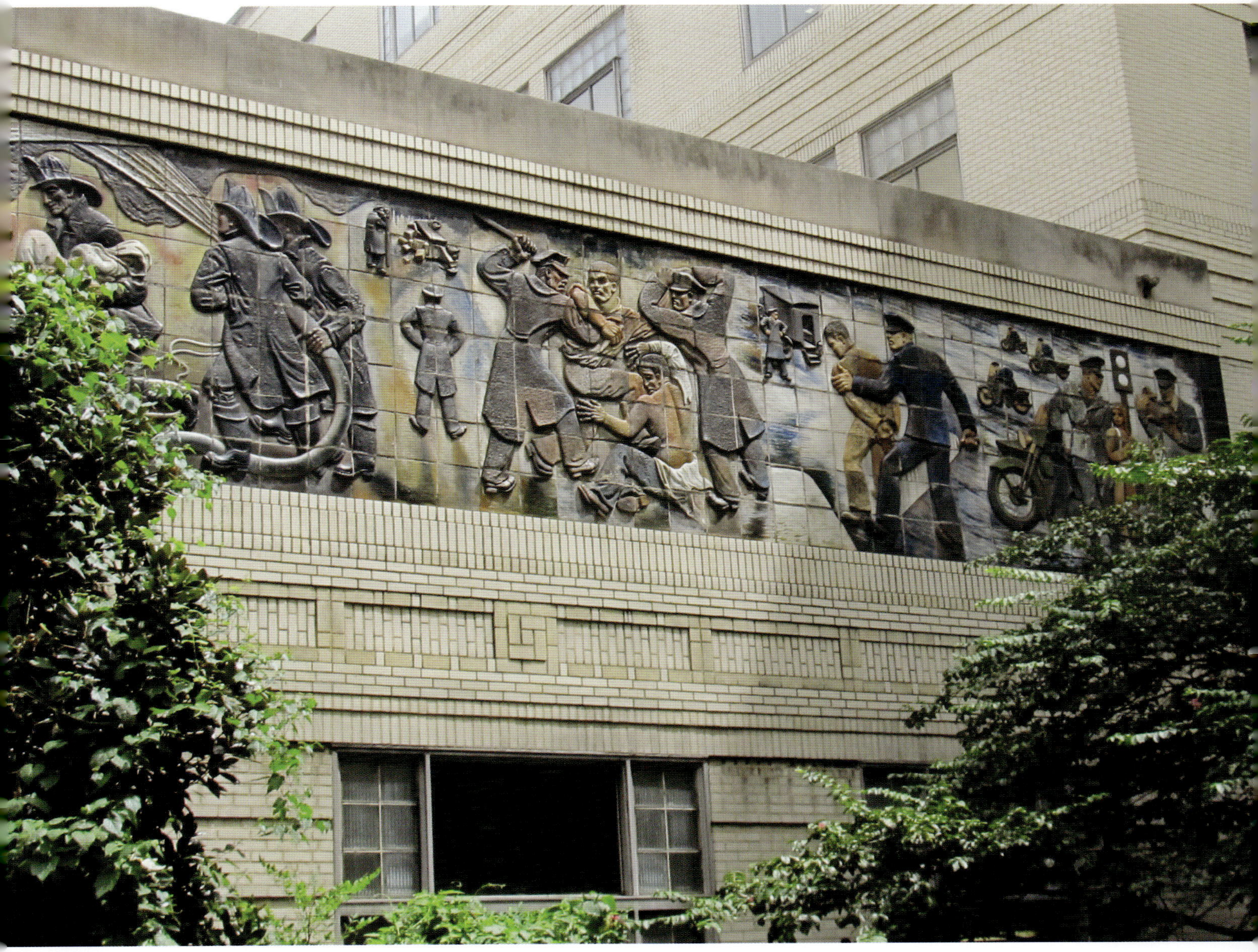

2.19 *Democracy in Action*, Waylande Gregory, 1941, DC's police and fire department HQ, photographer: Kent C. Boese

Viktor Schreckengost (1906–2008)

Viktor Schreckengost was a small-town American who grew up in a pottery town and 'had to get away'. In 1929 he went to Vienna to study at the *Kunstgewerbeschule* where he met and worked extensively with Michael Powolny, who became a major influence. Schreckengost was an immensely versatile artist. He designed tableware for mass production, made monumental sculpture for public places and table-top figures and animals for domestic spaces. He produced a vast collection of drawings and watercolours, devised costume and stage design for theatre and designs for ceramic decals and textiles.

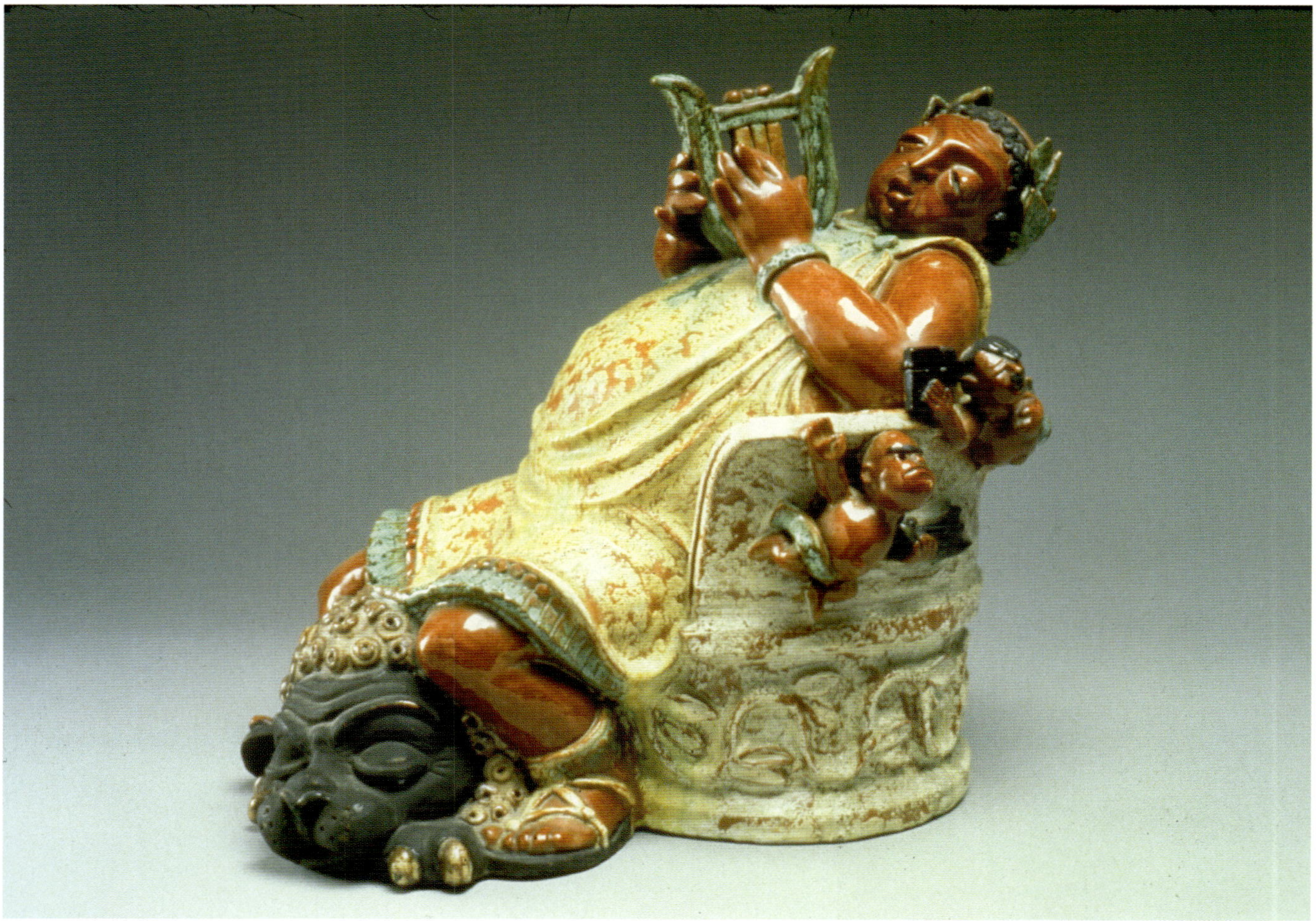

2.20 *The Dictator*, 1939, Viktor Schreckengost, courtesy of the American Craft Council

He designed and produced the famous Jazz bowl, commissioned by Eleanor Roosevelt from the Guy Cowan pottery and, a jazz lover himself and a frequenter of jazz clubs, he produced a large number of black American figurines, based on jazz songs. *Shadrach Mesach and Abed-nego* (1939, Metropolitan Museum, New York), for example, was based on a Louis Armstrong song. His figures, whether they represent black people or white, are cartoon-like. They are all stereotypical, with the result that the black figures read as racist, resembling the minstrel look. That said, he was one of few white artists in the twentieth century to represent black American culture or to represent black people – which he often did in mythological settings – with any degree of serious interest. He certainly inhabited a racially mixed environment and had a clear understanding of the meaning and impact of oppression, as some of the later works show.

In 1937 he returned to Europe, and in Berlin witnessed the meeting of Mussolini and Hitler. He saw them ride together in a motorcade down a main street and was 'roughed up', by the crowd because he did not do the Nazi salute. On his return, his work became more political. *The Dictator* (1939) is a highly satirical work depicting the Emperor Nero with the four dictators, Hitler, Stalin, Mussolini and Hirohito with swastika, hammer and sickle, fasces and rising sun, respectively,

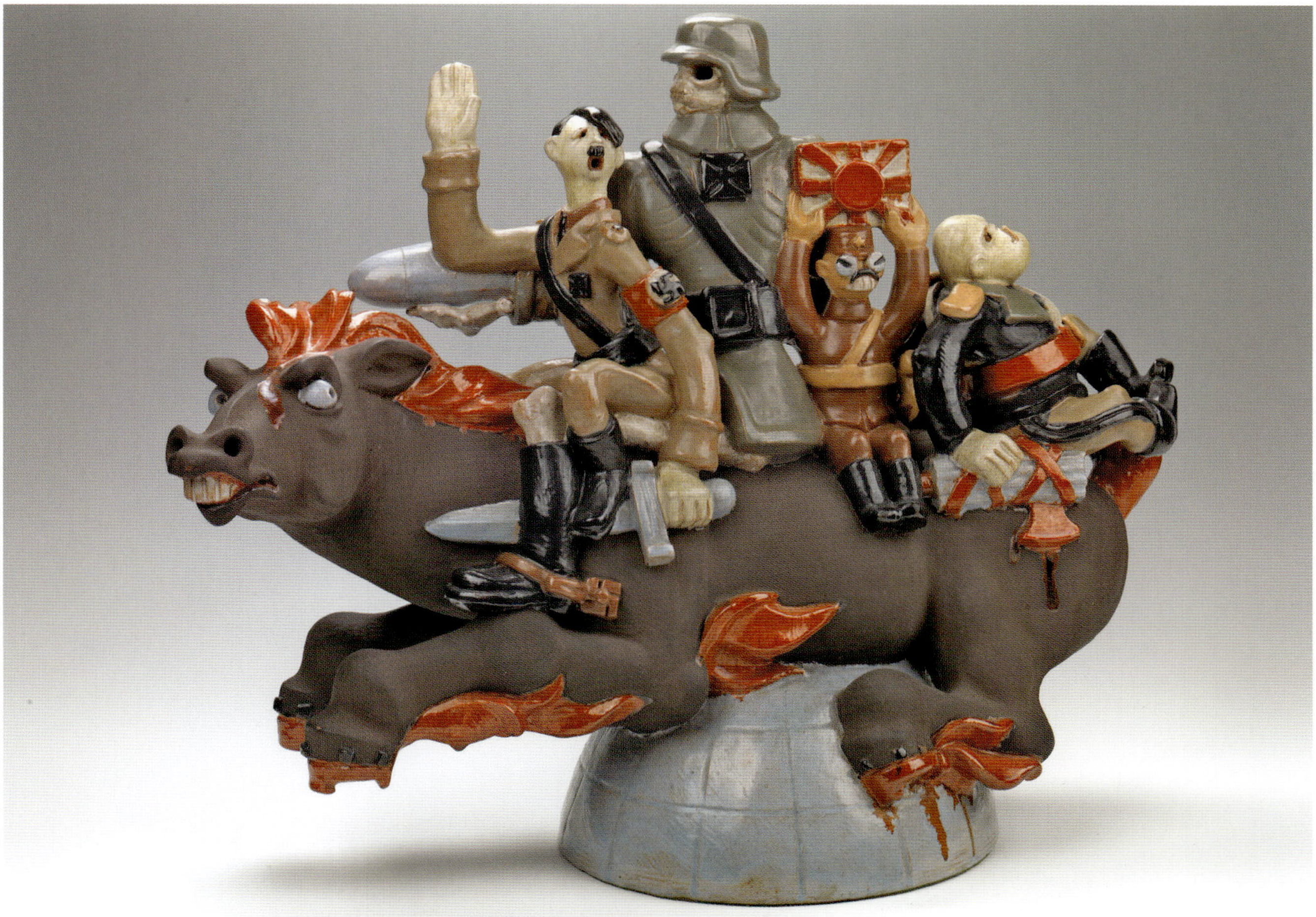

2.21 *Apocalypse '42*, 1942, Viktor Schreckengost, gift of the artist © 2014. Photo: Smithsonian American Art Museum/Art Resource/Scala, Florence

climbing up the throne on which Nero reclines. The emperor is playing the harp as fascism rises around him, and the British lion sleeps at his feet. It caused a furore when he showed it at Cleveland Museum of Art: the director, recently honoured by Mussolini, declared that Italian Americans would be offended, and that the subject had nothing to do with art.

Undaunted, Schreckengost went on to make *Apocalypse '42*. Completed in 1942, it shows Hitler astride one of the four horses of the Apocalypse. Behind him is Death in a German uniform; Mussolini is at the back and Hirohito in the middle. Red glaze runs in bloody suggestion over the globe on which the horse is poised. Schreckengost commented on this work: 'Perhaps it is humorous but I really believe it tells a true story.' Again his work caused controversy. Its imagery mixes the Book of Revelations with Christian folklore and global politics articulated through a cartoon aesthetic. According to Christina Corsiglia, the meeting of classical and religious mythology with high and low art, and a hint of the grotesque, is a typically American idiom.[29] It is a classic visual satiric formula and retains its force: the use of metaphor and allegory makes it less time-sensitive than much political art and also brings it to a wider audience.

[29] Christina Corsiglia, 'Viktor Schrekengost: Evolution of a Cleveland Ceramist', in *Cleveland as a Center of Regional American Art, Symposium*, Cleveland Artists Foundation, 1993, 91–100.

Conclusion

The brief histories examined here cannot do justice to the full history of the relationship between ceramics and political and popular movements. In Britain, as mass production and industrial processes developed through the nineteenth and twentieth centuries, so the volume of propagandist and campaigning imagery increased. Part two examines the growth of the studio pottery movement where potters returned to the studio or worked in small workshop groups rather than being part of the process of mass production. Political and social comment, therefore, became the work of individuals and part of their artistic identity rather than their being part of large-scale, organized political movements as we saw with the anti-slavery ware and Soviet porcelain. A 'honest pot' will introduce each of the three chapters to act as a foil – or not – to the ceramic practices under discussion. The next chapter looks at the use of satiric imagery and design by studio potters to 'subvert' well known ceramic archetypes and produce social or political comment.

PART TWO

BREAKING OUT: The influence of political and social movements on the studio potter and ceramicist

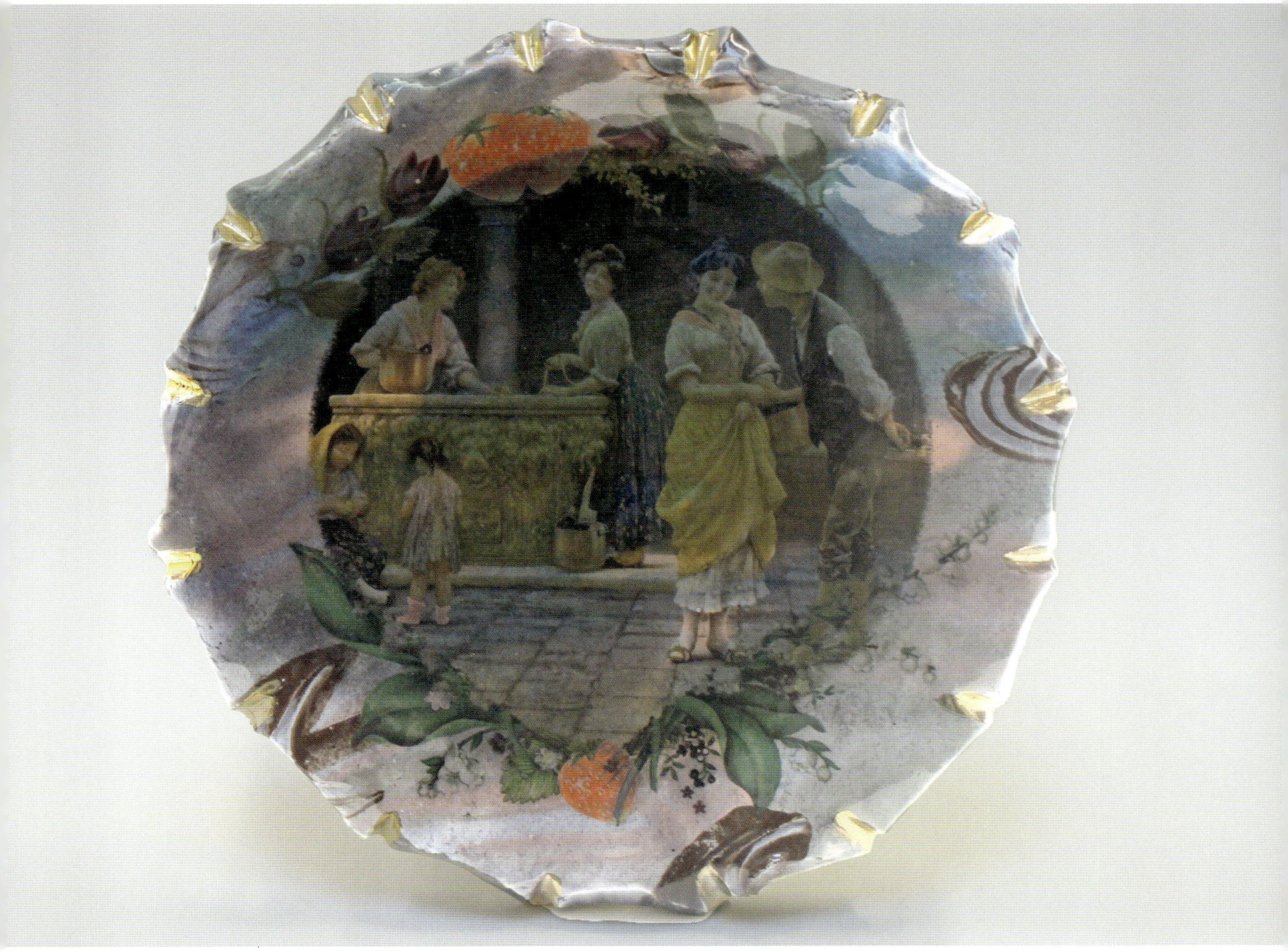

3.1 Previous page: Plate with decals, 1997, Philomena Pretsell, The Ceramic Collection and Archive, Aberystwyth University

3

The Peasants' Revolt: Form and message

The peasants

The 'honest pot' is the totem of the British studio pottery movement. These sturdy brown vessels, redolent of their muddy beginnings, unembellished save perhaps for an incidental honest hand-print, glimpsed through a rough and ready glaze, are the true descendents of the English country pot, or so the story goes. The 'peasant', in terms of this book, is the contemporary studio potter who makes them. Drawn predominantly from the middle class and urban elite, the twentieth-century studio potter regarded the traditional country potters with romanticized reverence, the rural working-class 'other', the very embodiment of what they regarded as the inherent moral virtue and authenticity of the 'simple country or "honest" pot'. The 'peasants' revolt', in Britain, could be said to have arrived with the modernist-influenced studio potters, whose revolt was not against the country potters, but the vile interloper, mass-produced industrial ceramics, with their 'bad forms and banal, debased, pretentious decoration – qualities that are perhaps most conspicuous in "fancy vases", flower-pots and other ornamental pieces'.[1]

Towards the end of the twentieth century, however, the studio pottery movement went into revolt against itself, following the process of the avant-garde set out by Griselda Pollock in her lecture, 'Avant-Garde Gambits 1883–1893'. Pollock proposes a three-part process which she defines as 'reference, deference, difference'.[2] The aspiring artist references a 'grand master', then shows deference to the same, and finally goes in for the kill, except that Pollock, in rather more restrained language, refers to 'the kill' as 'difference'. The 'difference' must displace the grand master but on his own terms, thereby ensuring that the young pretender is the new master of the recognized 'avant-garde' and will set its agenda according to the established pattern. Edmund de Waal's reference and deference was to the Leach school of thought. He then defiantly declared his difference and displaced the originator of the studio pottery movement, ushering in a new phase, which dispensed with the faux authenticity that had dogged the movement for years, allowing makers to concede that what they produced was artefacts – museum pieces – rather than strictly utilitarian pottery. It also liberated those who wanted to continue making tableware. The industrial

1 Bernard Leach, *A Potter's Book*, Faber & Faber, 1940, 3–27.

2 Griselda Pollock, *Avant Garde Gambits, 1883–1893*, Thames & Hudson, 1992, 14.

aesthetic was rehabilitated as was its process. Makers now deploy mass production techniques in tandem with their studio work, reducing unit cost, potentially resulting in a more viable practice overall.

The kitchen: Tableware

One has to wonder how it might be possible to subvert tableware that is going to be used. Would this involve making holes in it so it doesn't work, or is it subversive only when sporting a revolutionary political message? Tableware epitomizes what ceramics is thought to be. Whether industrial mass production or finely produced studio pottery, what instantly springs to mind is kitchen crockery: domestic and associated with women. Industrial tableware involved a division of labour with the forms made by men and the decoration by women. This probably helped to entrench the notion that decoration and ornament were feminine, and that proper, unadorned form was the domain of the male. Bernard Leach's dismissal of 'fancy vases' and 'careful painting' as a debased violation of the true pot, along with the inherent sexism in the language of modernism, persist in fixing a gendered understanding of what tableware and clay pots should look and even feel like. Descriptors such as 'prissy' or 'fussy' quickly attach to discussion of decoration, ornament or even pattern.

The language alone expresses the threat of pernicious incursions into the well-ordered modernist kitchen by purveyors of ornaments and roses. Philomena Pretsell defied the norms of British studio pottery in the late twentieth century when she started raiding open stock industrial transfers and adding them randomly to handmade mugs. These were slab-built confections, not even properly made on the wheel. Worse, they had fancy extruded handles topped off with gold blobs, and decal roses emerging from the sides. Her plates sported ribbons and 'fussy' folded edges, like linen napkins or pastry craft. Even her clay was like pastry, rolled out over paper doilies to imprint the pattern, a practice reserved for night-school amateurs. The finished ware was adorned with transfers – strictly for charlatans – of pretty ladies in gossipy conference, all petticoats and bows, balconies and flowers. It was nothing short of a travesty, a vulgar assault on the propriety, taste and manners of modernism, but her work has made its way into public collections.

Linda Bloomfield's attack on the guardians of design and their rigorous policing of taste was, possibly, even more insidious. She infiltrated the territory of handmade studio domestic tableware, barely detectable at first. She threw her pots on the wheel, roughly and simply, no fuss turning the bases, just straight off the wheel and onto the plank for drying. She mixed her own glazes and pulled her handles in the time-honoured manner. It was a brilliant disguise until she declared, 'I want to be a brand name.'[3] She was publicly cavorting with capitalism. To the studio pottery movement, with its avowedly anti-capitalist, bohemian, alternative roots, this was tantamount to a thought crime. Bloomfield works in London, but makes 'rural pottery' in every

[3] Conversation with the author, 24 September 2011.

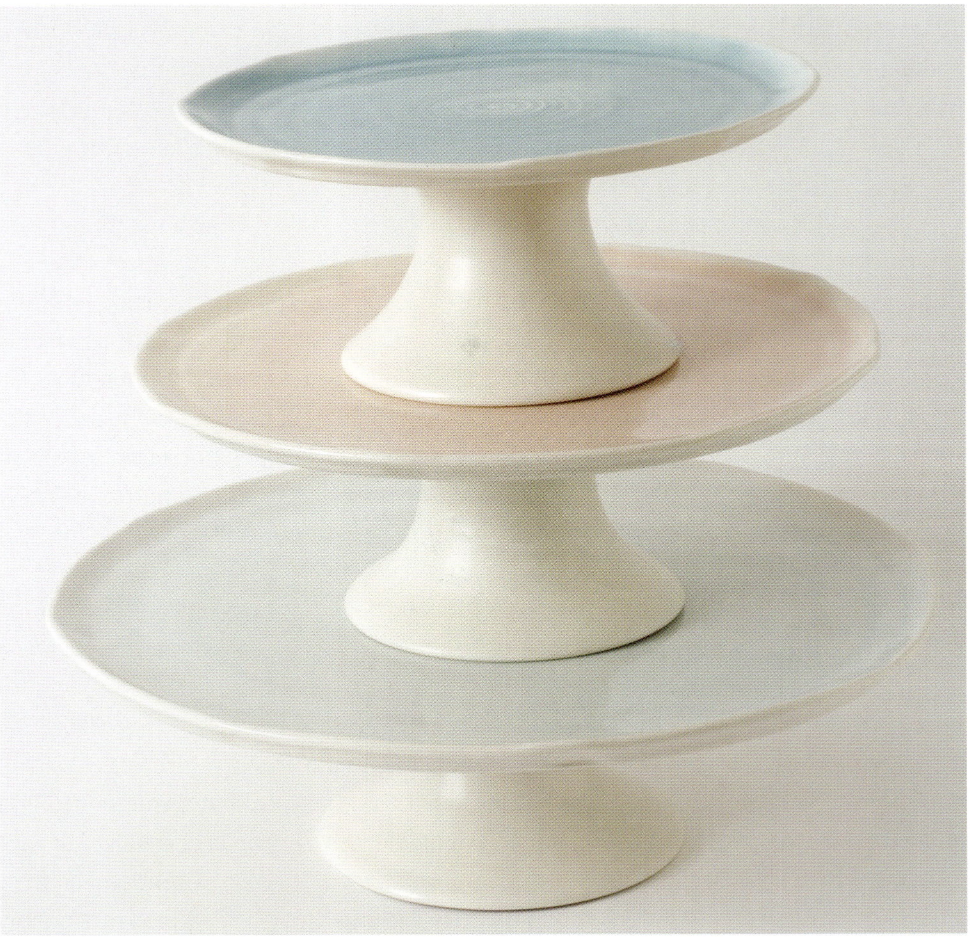

3.2 Cake stand, 2014, Linda Bloomfield, photographer: Henry Bloomfield

sense, except that it is suspiciously smooth, satiny almost. Her tableware is certainly more milkmaid than noble peasant but, happily, this is a milkmaid of dubious moral virtue. Making good, serviceable butch mugs partially redeems her, but she betrays her dangerously 'feminine' intentions by glazing them in pretty, ice-cream colours: shell pink, mint greens, yellows, turquoise and powder blue.

Bloomfield availed herself of Edmund de Waal's notion of 'kitchen porcelain', and set out to make a good business. Pretsell set out to produce a pastiche that parodied studio pottery and simultaneously ridiculed it. Bloomfield's work is a paradox, technically a branch of satire, but there is nothing satirical in her intention. Rather she robustly rejected the established conventions of the movement, particularly those of the muddy brown pot, and rewrote the rule book, introducing the F word, the 'feminine' in this case. She still does not find favour with those who regard themselves as serious ceramics aficionados, but the market is delighted.

It is the great paradox of ceramics that, as a craft, it is perceived as feminine, but traditionally in Britain it has been made by men. Although the studio pottery movement brought in many more women, its design principles were commandeered by modernism, with its overweening concerns to obliterate ornament and decoration, both of which are still understood as feminine – plainly absurd but, nonetheless, the belief persists. Pottery, and particularly studio pottery, is undeniably associated with domesticity, nurturing and hospitality, all of which are also still gendered; yet the act of 'feminizing' ceramics is regarded as an act of sabotage. There is an extraordinary fear of 'the feminine' among makers, particularly among women makers, yielding to internalized sexism. There are more industrially produced ceramics – mostly tableware – adorned with roses than with almost anything else, but pots with roses on are derided and denounced as kitsch or 'fussy', unless, of course, it is ironic, in which case it is permitted, particularly if it is exposing the vice and folly of women. Conversely, ceramics, particularly those which have come to be known as subversive, can be profoundly reactionary when scrutinized through the lens of feminism. That either colour or decoration should be gendered in such polarized terms is ludicrous, but they still are, and in spite of numerous attempts to overturn this, it is proving stubbornly persistent. One only has to glance at the marketing of clothing and toys for children for this to become blisteringly obvious.

From kitchen to living room

In the realms of disobedient women, few are more disgraceful than Rose Wallace's. Strictly speaking, we're moving from the kitchen to the living room now. Wallace deploys well known, domestic ceramic forms, both tableware and the figurine, and has produced a number of works commenting on the British love of alcohol and partying, particularly among young women. These are works for display rather than use. The subversion is therefore not so much in the use or misuse of kitchen crockery but rather in the story she tells and the tone or register of her comment.

In two groups of work, *WKD Women* (2011) and *Bingeing Britain* (ongoing), she depicts groups of women having a night on the town. Public commentary, across all media platforms, about British drinking habits, tends to be either damning or celebratory. The former disapproves of bad behaviour in public and deplores the negative impact on health and resulting costs to the National Health Service. The latter applauds the brazen antics of loud and public debauchery as a sign of a nation at ease with itself and wholly unconcerned with the sideways glances of more self-disciplined neighbouring nations. Wallace, with extraordinary skill, presents an entirely different narrative, balanced somewhere between these two extremes.

WKD Women, made for the Bluecoat gallery in Liverpool, uses that city as the context for a group of three women, probably low-waged, in low-status jobs, who are setting out with great purpose to enjoy a night of sheer dissolute pleasure – a complete break from a life limited by lack of money and opportunity. *You'll Never Walk Alone* and *The Three Graces* are both the titles and the inscriptions on plates depicting a group of three women dressed up for an evening out, propping each other up, bottles in hands, leaning into one another as they totter down the street on the edge of their precipitous heels. One title is the motto on the gates of Liverpool football

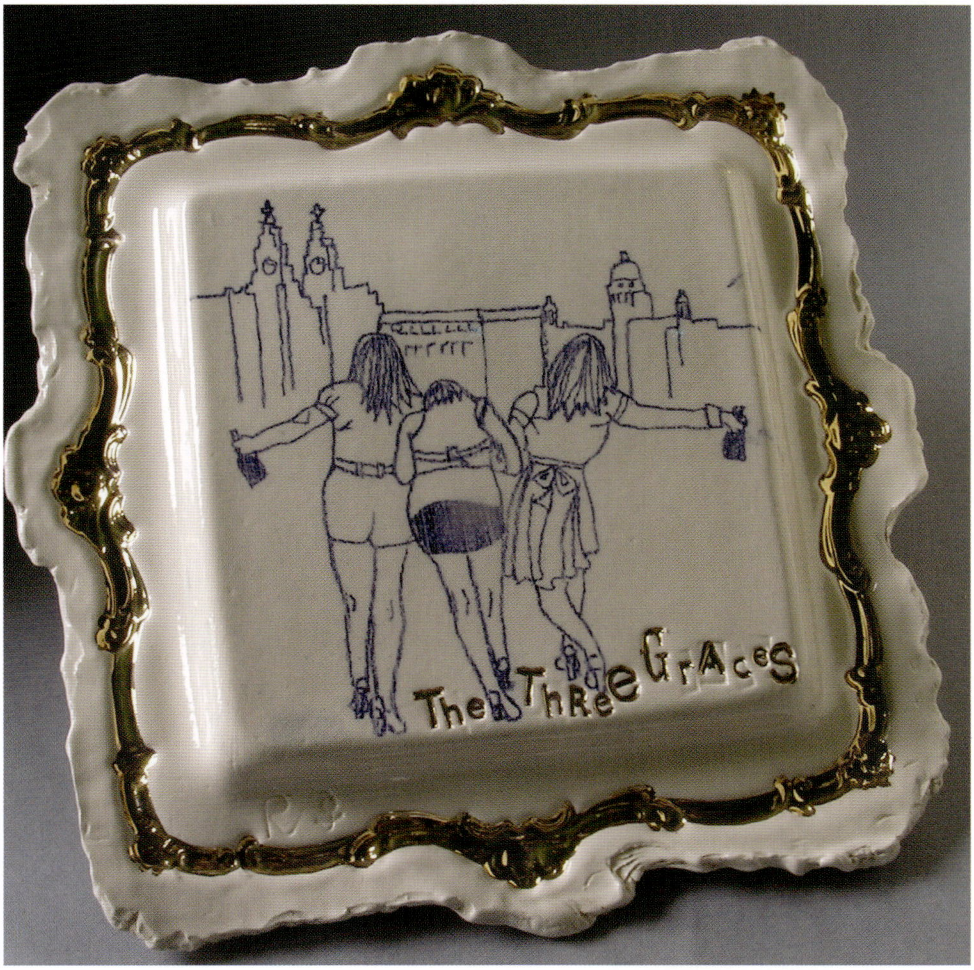

3.3 *The Three Graces*, 2011, Rose Wallace, courtesy of the artist

club; the other, *The Three Graces*, is the local name for three of the buildings in the Liverpool skyline against which our 'Three Graces' are depicted. Both are a statement of the group, of sisterhood and mutual support. *Liverpool Lou*, a reference to a well known Liverpool folk song, as well as a pun, depicts – in delicate blue lines on a white serving dish – a woman vomiting into a toilet while her friend holds back her hair. Many an English woman will see this image and flinch at the memory of her own dissolute youth, even if it was only the once. *Hold my Hair*, which is also the title of a figurine, is the battle cry of a woman who has drunk herself sick, and resembles a tribal call for young British women 'on the lash'.

What indicates that these are working-class women? The middle classes drink as much and in public, at least when young. In a society marinated in class concerns, the visual signs are minute but readable to anyone who looks. Young middle-class women who drink in public are not dressed up this way. The dress code for excessive drinking among the middle classes and elite is either torn jeans or a ball gown. The ball gown indicates a private event that becomes public because someone has published the photograph, either on a social network or in the newspapers. Torn jeans

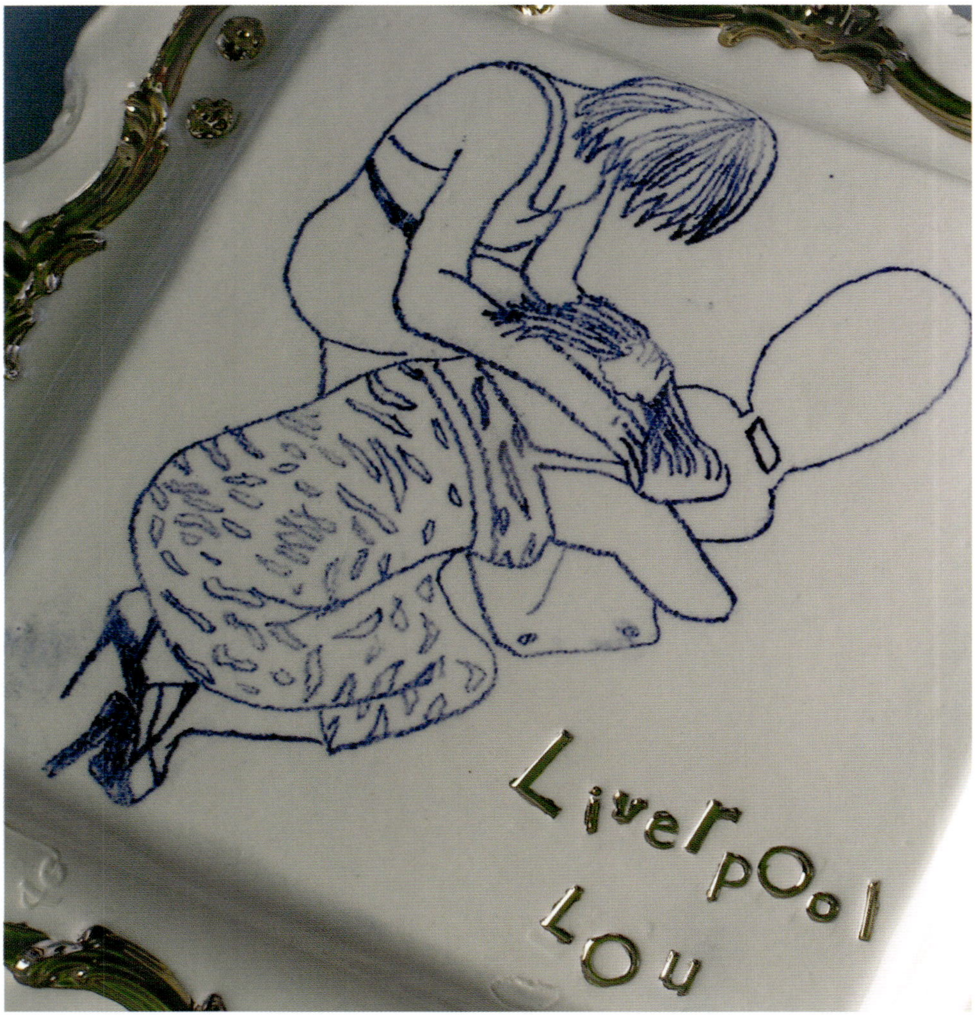

3.4 *Liverpool Lou*, 2011, Rose Wallace, courtesy of the artist

are for more casual public imbibing. The *WKD Women* are clearly dressed up in their best, and their best is not expensive finery, it is high street. They do not look like students, they look like escaped call-centre workers.

The overall effect of these works, both the plates and the figurines, is one of warmth, compassion and familiarity: the women are both likeable and recognizable, an effect achieved by the combination of words and imagery. The sense of the group, of togetherness, suggests that the work is made by one who is 'of' the tribe, and regardless of her own drinking habits, knows its ways. The artist likes these women, she does not either condemn or unduly celebrate their antics, she is laughing with not at them and enjoins the audience to do so too. The 'voice' in these works is female and working class. It is also feminist, in that Wallace has successfully circumvented and, effectively, undone a host of available negative stereotypes by locating the humanity in the women she depicts. Working-class women are, invariably, stereotyped in public discourse and presented as caricatures, but Wallace has presented us with a group of women we might either know or be ourselves.

Tea rooming with Matt Smith

An elegant Wedgwood-style creamware teapot has a double-headed lid and two spouts. It is a cheerful, if nostalgic, reminder of gay sexual promiscuity before conformity set in.[4] 'Tea rooming' is American gay slang for anonymous sexual encounters in public places. Made in 2010, *Double Spouted Teapot* (Figure 3.5) has multiple meanings, both contemporary and historic, which vary depending on context. Matt Smith is a British artist so the context set out here is British. It recalls a time before gay male relationships were decriminalized, when gay men frequented 'cruising grounds' for sex, known in Britain as 'cottaging'. This has always been and still is part of gay male culture in Britain, as it is in many countries. In Britain, however, social norms have changed dramatically in the last fifty years, superficially at least, and particularly so in the last decade. It is now legal to marry and have children, something which was considered unthinkable as little as twenty years ago. The 1970s Gay Liberation Front did not even wish for such things. It was an emancipation movement, allied to feminism, which aimed to deconstruct marriage and family and open up new ways of living not solely dependent on monogamous couple relationships, and certainly not just reproducing heterosexual norms.[5]

[4] Julie Bindel, *Straight Expectations*, Guardian Books, 2014, 189–191.

[5] Bindel, 12.

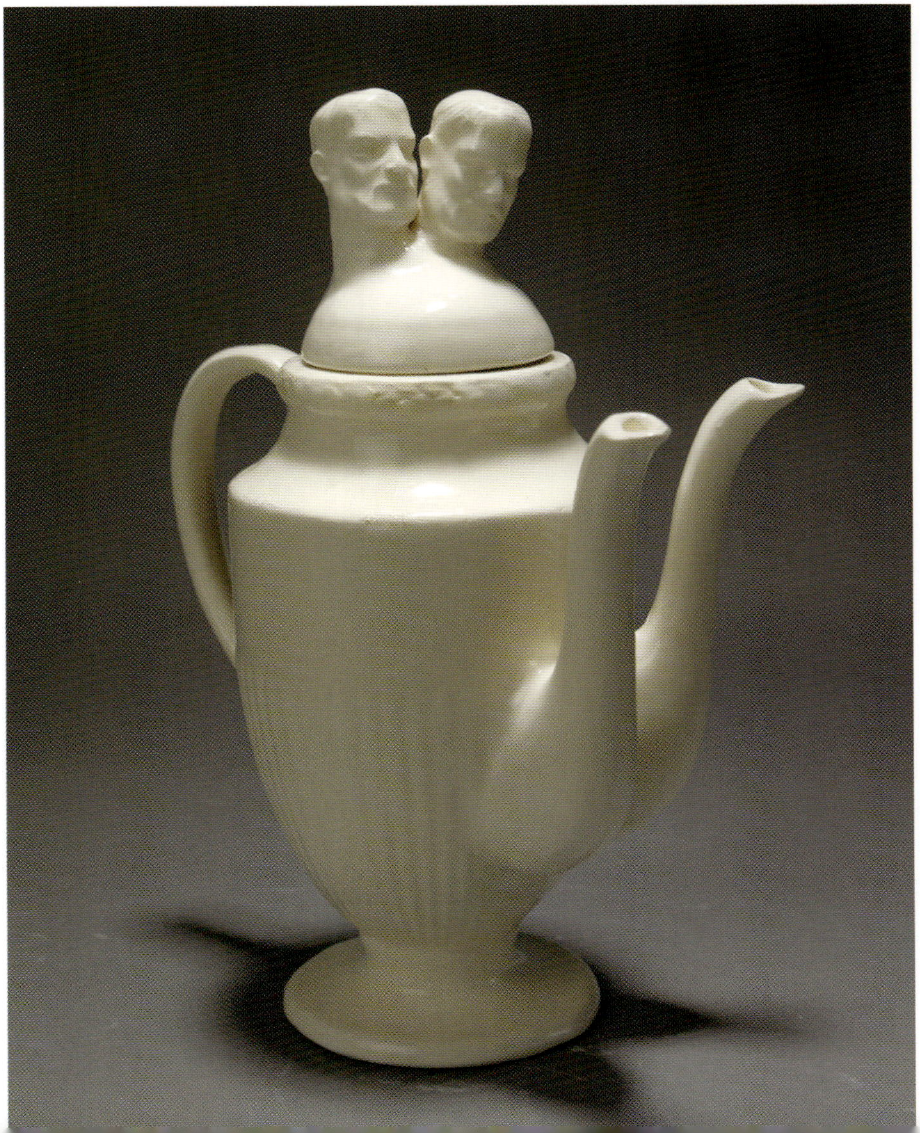

3.5 *Double Spouted Teapot*, 2010, Matt Smith © Matt Smith, photo © Birmingham Museums Trust

Double Spouted Teapot was made as a faux museum object for 'Queering the Museum', an exhibition at Birmingham Museum that aimed to interrupt the museum's ways of categorizing objects and to present them with a different, 'queer' narrative. As part of this process, Smith placed some of his own work among the museum objects. Depending on your point of view, and probably your experience, this teapot is a wonderful blast from the past, a reminder of the heady days before the gays were tamed, co-opted, defused and made safe. In other words, before we were subject to a thoroughly British establishment stitch-up. Marriage equality has been welcomed by the vast majority of gay men and lesbians, but not by all.[6] The LGBT community as it is now called, has become deeply conservative – perhaps it always was – but either way, Smith's teapot evokes these complicated and conflicted meanings very successfully.

The living room: Vases

A vase is an ornament; its purpose is to be admired. It belongs in the room that is kept clean and tidy for visitors, a status object that tells the guest something about their host. It may have been bought from a junk shop, an antique shop, a department store, a market stall or, if you are visiting someone from a family with 'background', it will be inherited. If your host is 'well travelled', it may well be a souvenir of 'ethnic craft'. If they belong to the haute bourgeoisie it may have come from an exclusive craft gallery, an upmarket craft fair, or if they're very upwardly mobile, an art gallery. It may be a gorgeous slipware jug rather than a vase, and it may have been bought online from any of the above. Wherever it came from, it says something about both the purchaser and the maker.

Mary Morgan made the *Seven Ages of Woman*, a series of seven vases, in 2013, based on a rereading of the 'seven ages of man' speech in Shakespeare's *As You Like It*. Morgan has matched words from the speech with her depictions of the corresponding passages in the life of 'everywoman', fusing the grand scale of Shakespearean drama with the banality of everyday life. Except, of course, Shakespeare's great strength was his grasp of intimacy and human sensibility, which animates his plays no matter how grand the scale of the subject matter may be. The result is a quietly sardonic rendition of a woman's life in the context of family. The baby girl is presented in a background of blancmange pink alongside Shakespeare's apt description of the 'mewling and puking' infant – the words threaded round the rim like a necklace. The decals accompanying the charming, time-honoured image remind us of infanticides of baby girls and foetuses, and namechecks the pressure group Pink Stinks, which campaigns against 'pinkification' of childhood and the limiting and damaging stereotypes foisted on girl children from the day they are born. As baby photographs go, this is some way from the framed newborn taking pride of place on the mantelpiece in the average family home.

In the most polite, drawing room-friendly way possible, Morgan continues her laceration of conventional 'family values', through the high achievement of

3.6 Opposite: *Seven Ages of Woman 1*, 2013, Mary Pamela Morgan

[6] Bindel, 126–128, 140, 176.

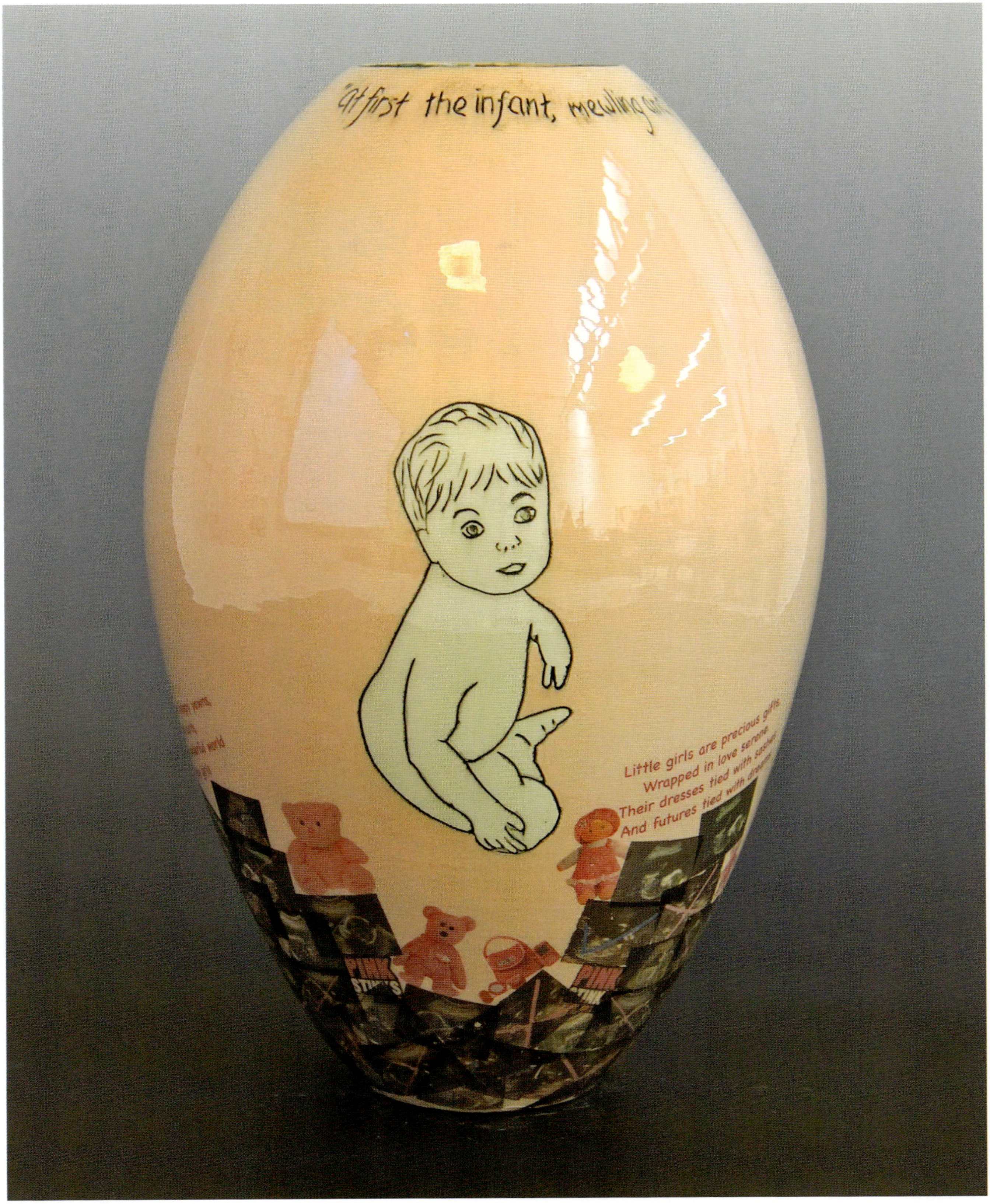
"at first the infant, mewling
Little girls are precious gifts
Wrapped in love serene
Their dresses tied with sashes
And futures tied with

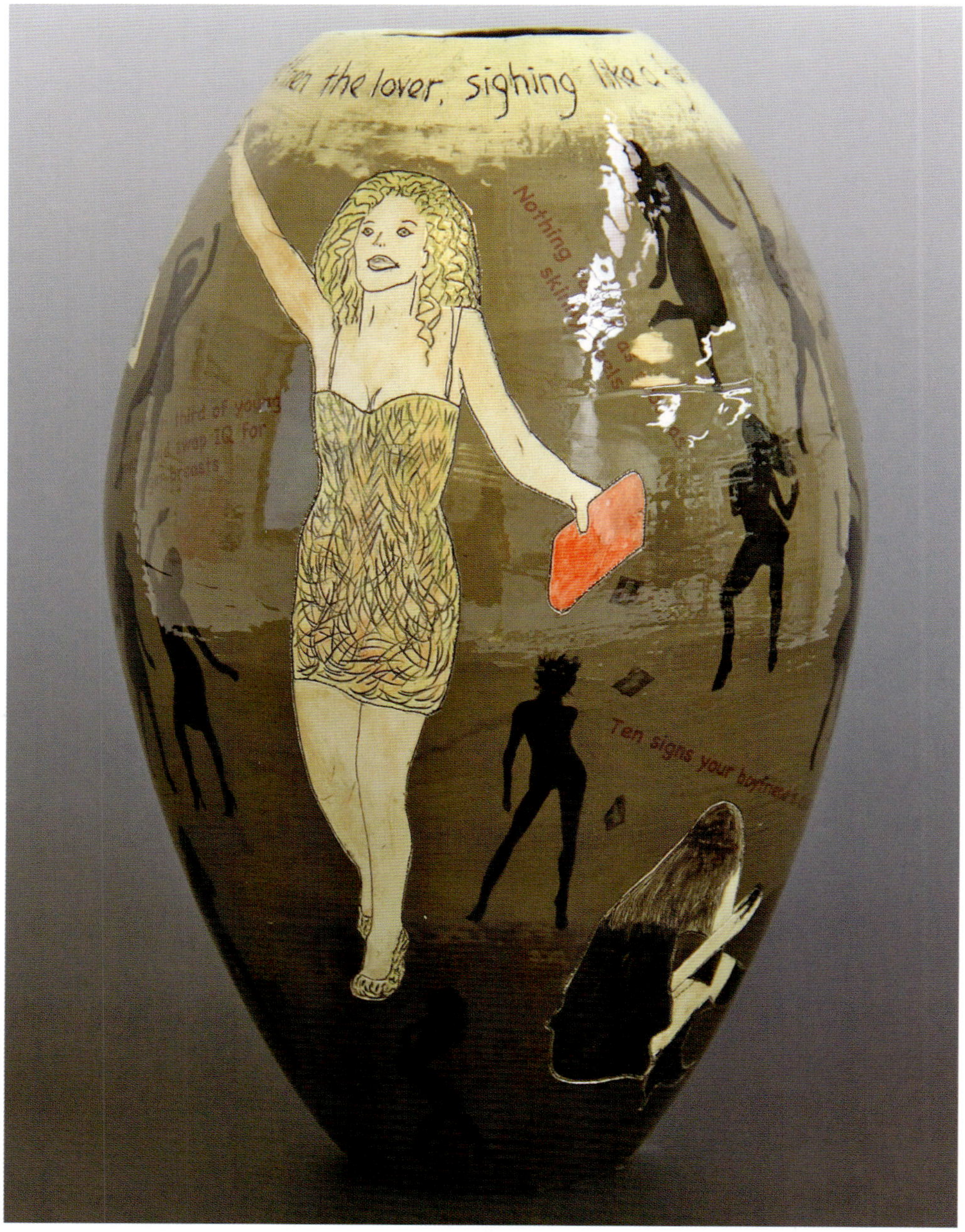

3.7 *Seven Ages of Woman 3*, 2013, Mary Pamela Morgan

schoolgirls, set alongside cyber-bullying, to the young woman, where she launches a broadside on the double standards applied to the sexual and social conduct of young women as opposed to that of young men. Again we see an image of young women 'on the lash', sexily dressed and 'on the pull', properly obedient to the mandatory regulations set by celebrity and mainstream-media cultural norms. Having partied it up a storm she is then roundly condemned by the same purveyors of proper conduct and, as often as not, publicly shamed via social media. Interestingly, Morgan briefly departs from Shakespeare at this point: 'the lover, sighing like a furnace', is followed by 'yes', in Morgan's voice, 'girls just wanna have fun', in the voice of the eponymous

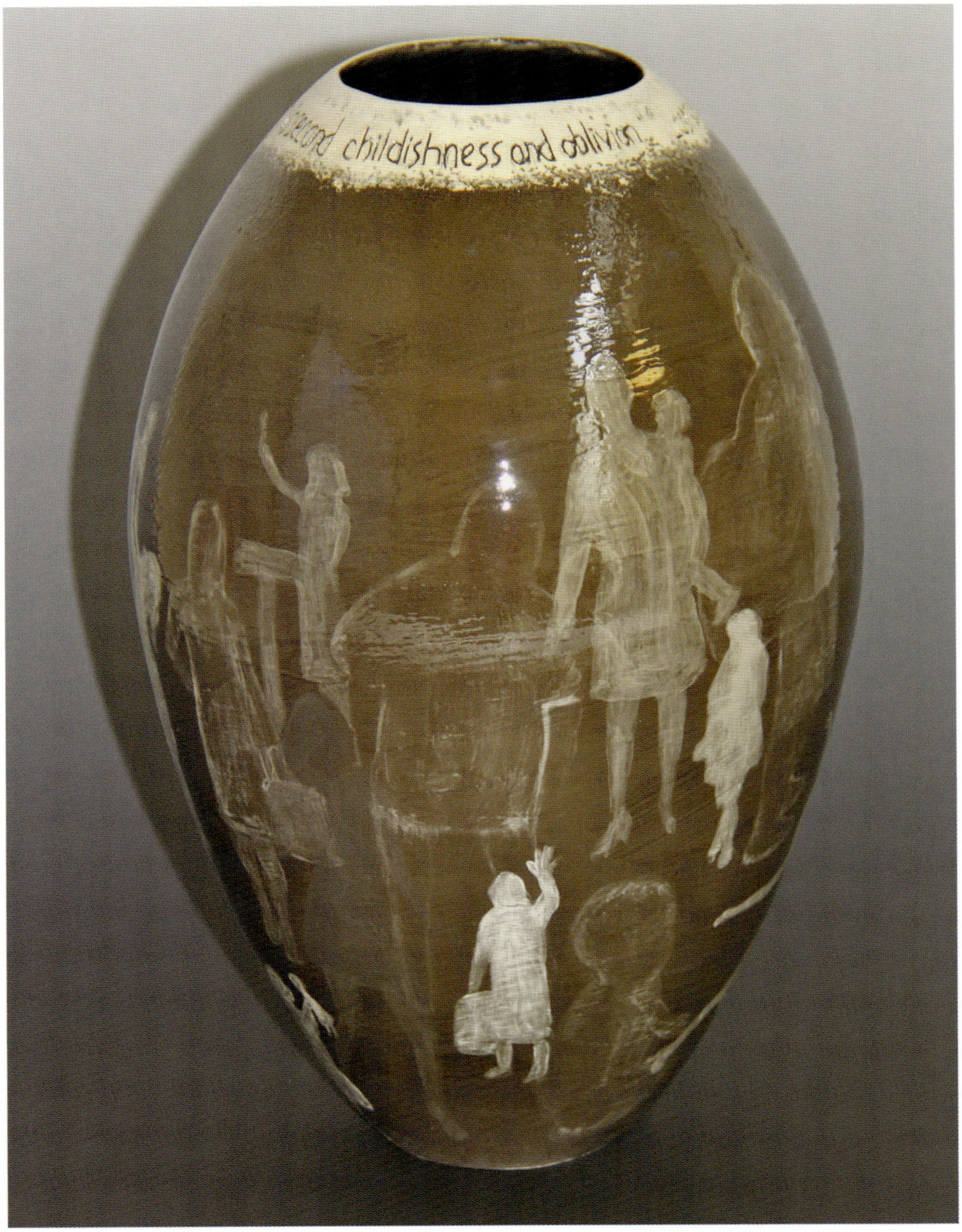

3.8 *Seven Ages of Woman 7*, 2013, Mary Pamela Morgan

pop song. The fourth phase, the soldier, has been reinvented as the peacemaker, endlessly engaged in resolving conflict, both family and social, while struggling to make ends meet, and the fifth, 'the justice', applies these skills to wider society, from the local to the international, using images of women in positions of leadership and influence as well as in support roles. 'The slippered and spectacled' is the sixth vase, where Morgan depicts the army of grandparents doing childcare to support younger workers in the family. The final vase of the series, shows the elderly dying woman and the slow deterioration of memory: no drama here, just the slow, aching, painful ghastliness of dying.

In this series, Morgan has produced a contemporary fable, a portrait of family life that is unequivocally feminist: critical of the authority and of patriarchal social norms and pressures. She holds up the mirror of irony to the family and exposes its untruths, its drudgery and some of its horrors as well as its strengths. She parodies the front room vase, invading it with sardonic humour. Combining feminism with satire, particularly irony and parody, is not easily done because of the problems of reproducing the very same damaging stereotypes that we seek to undermine. Morgan has pulled off an unusually successful drawing room coup in this series.

Avital Sheffer's pots all look innocent enough, to Western eyes, anyway. They might be serendipitous antique market finds, or lovely 'ethnic' pots brought home from travels in the Middle East. Graceful forms, in soft sandy colours and decorated in twirling arabesques, they all have panels and seams of text in what turn out to be ancient or historic versions of modern Middle Eastern languages. Some have fallen out of use, others simply mutated. *Etrog 1* is one of a number of pots bearing the ancient but now disused and largely denied Sephardic Hebrew, spoken and used by Spanish Jews in southern Spain, in religious contexts and written in the dominant script of Arabic. Known as Judeo-Arabic it evidences the migratory history of both Jews and Arabs and is politically immensely inconvenient for almost all the warring parties of the Middle Eastern conflicts. It betrays, with utmost eloquence, the peaceful cohabitation of Arabs of all religious denominations with Jews of all ethnic backgrounds in lands as far apart as southern Spain and western Iran. That one small pot can drive a coach and horses straight through the grotesque rhetoric of pan-Arab, Israeli and Iranian nationalism and their bogus land, site and memory claims, is an extraordinary achievement.

Sheffer's pots excavate language and pattern with the ceaseless attention of an archaeologist to minute details, matching pattern together with the language and story. Another pot uses a translation of *Almagest*, 'The Great Book', a second-century treatise on astronomy and mathematics by Ptolemy of Alexandria. According to Sheffer, it is one of the most important documents to date to shed light on Greek mathematics and sciences. The document was translated into Judeo-Arabic by a Jewish scholar from Kalatayud, northeast Spain, in 1475 – seventeen years before the expulsion of the Jews from Spain. Another pot uses lines from the love letters of a thirteenth-century merchant to his wife – promising to come home and failing consistently – surrounded by the tragically optimistic pomegranate designs. It brings a note of intimacy to the vast historical and political terrain that Sheffer's work treads.

Land, memory and minoritized languages are also the not-so-distant hum beneath Susan Folwell's pots. Folwell is a Santa Clara potter from a large and successful pottery family. She uses her established Native American ceramic methods and forms to critique the dominant American culture that excludes and systematically deprives native people, which results in corrosive poverty and social and economic exclusion. *Photo-Op Jar* (Figure 3.10) is based on a black and white photograph

3.9 Opposite: *Etrog 1*, 2010, Avital Sheffer, photographer: David Young

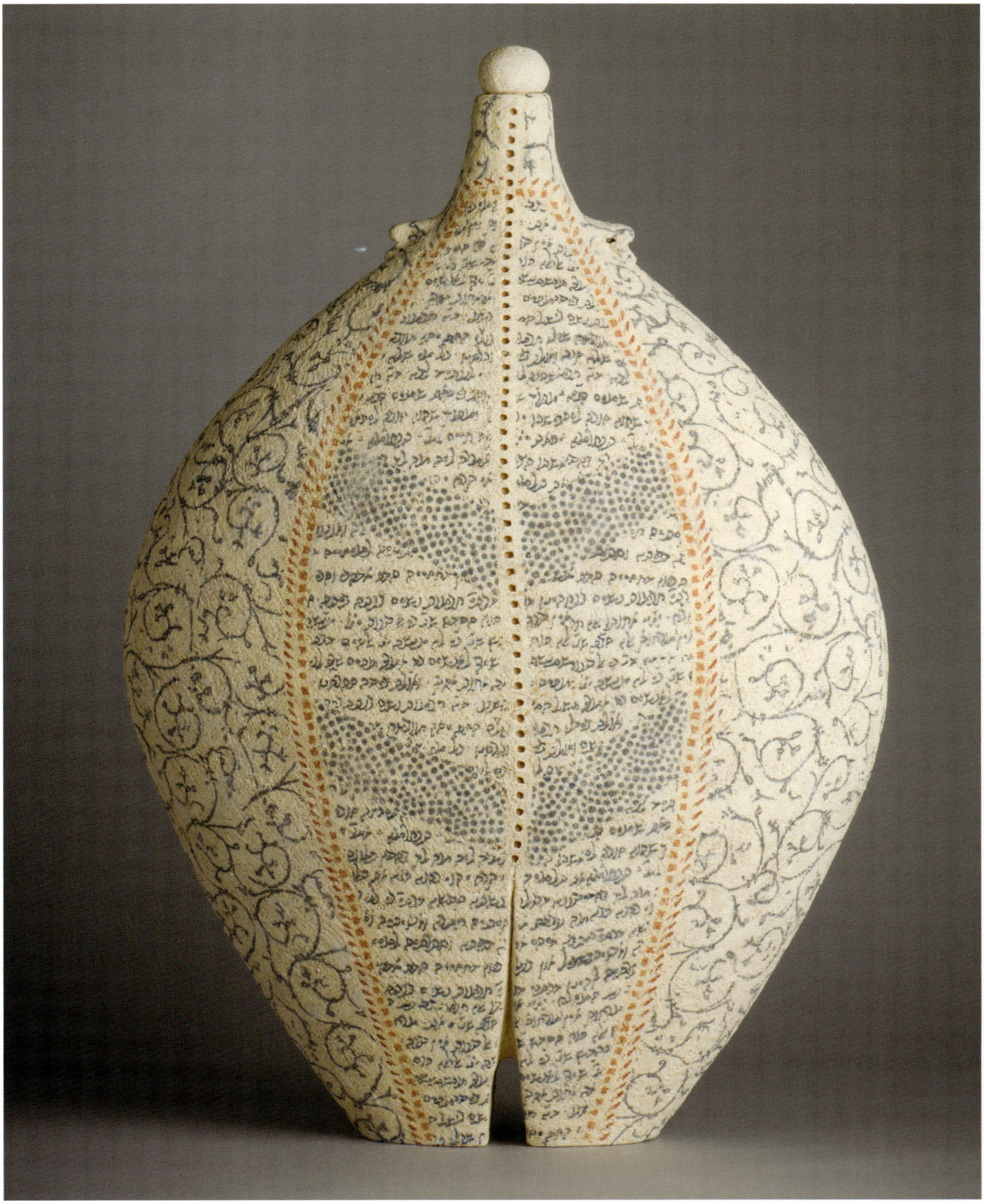

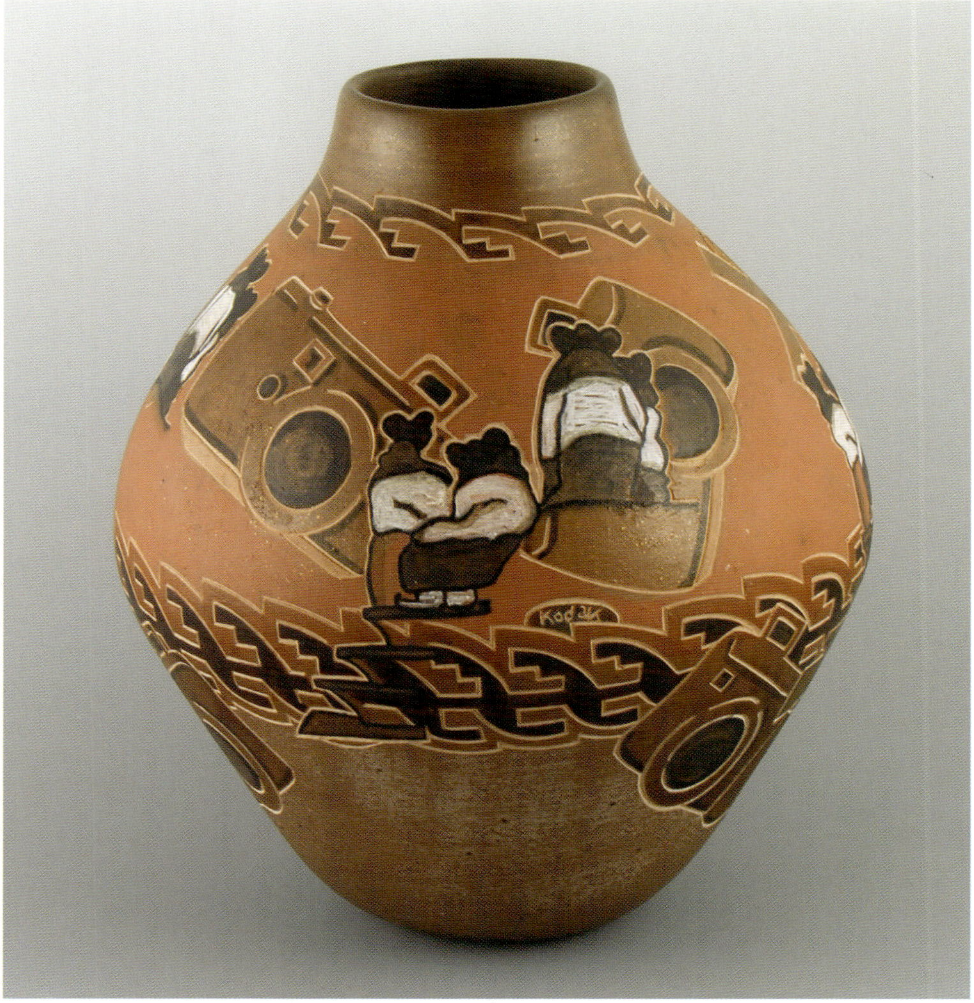

3.10 *Photo-Op Jar*, 2014, Susan Folwell, courtesy of Charles King

by the renowned American ethnographer, Edward Curtis, who photographed some eighty Native American tribes in the early twentieth century as part of a detailed study including over forty thousand photographs. Folwell's jar turns the lens around and depicts the Hopi women he photographed watching the tourists. She questions whether they themselves are looking for a photo opportunity, affected by celebrity culture as much as any other modern American, or if they intend to snap the tourists. Hopi women were irresistible as images to photographers of the early twentieth century because of their highly distinctive hairstyles: long hair is twisted in a rope and tied around the ears. It is a wryly humorous critique of the unequal power dynamics in both ethnography and tourism, while also presenting the possibility that native women may be able to turn the situation to their advantage. In *Collab Bowl 1* she does exactly that. She uses the white American cartoon image of Wonder Woman and recreates her as Pueblo Wonder Woman, armed with magic pots and the force within her, ready to take on the adversary. Folwell speaks in an interview of the precarious nature of the lives of native women, and has produced a series called *Cry Baby* about

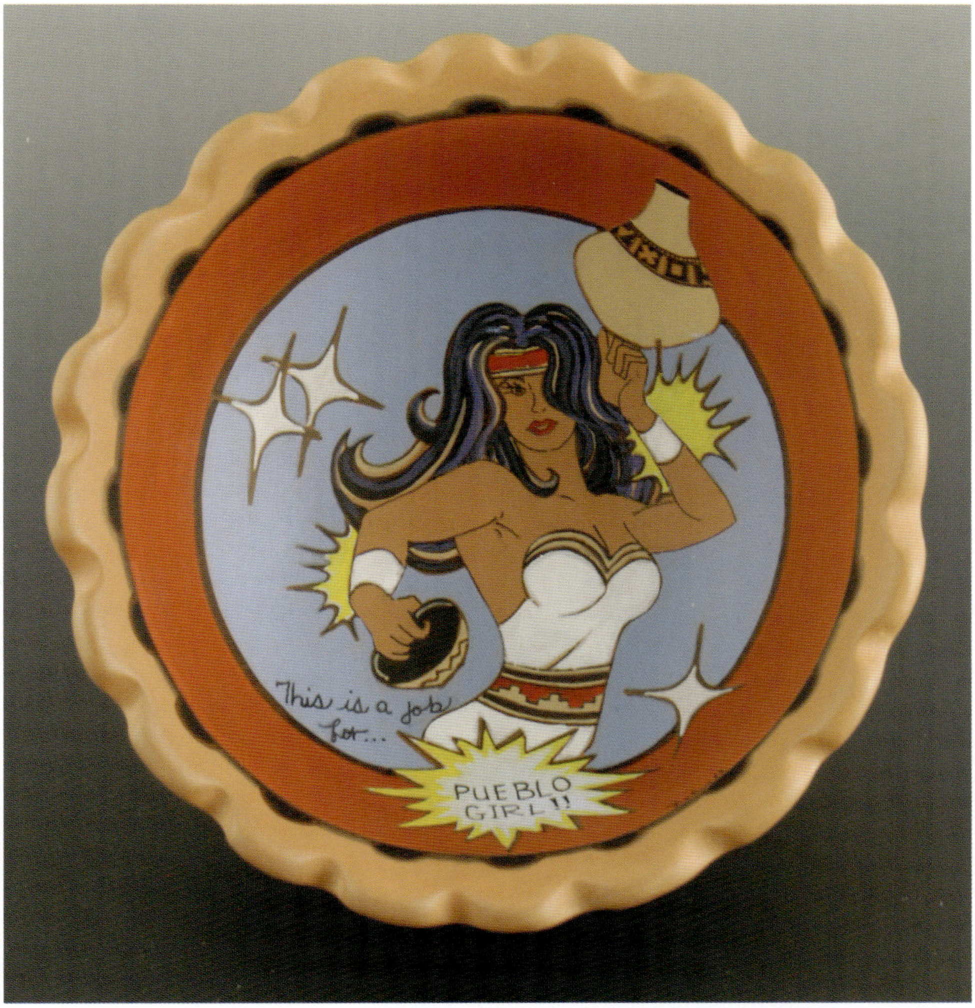

3.11 *Gun Love*, 2013, Susan Folwell, courtesy of Charles King

the ongoing catastrophe that is American gun culture (Figure 3.11). She mobilizes her formidable skills as a potter to chronicle a time and culture that is both threatened and, simultaneously, a significant, growing and changing cultural force within the American body politic.

North American Conchiti potter, Virgil Ortiz, son of the potter Sefarina Ortiz, is an outstanding virtuoso maker who excels in the unlikely mix of pottery and fashion design. Achingly cool and utterly beguiling he has reinvented both the much disparaged pueblo figurine and the clay pot. The latter in his hands is an elegant, satin smooth creature, adorned with fashionably sadomasochistic figures attired in leather and studded collars, blindfolds and fetish-wear, the uber-cool version of 'playing against convention'. Like Folwell, he asserts his American-ness, his claim to the cultural iconography of the white dominant culture, and simultaneously declares his unique brand of pueblo-chic. A black and white photograph of a model wearing Ortiz-designed trousers and sporting a *Clay Canteen with Leather Strap* (Figure 3.12) demonstrates the urban warrior nature of these vessels. The canteen is based on

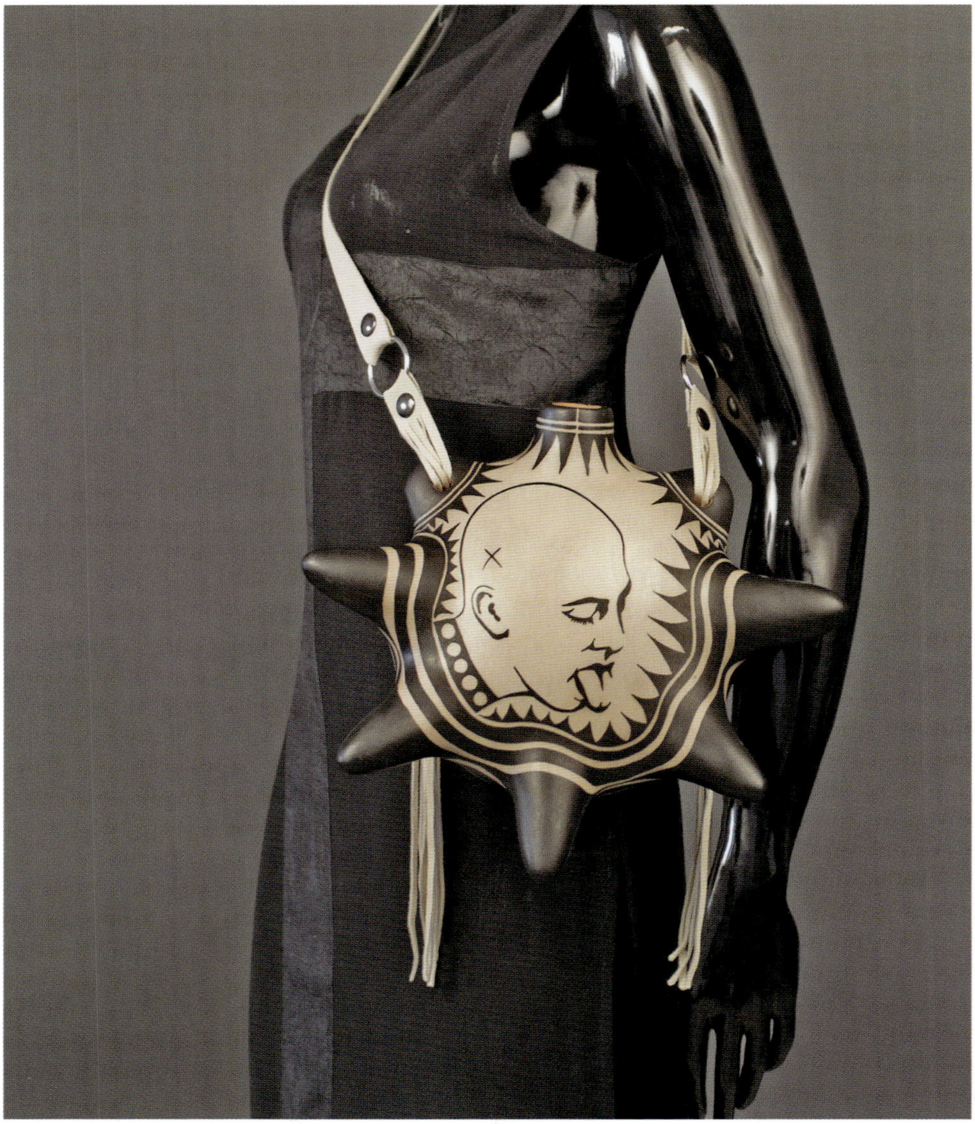

3.12 *Clay Canteen with Leather Strap*, 2011, Virgil Ortiz, courtesy of King Galleries and Virgil Ortiz

the pilgrim pot form, but imitates the leather and rubber look of fetish gear and features a naked head, collared, with tongue protruding in the direction of the spiky motif. The fashion-photo style presentation, showing the canteen worn by the model, emphasizes the sexual connotations of the design.

'Zipora, if Eitan were a girl, I would wait for him' was the title of an exhibition by Eitan Gross (Museum of Israeli Art, Ramat-Gan, 2006). According to curator Shlomit Bauman, who is also a maker, ninety per cent of Israeli potters are women, so for a man – a former soldier – to be a potter is a statement on gender by itself. Gross lived and worked in Jaffa, an area with a mixed population. Though Israeli Jews form the majority, there is also a significant population of Arab Muslims and Christians, the latter mostly Orthodox. Gross inhabited a mixture of often conflicting identities in his surroundings, in his family and in himself. In this body of work he explores his

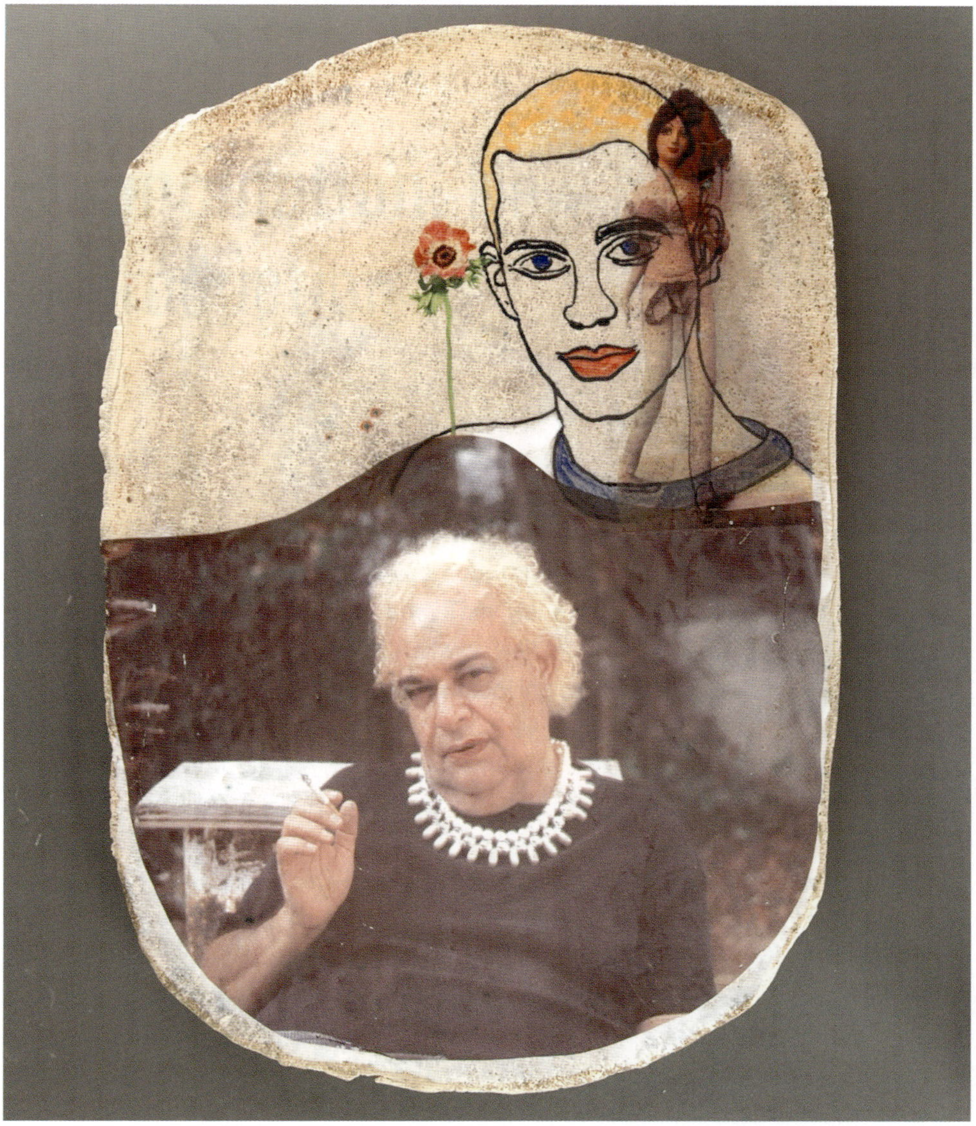

3.13 *Self-portrait*, 2006, Eitan Gross, photographer: Shay Ben Efraim. From the exhibition 'Zipora, If Eitan was a girl, I would wait for him', The Museum of Israeli Art, Ramat-Gan

transgendered self and his relationship with family, with Israel and with craft. He is depicted as an elderly man, dressed in women's clothing, an aging transwoman, comfortable as a mixed self. He also appears as a child, outlined in a cartoon-style drawing. Here he is the young, blonde, blue-eyed boy who first began to think of himself as both boy and girl (Figure 3.13). He includes an image of a childhood doll, a stereotyped representation of a woman, a cartoon extreme resembling no one. He also depicts his fantasies using similarly idealized, comic-strip cartoon gay men, super-sexual studs equipped with giant erect phalluses, absurd confections, a million miles from the image of the artisan potter in Jaffa.

Gross was a highly skilled craft potter who made a living making and selling decorated functional ware for use and display. One of the forms he concentrated on was the Palestinian water jar. According to Nurith Kenaan-Kedar, the water jar

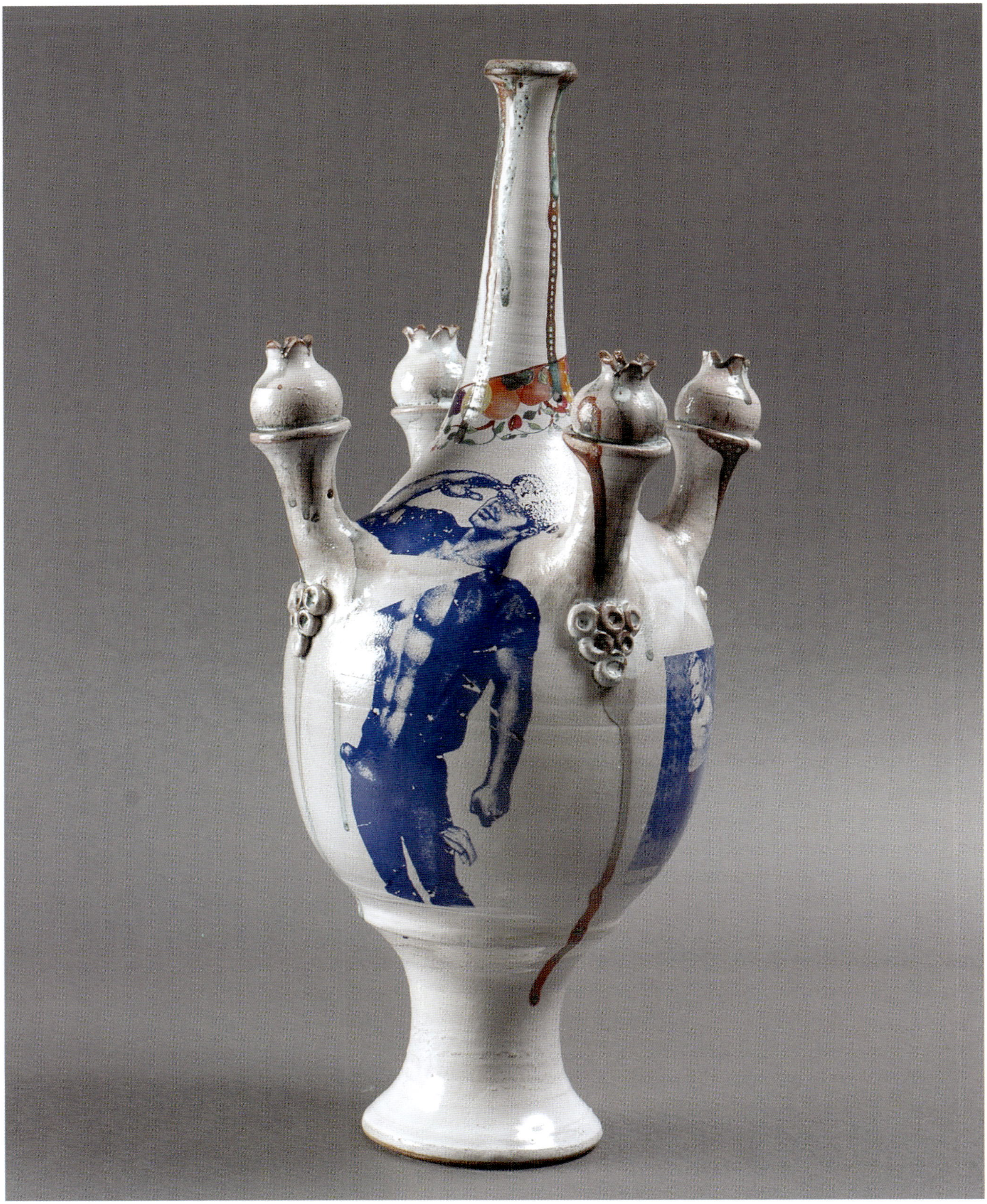

is a highly symbolic image for both Israelis and Palestinians, and has undergone numerous incarnations in its depiction and meaning. As a carrier of water, it was symbolic of everyday life in a dry land, where water was scarce. Palestinian women with water jars were photographed by ethnographers, reimagined as tourist images and romanticized by artists. Yet the jar itself maintained its own integrity, despite being subject to endless prettifying, not least because it continued to be useful until water was piped into villages, at which point it was modified for other, still utilitarian, purposes. The form of jar that Gross favoured was a ceremonial version, traditionally used for weddings. It is a complex form with a central opening on a long neck, and four more spouts coming out of the shoulder. His jars were often highly ornamented with fruit or birds and brightly coloured glazes.

For the 2006 show, he used a white tin glaze, collaged with cobalt blue decals of the hypermasculine gay male and an image of himself as a child. A band of fruit winds around the neck, which operates as a pun for a gay man in English, and the four short spouts are also finished with fruit: pomegranates, an ancient symbol of fertility and prosperity, which look oddly phallic in this rendition (Figure 3.14). According to Bauman, Gross made this jar for his own imagined wedding. It contains the many conflicting parts of Gross's identity in one object, the traditional Arab-Palestinian jar, adopted and remade as an Israeli craft artefact, turned around and against the macho Israeli social and gender norms. It is a peculiarly dissonant but endlessly fascinating and absorbing object. The tourist artefact fights with the comic-strip decals, which fight with the industrial tableware decals, all of which fight with the highly crafted aesthetic of the red clay, visible where the glaze is thinner. It is neither harmonious, nor particularly 'pleasing', which sets it at odds with the aesthetic norms of twentieth-century studio pottery. It is a highly accomplished and somewhat anxious object, expressive of the discomfort of living in a conflicted land where mixed identities can be immensely challenging.

3.14 Opposite: *Wedding*, 2006, Eitan Gross, photographer: Shay Ben Efraim. From the exhibition 'Zipora, If Eitan was a girl, I would wait for him', The Museum of Israeli Art, Ramat-Gan

The *Wunderkammer*: Figurines

Figurines are knick-knacks. They live on the shelf or in a cabinet, a gross distortion, as often as not, of the Renaissance *Wunderkammer* or cabinet of curiosities. There is, on the whole, nothing wondrous about figurines. They are mass-produced, mildly nauseating stereotypes. Ceramicists and other artists have tended to parody the figurine. Tempting though that is, it has resulted in quantities of work that reproduce the stereotype without presenting a particularly vital alternative. Parody can be limiting, it tends to restrict the narrative to that which is prescribed by the object being parodied. In this section, the potters are in absolute revolt against the tedious figurine and have completely remade it. The reference may be present but the remaking dominates and produces a narrative that leads in an entirely new or different direction, often undercutting, attacking or mocking the original debased form.

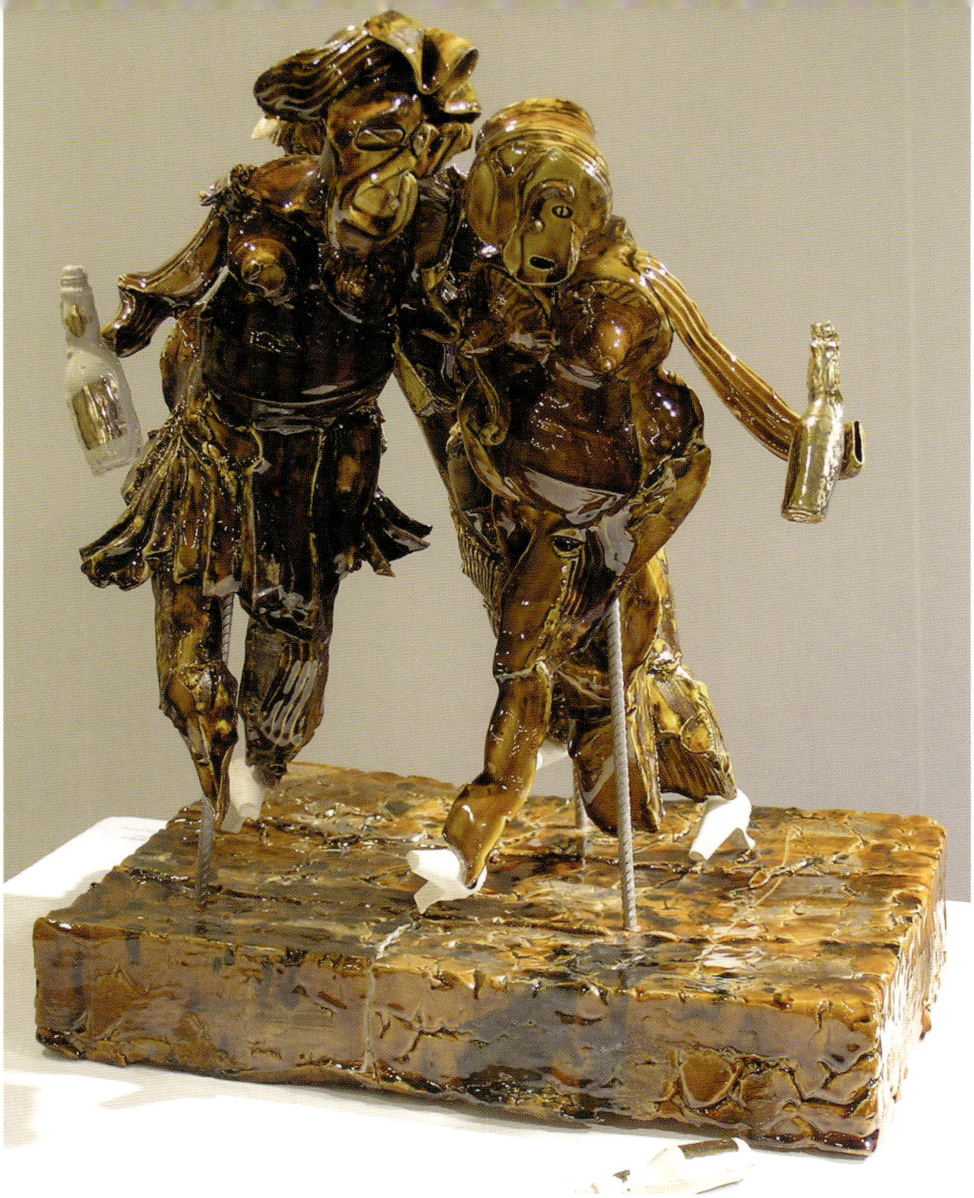

3.15 *The Three Disgraces*, 2008, Rose Wallace, courtesy of the artist

While the plates in Rose Wallace's *WKD Women* series have a cartoon-like but also naturalistic quality, her figurines are more allegorical in spirit. *The Three Disgraces* (2008) (Figure 3.15), a treacle-glazed group of three heavy-drinking figurines, assembled from pieces derived from drink cans and bottles, with glistening brown surfaces, protruding bosoms and grotesquely distorted faces, represent the polar opposite of the neoclassical *Three Graces* from which they take their name. This is a 'kinetic' work, where the discernible movement in the figures emphasizes their state of inebriation. With ill-fitting clothes and shoes made of kiln furniture, theirs is an uncertain, tottering gait. *The Three Disgraces* is a sister piece to *The Three Graces* (Figure 3.3), which shows our revellers setting out while the night is still young. The 'Graces' have not yet reached the point of saturation implied in the *Disgraces* or in *Liverpool Lou*, the vomiting party animal preparing for the next round. Wallace's figurines are a tour de force of British farce combined with wry social comment. Pastiche meets burlesque with a hint of grotesque, but the dominant satiric trope is irony, that highly equivocal social mirror that exposes folly but does not condemn, or not in this case, anyway.

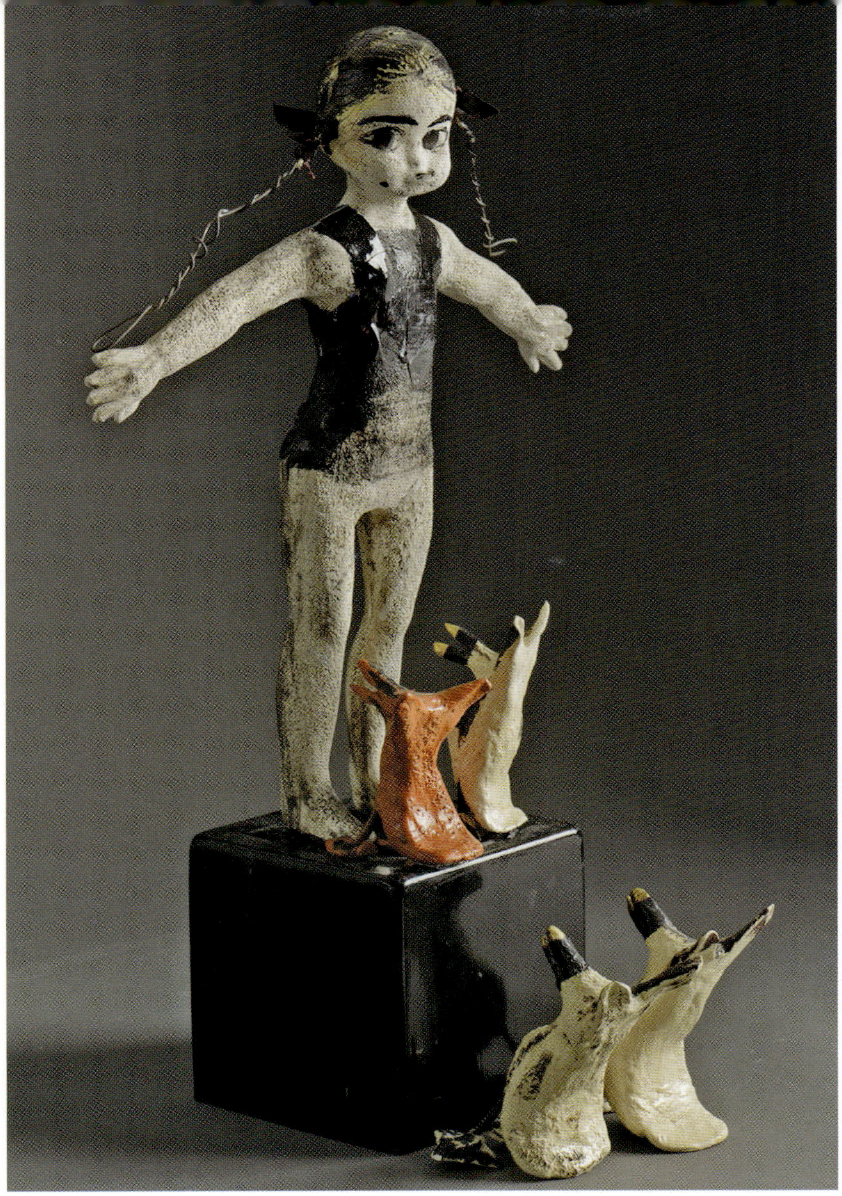

3.16 *No Trespassing, Boys!* 2003, Consuelo Radclyffe, photographer: Sussie Ahlburg

The favelas of Rio de Janeiro are home to most of Consuelo Radclyffe's girl figurines. She makes boys too, but girls, both children and teenage, are her main concern. It requires a steel nerve to take on this subject untouched by the vast majority of artists. Undaunted, Radclyffe creates girl figures and places them in groups or singly, sometimes with imaginary friends. Not a whiff of sentimentality emanates from these mini-dramas. The characters conspire with each other, whisper, exclude first one and then another, one minute the best of friends, the next minute worst enemies. Older girls compete sexually with one another, taunt boys or are furious at being taunted by them. Social politics of both class and race and the sexual politics of appearance jostle for position in these pairings. All manner of inclusions and rejections disturb the pleasures of playing on the swings. A glance or a gesture, the positioning of one figure in relation to another can radically alter its message. We are invited into these gatherings, as participants rather than observers. It is almost impossible not to identify with them.

A tall, determined-looking child instructs her imaginary underlings, the unsuspecting dog creatures who gaze up at her, adoringly. Another confides in a beaked friend, still others perch on the edge of a bed or chair, while an abandoned

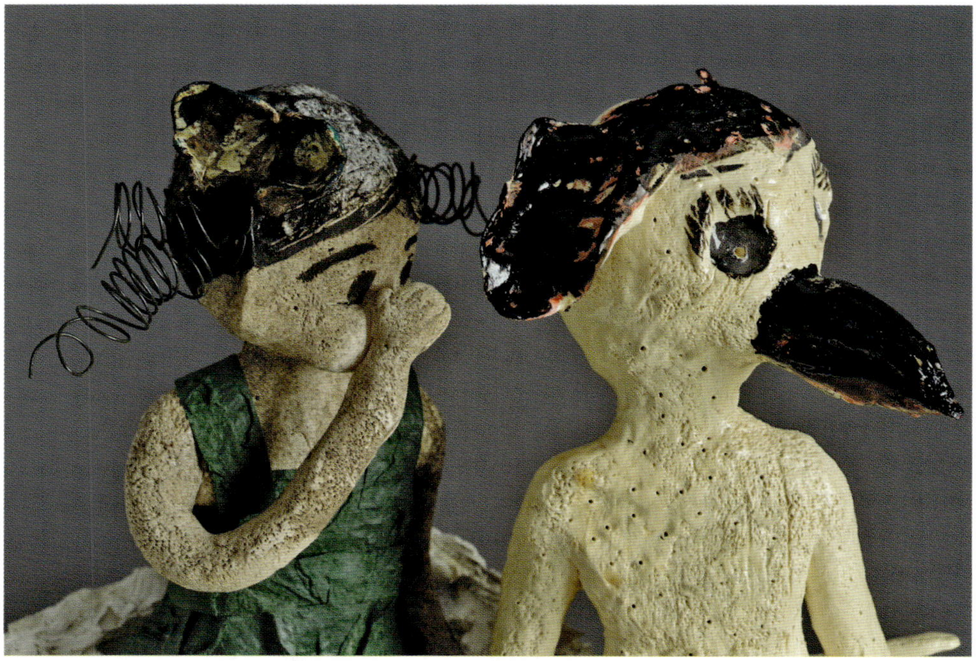

3.17 *Secrets and Lies*, 2002, Consuelo Radclyffe, photographer: Sussie Ahlburg

doll lies discarded to one side. The otherwise lone child might be thinking anything from absorbing major trauma to wondering where she put her socks. These cameos capture perfectly the subtle and varied shades of emotion and expression in the behaviour and gestures of children, who are often such consummate and practised survivors, all too eager to protect their adults from knowing that anything might be wrong. Radclyffe's explorations of the psychological terrain of childhood in these pieces recognizes its everyday pains, the rejection and sense of loss, as well as the more complex or deeper trauma, and also the moments of joy and adventure. These apparently simple figures are steeped in the light and shade of human experience.

Teenage life also preoccupies Jo Pipkin, along with the fairy tales that play a formative role in the life of a child. Reading to her own children, she grew impatient with the limited range of female characters in these tales, all either 'the wicked stepmother or the hapless victim whose only hope of salvation is the intervention of a handsome prince'.[7] She investigated further and found that the original tales were much tougher than the modern, sanitized versions and were used not only to entertain but as moral tales that cautioned the socially wayward. *Red Riding Hood* is a teenage school girl, becoming sexually interested in and attracted to a male teacher. It is a simple image of a well known and popular tale, but deeply disturbing and grotesquely pertinent to the growing awareness of widespread child sexual exploitation throughout the UK.[8] At first glance we see a cheerfully flirtatious teenager in school uniform, still very much a young girl in her white ankle socks. The teacher looks like Mr Normal, until we see his copy of *Great Expectations* and the wolf's tail peeping out of the back of his coat. It is a truly hideous image in the best possible sense of that word. It shocks because of its accuracy, not because Pipkin has used any imagery that is inherently shocking.

[7] Joanne Pipkin, Artist's statement, 2013.

[8] Anna Hall, *Edge of the City*, 2004; Julie Bindel, 'Mothers of Prevention', *The Sunday Times*, 30 September 2007; Julie Bindel, 'The Victims of Sex Gangs are Never Heard', *The Guardian*, 9 May 2012; Samira Ahmed, 'Widespread Sexual Abuse in Rotherham has Caused Outrage – But Little Action', *The Guardian*, 6 October 2014.

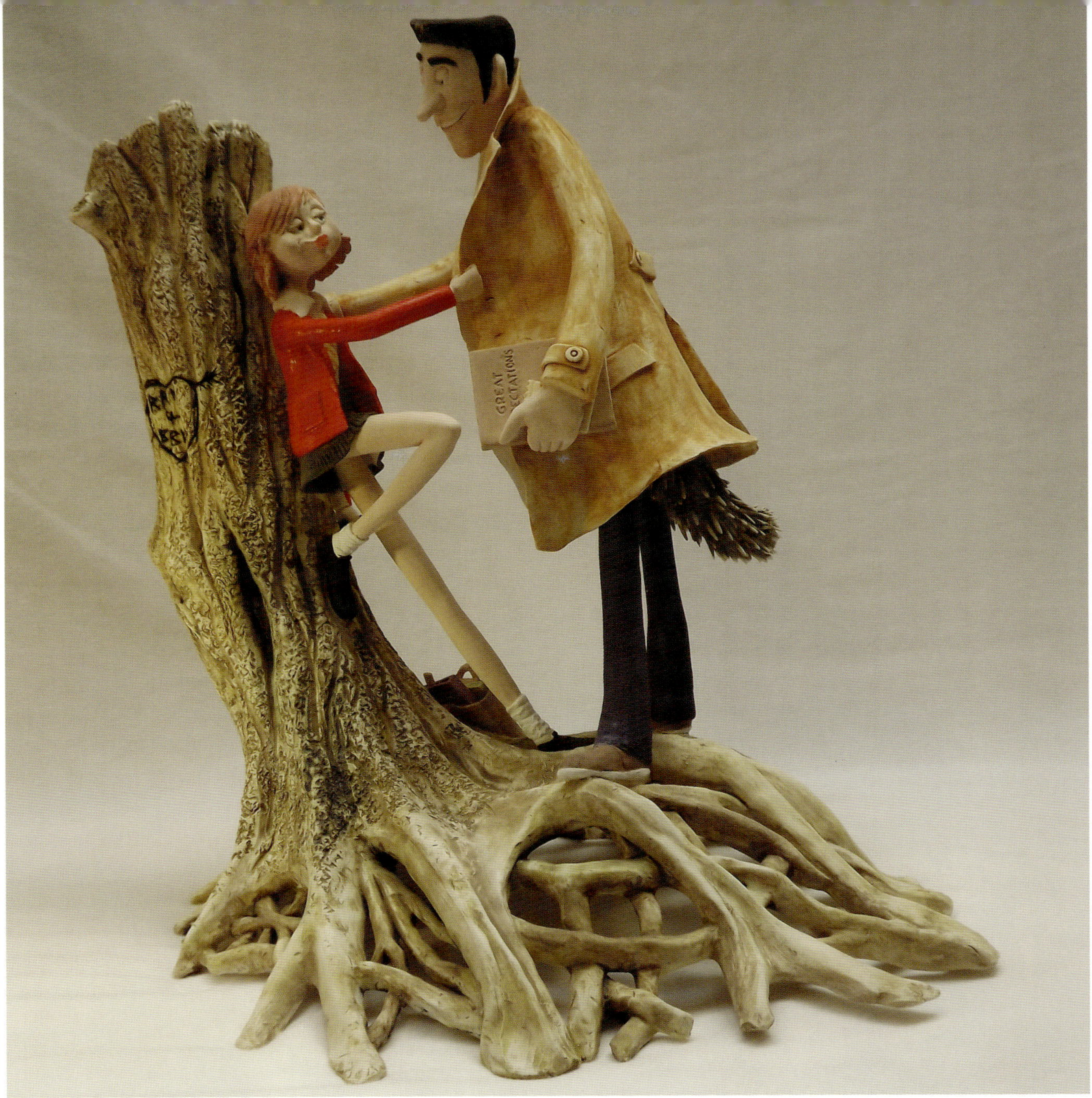

3.18 *Red Riding Hood*, 2013, Jo Pipkin, BA Ceramics

The girl is at the age of puberty, a time of heightened sexual curiosity. The teacher is a trusted authority figure: so easy for him to abuse and such an absolute violation of the position of trust. The shock hits home also because Pipkin is so clear and unequivocal about where the blame must be apportioned, about whose responsibility this is, which liberates her to produce an image of the man which, momentarily at least, makes him seem 'perfectly pleasant'. Similarly she shows this very young teenage girl as flirtatious, flattered, even tempted, without producing an image that would ultimately betray her, by suggesting she is somehow to blame for her own abuse.

Attempted 'subversions' of childhood imagery have often resulted in presenting the child as 'evil', the author of their own misfortunes, sexually knowing, manipulative, cunning and calculating. While many artists fondly imagine they are undoing the idealization of children,[9] in reality the images of children produced are often

9 James Reilly, *Casual Influences*, Oriel Mostyn, 2000.

consistent with one that blames girls for being raped and abused, and configures the perpetrators as unwitting victims of sinister childish scheming. Radclyffe is not coy about the petty cruelties of children towards each other but, where others have failed, she succeeds in making images of children that are complex and human while still being an artifice, a fiction based on the figurine. Pipkin like Radclyffe has used her knowledge, intelligence, courage and an almost wilful commitment to truth-telling, to portray a freeze-framed moment in the process that has come to be known as 'grooming'. Without the small but vital elements she includes – the girl's youth and her tentative smile, the teacher's 'pleasantness' and the wolf's tail – the image would be either only a partial exposure of the social ill or, in the wrong hands, would result in a victim-blaming image. As it is, it is an extraordinarily simple, restrained but blistering piece of social commentary, much needed in times of fear of 'causing offence'.

Baps and Buns is a social critique but in a completely different register from *Red Riding Hood*. Here we see a young woman, perhaps still a teenager, pondering which breast size to select from those on display in a slot machine. It is an ironic twist mocking the absurdities of the beauty industry and our own susceptibility to its worst excesses. Our huntress for the perfect body already has ludicrously elongated, Barbie-doll proportions, complete with pumped breasts. It is a comic take on a highly oppressive force that threatens the lives and well-being of a great many girls, women

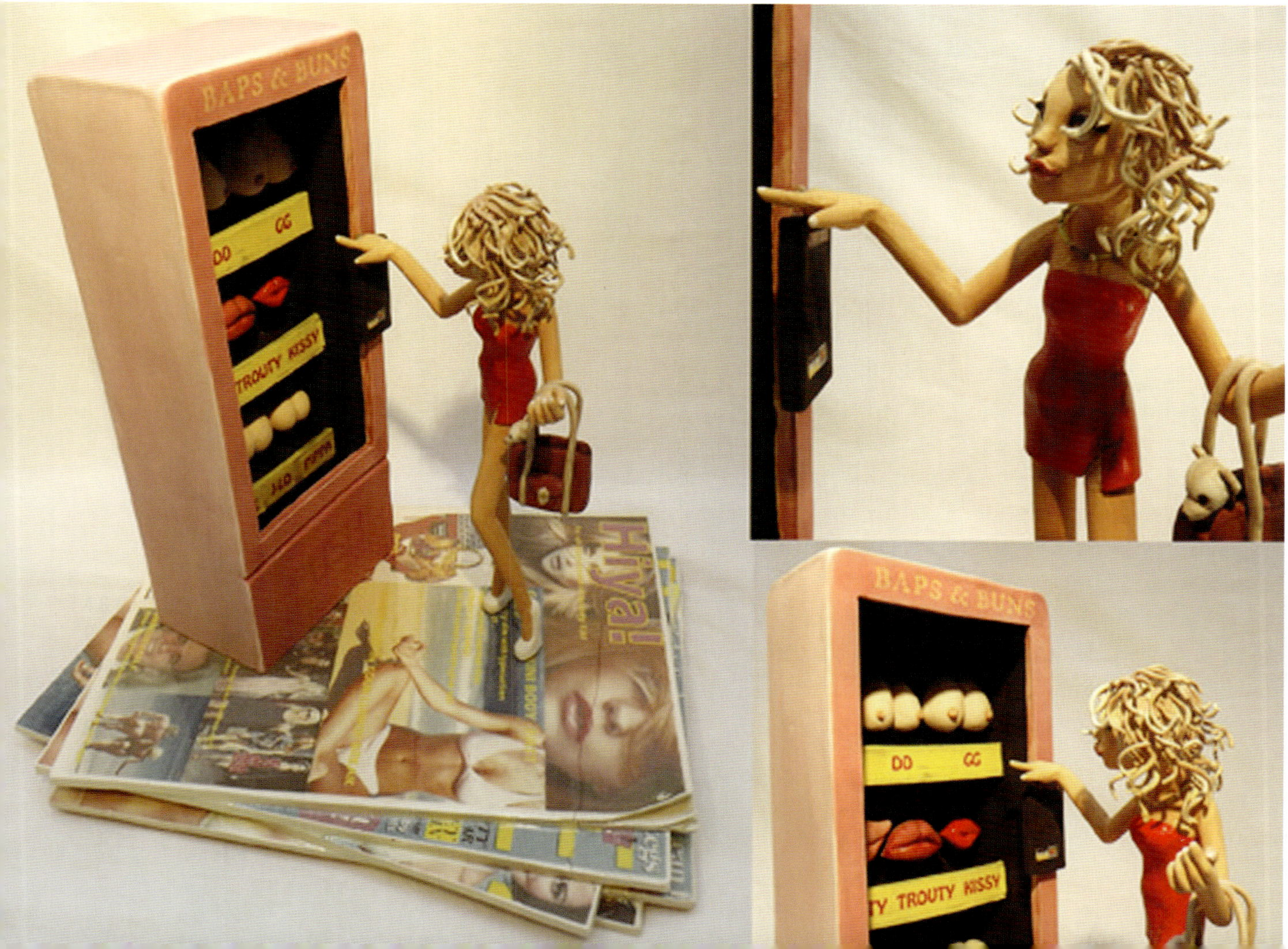

3.19 *Baps and Buns*, 2013, Jo Pipkin, BA Ceramics

and some men. The grotesque extremes of the image, disembodied breasts, buttocks and lips, for sale from a machine, make the point very effectively.

Absurdity and the grotesque are also Louise Hindsgavl's approaches to human relations, combined with allegory and comedy. Her most recent work, *Power, Porcelain, Poetry* (2014), is as the title suggests, a highly poetic, if, on closer inspection horribly brutal meditation on violence, depravity, corruption and all things vile and human – some of the time, anyway. It is a disaster zone of human relations. It may be a response to war, to domestic violence, or to mass political corruption – of the sort that depraves an entire nation, destroys its people and leaves them without a shred of human dignity. There are suggestions of torture, massacre, execution and rape, of every sort of violation and assault imaginable: all are present in this melee of figures, arranged in various tableaux. Some are obscured from view in frosted vitrines, others are eerily lit, others appear at the edges of upended furniture, and all the while the small creatures Hindsgavl presents to us are disturbingly loveable. They have sweet faces, even as one picks up a pair of scissors and cuts off the snout of another (Figure 3.20). One cannot write about it without recourse to picaresque language. These are sweet, if roguish, little animal-like things, part human part beast, with all the innocence that implies. Their actions, however, are anything but sweet and roguish: they are caught in a maelstrom of horror. There are perpetrators and victims, certainly, but also present is the certainty that, at any point, a perpetrator could themselves

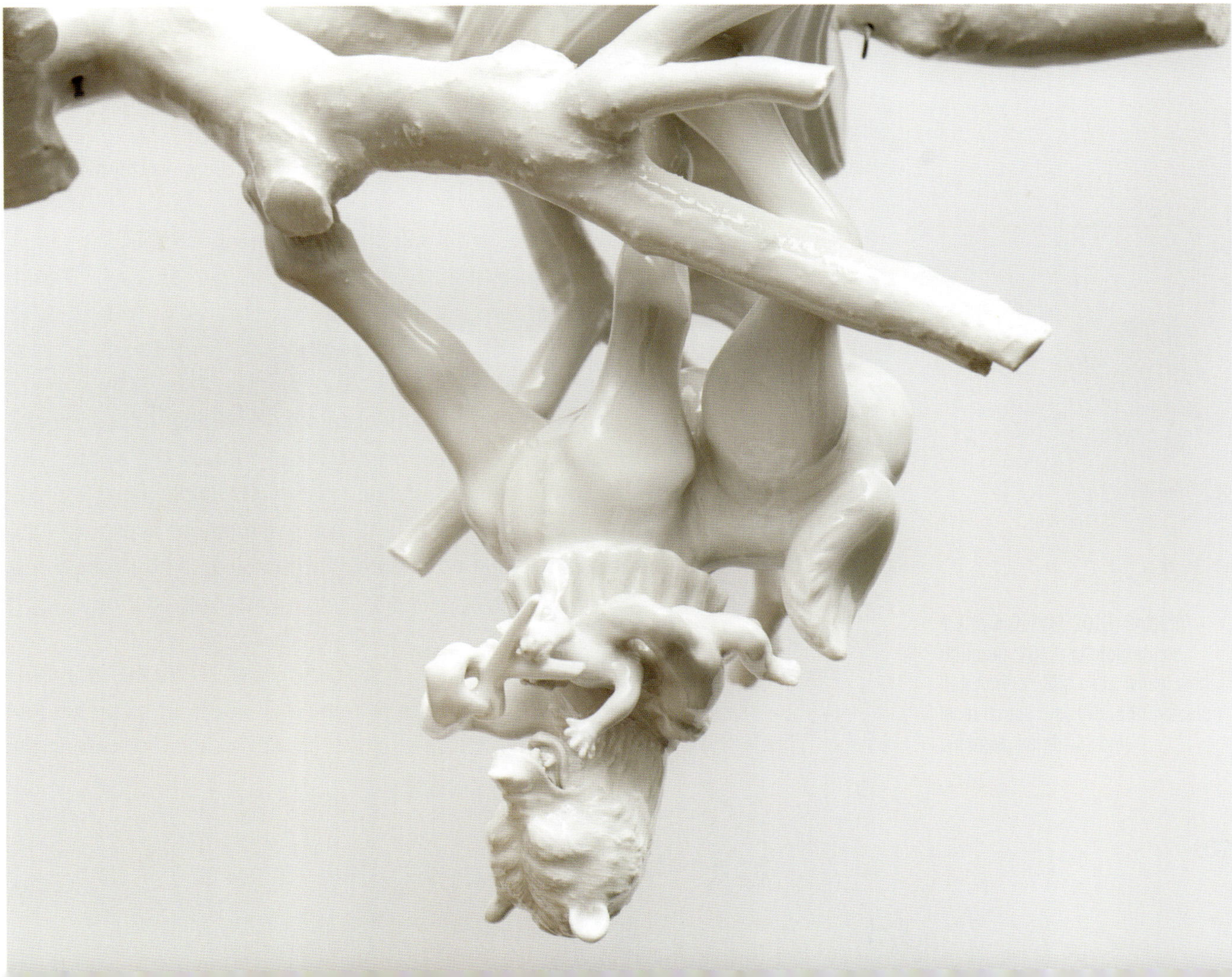

3.20 *Power, Porcelain, Poetry* (detail), 2014, Louise Hindsgavl, courtesy of the artist

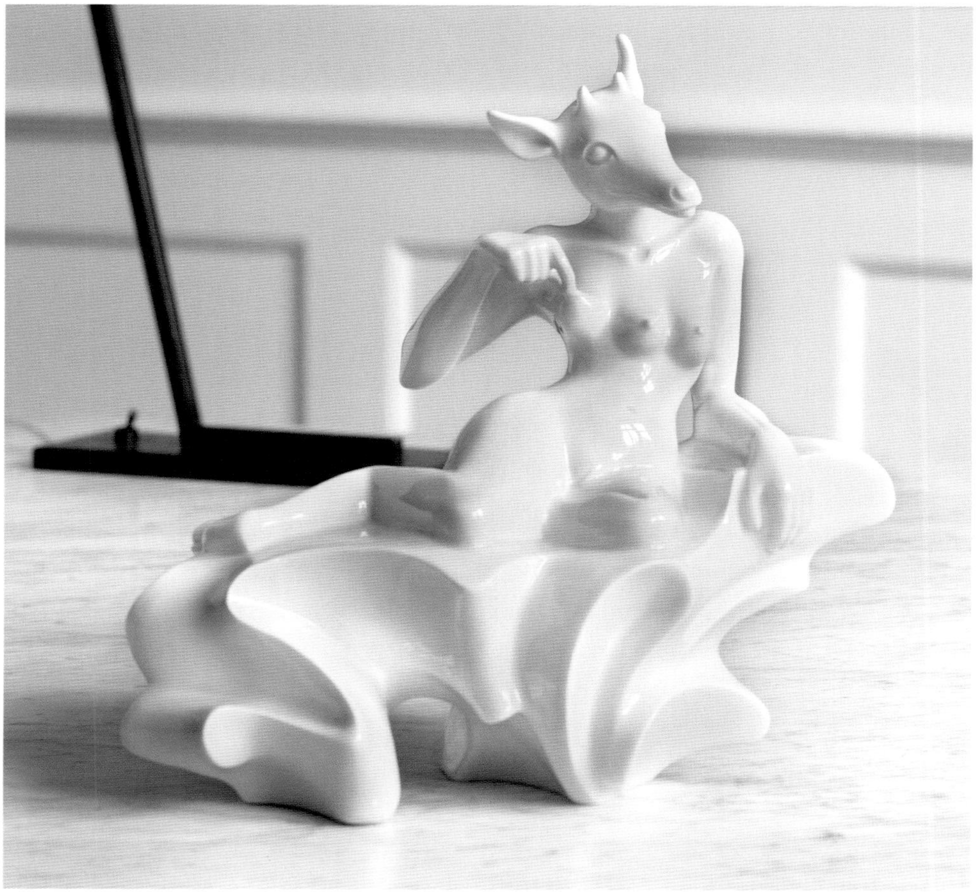

3.21 *Happiness*, 2012, Louise Hindsgavl, Kähler Design

be victimized. This is what makes this work almost unconscionably disturbing, but acts as an intensely moral tale, one that warns against politics being enough to guide moral principle or action.

Hindsgavl is not afraid to take on either the big subjects or the tiny tender moments. She executes both with equal conviction. *Stories of Eve* includes *Happiness* (Figure 3.21), *Love in Motion* and *Tenderness*, all three of which live up to their titles. *Happiness* is ridiculous, hilarious and imbued with no small sense of pathos. Three breasts? Oh the irony! Is this a comment on the insanity of the beauty industry, or the even greater insanity and absurdity of pornographic imagery? Is she ridiculing heterosexual men, or female breast-anxiety? Given the added twist of the charming deer head, it could be any of them. *Love in Motion* shows a roller-skating horse-headed adult figure with infants in its arms, a moment of exquisite joy encapsulated in the unfettered speed associated with the image, while *Tenderness* shows a horned figure stroking the bunny ears of a youngster who stands on hind legs to be so cosseted.

Brutality meets vulnerability in *You'll thank me later (I Hope)*, a brutal, unflinching image that condemns the practice of female genital mutilation without reserve. Hindsgavl presents the image of three older female 'mutilators' cutting the

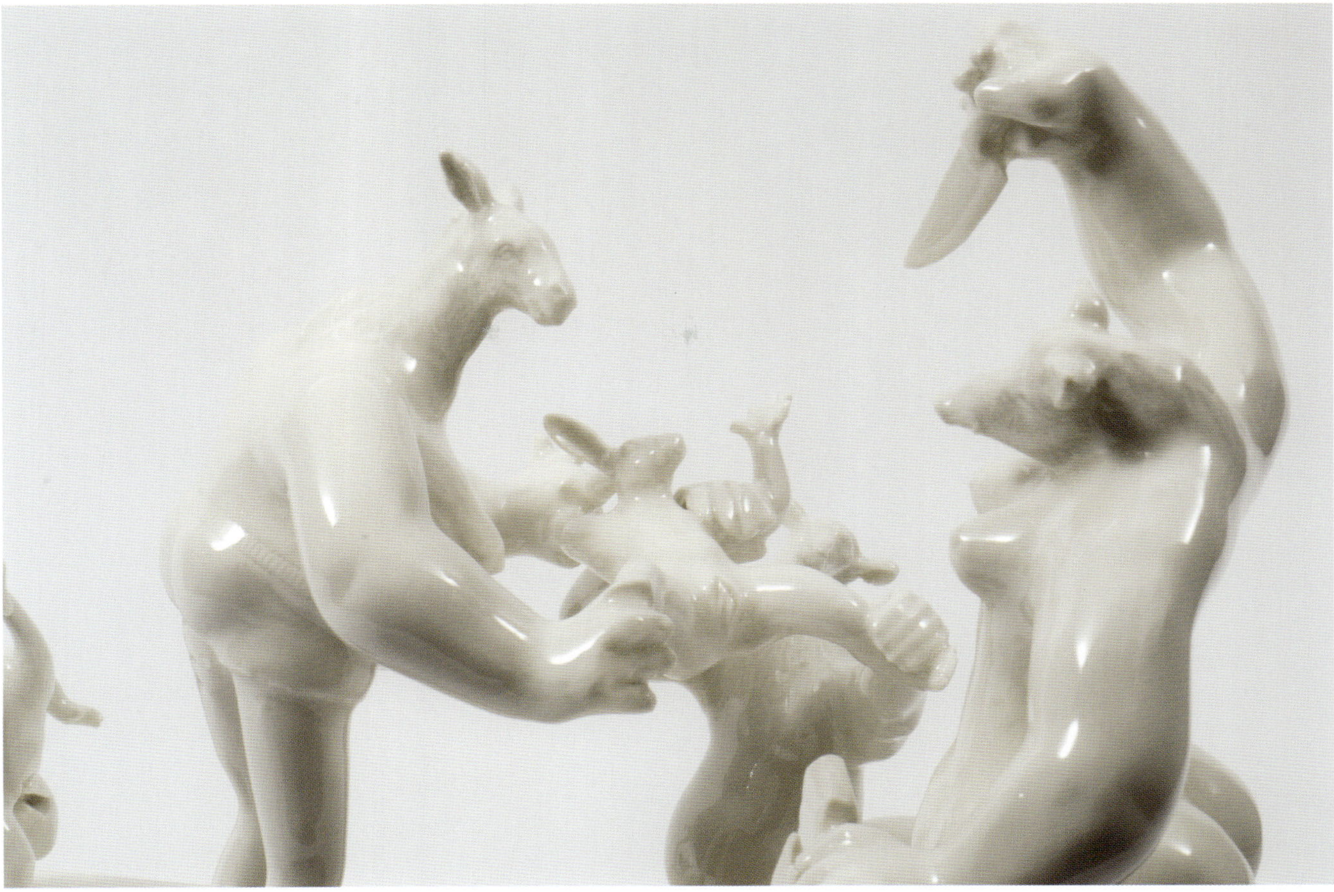

3.22 *You'll thank me later (I hope)*, FGM series, 2010, Louise Hindsgavl, courtesy of the artist

vagina of their young charge. She portrays the superior strength of the cutters, two holding the struggling child in place while the other wields a vast and hideous knife. One would wish there to be nothing subversive about such an image, but feminism and wider liberal thinking in Denmark, the UK and elsewhere in Europe has been plagued by a pernicious cultural relativism, a profoundly reactionary force, which suggests that FGM is a 'cultural' practice and should, therefore, be 'respected', or at least not condemned.[10] In the face of such collusion, it is a bold and welcome statement.

Kate McBride specializes in the imagery of excess. Tea sets become objects of decadence, festooned with cavorting women, snorting lines of cocaine and smoking spliffs, two at a time. Indulgence is matched only by the outrageous extent of the gold ornamentation and cascades of floral detailing. McBride's figures are craftily handmade, slightly awkward with their absurdly pointy, gold-tipped breasts. No more than stick figures, they are freely fashioned, gestural and wholly expressive of their decadent abandon. She uses the same approach to making for the figures in her Rainbow Chess Set. This is the anti-war chess set: it lampoons and renders absurd the entire meaning and purpose of chess to the earnest and military mind, and disrupts the strategic logic that divides humans into blocs, stubborn partisan binaries,

[10] Julie Bindel, 'The Ordeal of Muslim Women: No More Excuses', in *Standpoint*, March 2014.

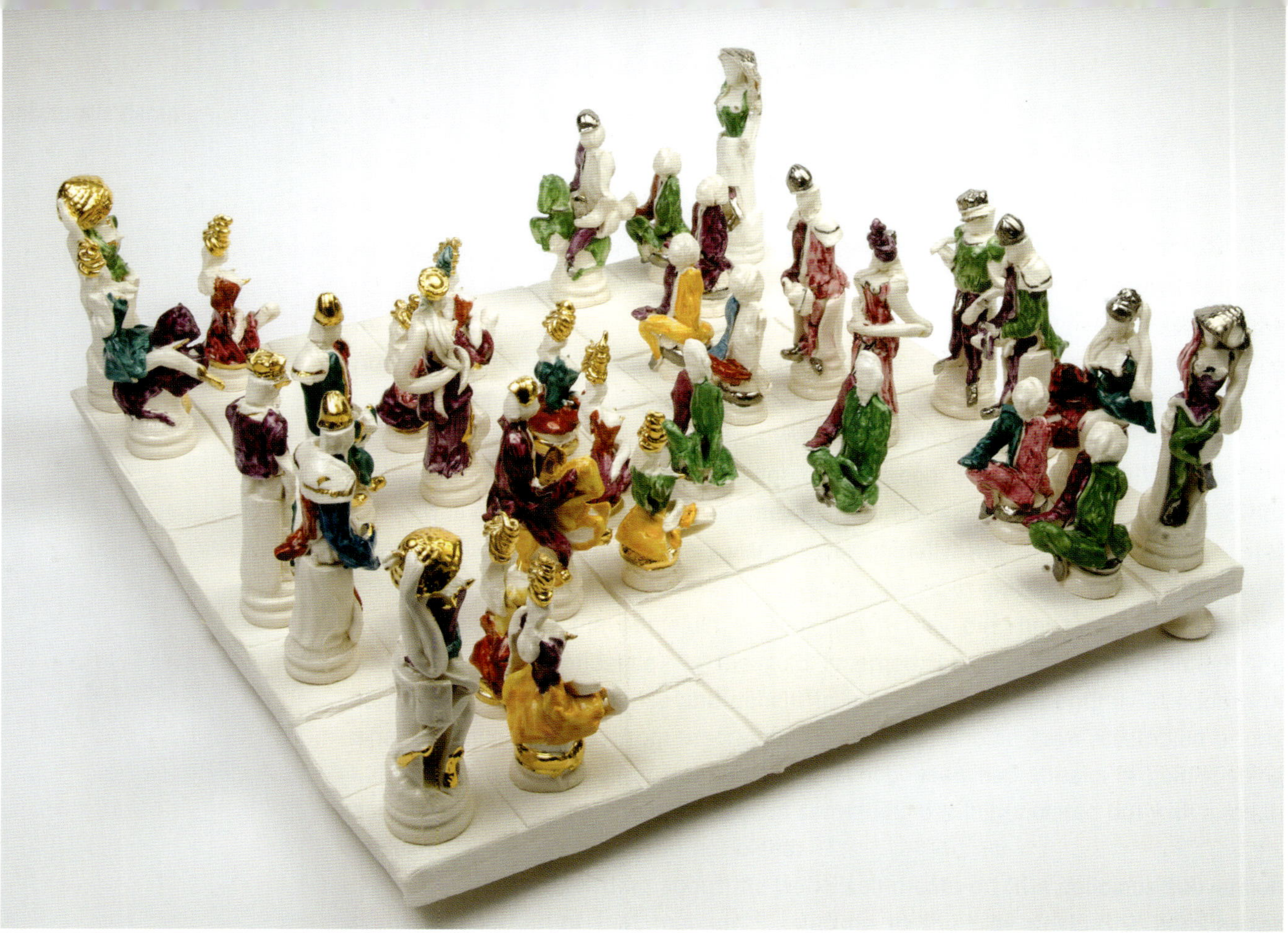

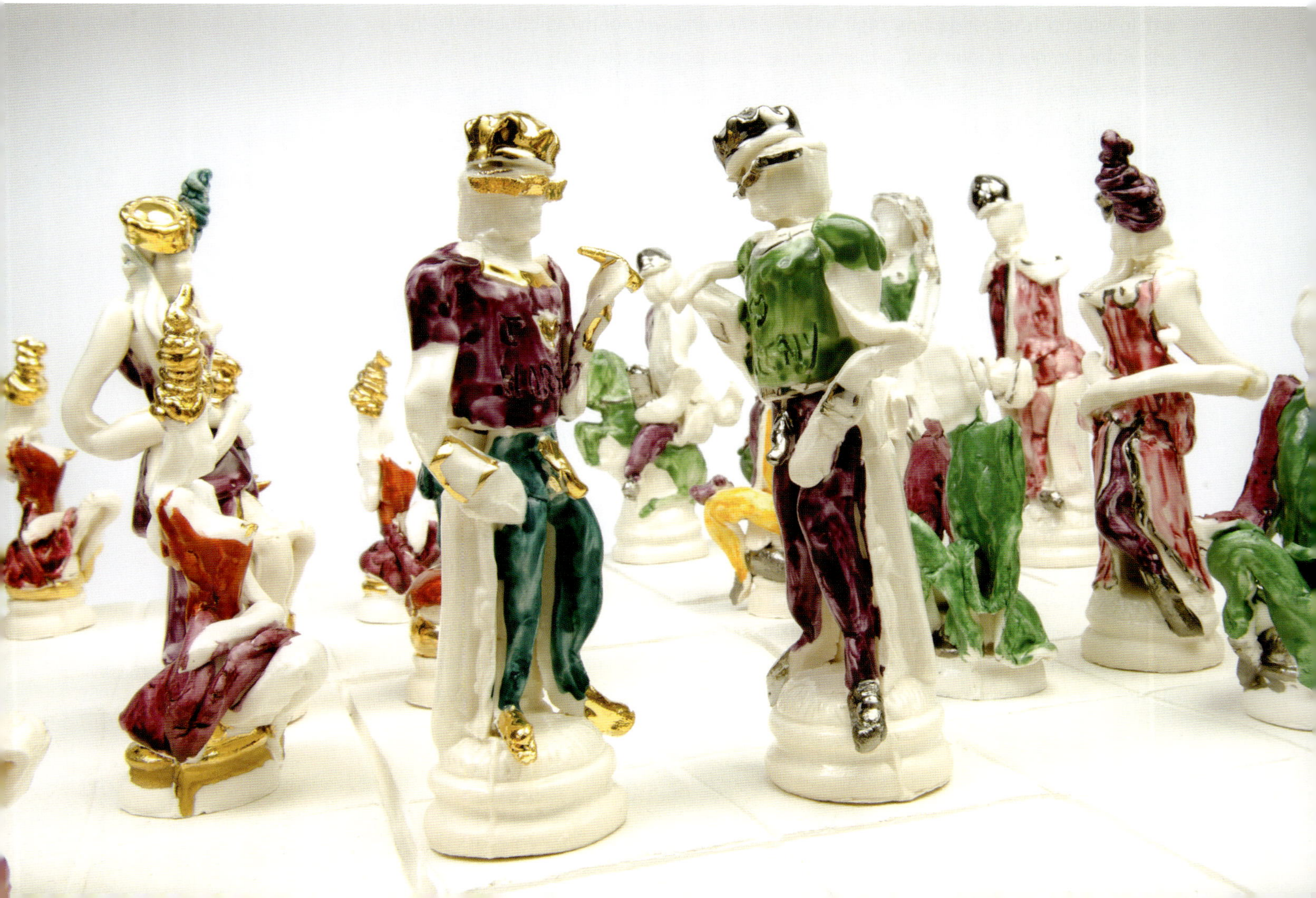

and devises reasons to kill and maim in vast numbers. An ingenious idea, this set comprises pieces that look suspiciously similar. As the game progresses, it becomes increasingly difficult to discern which piece should be moved by which player. Once again her making technique, freely expressive, unencumbered by anxieties about carefully made forms, emphasizes the chutzpah of these saboteurs and refuseniks of the military project. As a subversion of an archetype, this is one of the most impudent I have encountered in ten years of research. It is easily the most convincing anti-war statement I have seen in ceramic form, where the tendency has been to make protest work – which is perfectly valid, but not subversive by any definition.

3.23, 3.24 Opposite: *Rainbow Chess Set*, 2014, (detail below). Kate McBride, photographer: Martin Bramwell

Where outrageous cheek is concerned, Virgil Ortiz's figurines also take some beating. The traditional pueblo figurine had been largely ignored but has recently seen a revival. Ortiz has completely reinvented it as part of his new pueblo-chic urban-warrior project. His figurines, like his pots, are swathed in the latest fashions but with animal or bird heads, or the body of a horse (Figure 3.25). Some have two heads and accessorized futuristic 'pets', others are part reptile, or anthropomorphic beasts. There are acrobats performing elegant if almost inhuman feats of contortion and there are figures in pairs and threes engaged in bizarre ritualistic behaviour. Though Ortiz is at the leading edge of rethinking Native American ceramics, he acknowledges his predecessors and builds on their aesthetic. A recent post on his Facebook page,

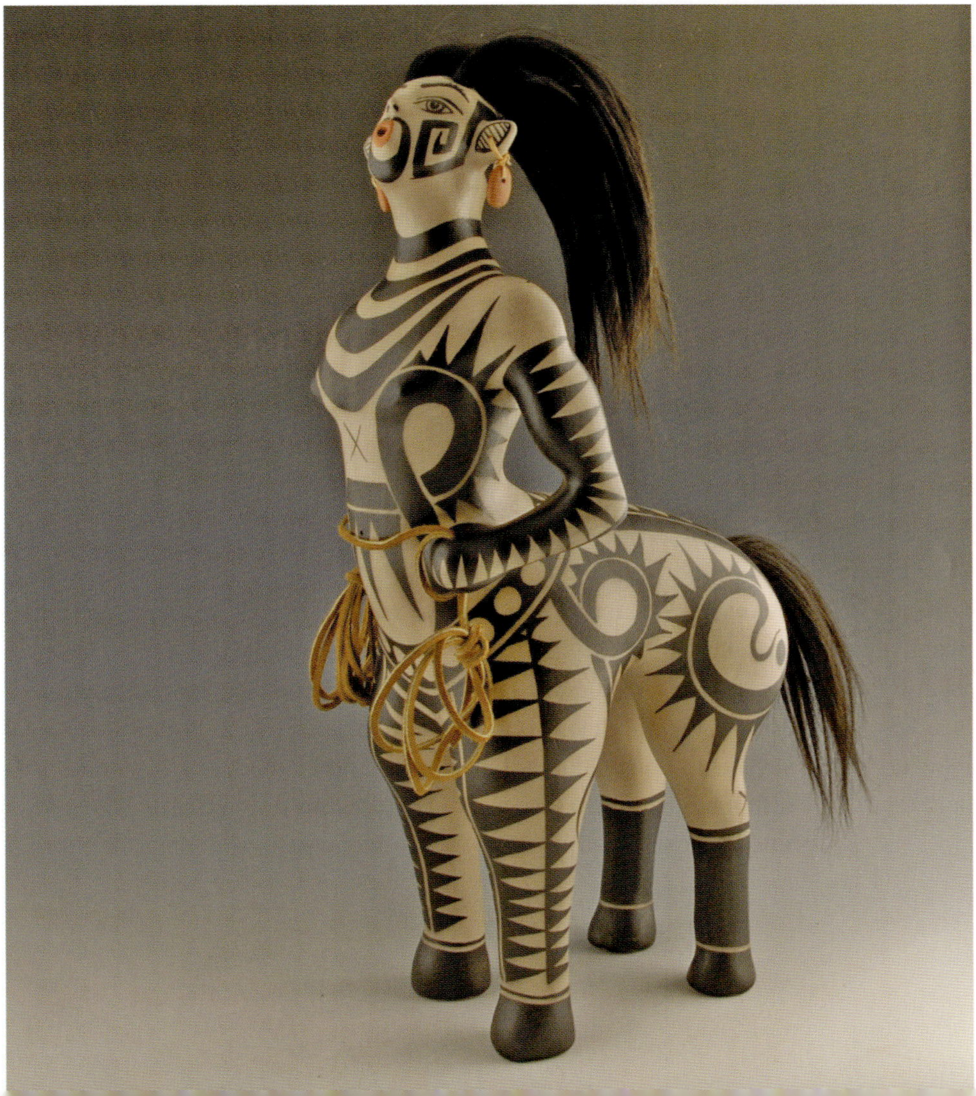

3.25 *Centaur*, 2011, Virgil Ortiz, courtesy of King Galleries and Virgil Ortiz

of an elegant shallow dish by his grandmother, Laurencita Herrera, shows clearly from where his knowledge and understanding of pattern, form and design were derived, deepening the richness already apparent in the Ortiz revolution.

Also honouring an ancient material and form, and also in anti-war mode, is Syrian ceramicist Zahed Tajeddin. According to Nigel Woods, the type of Egyptian faience that Tajeddin works with predates both glass and conventional glazed ceramic. It is, in effect, a modelling recipe that does not include clay and, therefore has very little plasticity. Woods likens it to working with 'fine wet sand'. The original Egyptian faience recipe was mixed with a small amount of copper, which produced the blue, comparable in colour to the highly prized and valuable lapis lazuli, but made from simple, relatively cheap materials. It was used to create, among other things, the ushabtis, small figurines that were buried in vast numbers in Egyptian tombs to serve the occupant in the afterlife.

Using this seven-thousand-year-old technique, Tajeddin has produced an entirely new population of figurines, the 'Nu-shabtis', who, in the most delicious twist of fantasy have escaped eternal entombment and, finding no master to serve, no pharaoh – not one instantly recognizable as such, anyway – to venerate, have

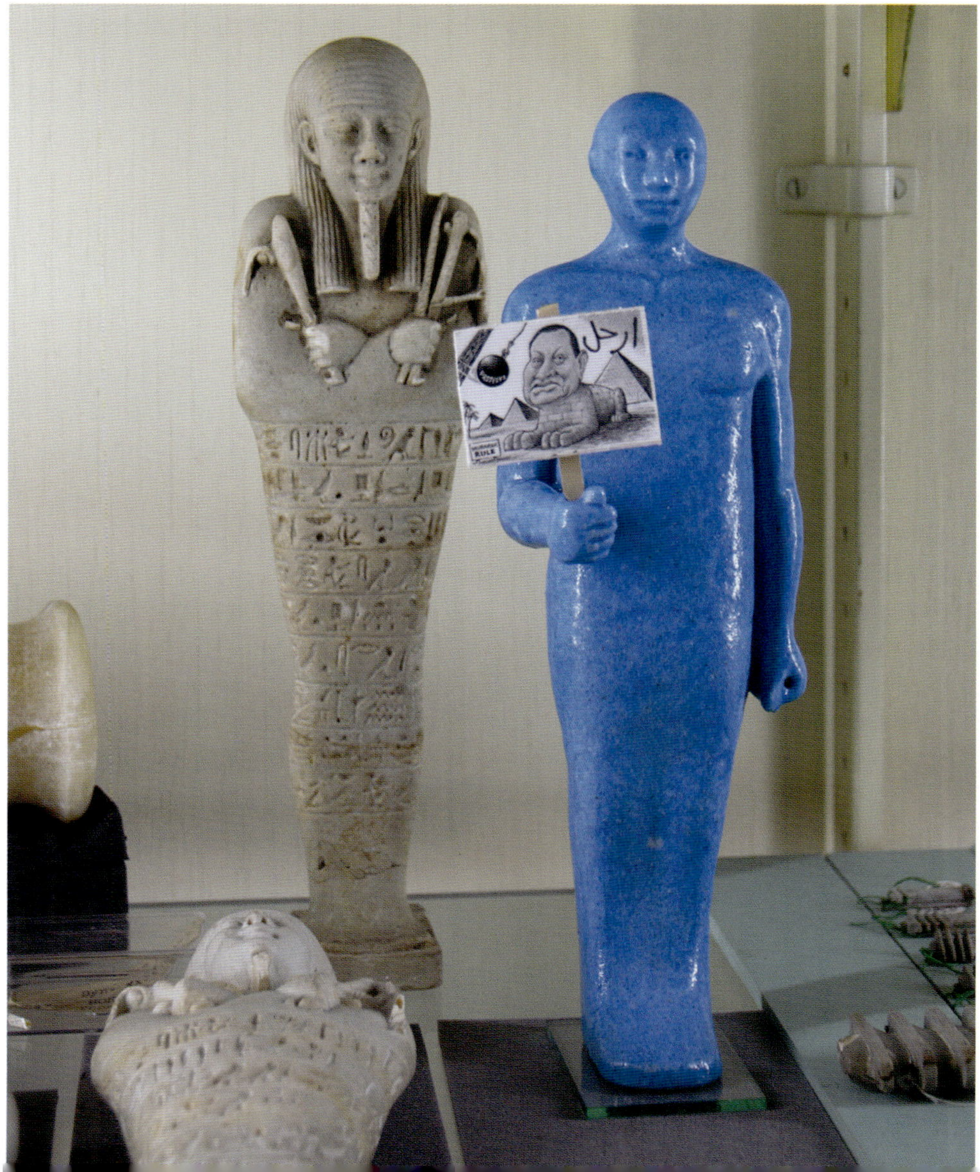

3.26 *Nu-shabti protester*, detail from 'Nu-Shabtis, Liberation', shown at the Petrie Museum of Egyptian Archaeology, London, 2014, Zahed Tajeddin, courtesy of the artist

melted into everyday life in Europe and the Middle East and found new interests and occupations. With the addition of a few plastic props, some of the Nu-shabtis have conformed to a Western consumer and commuter lifestyle, with brand-name carrier bags and phones permanently clamped to their ears. Others are pursuing the arts and literature, or have become 'citizen journalists' and commentators. A few have joined the demonstrations of the Arab Spring, and one, perhaps with a distant memory of life as a ushabti, carries a placard showing President Mubarak as an Egyptian pharaoh, with 'Just GO' (Figure 3.26), one of the widely used slogans during the 2011 demonstrations, written in Arabic above the pyramid on his placard. Another demonstrator carries a placard with a picture of President Bashir Al Assad, 'Assad Murderer' is written on this one; another wears the mask of the 'Anonymous' movement, an 'internet gathering' of protestors, 'activists and hacktivists', whose main aim was to disrupt the activities of government, religious authorities and multinational corporations by disabling their websites.

Fired in shades of copper blues and greens, Tajeddin has fashioned this notoriously difficult material into finely modelled figures with facial features and cast them in series. He has created groups, crowds and individuals, some of whom stand

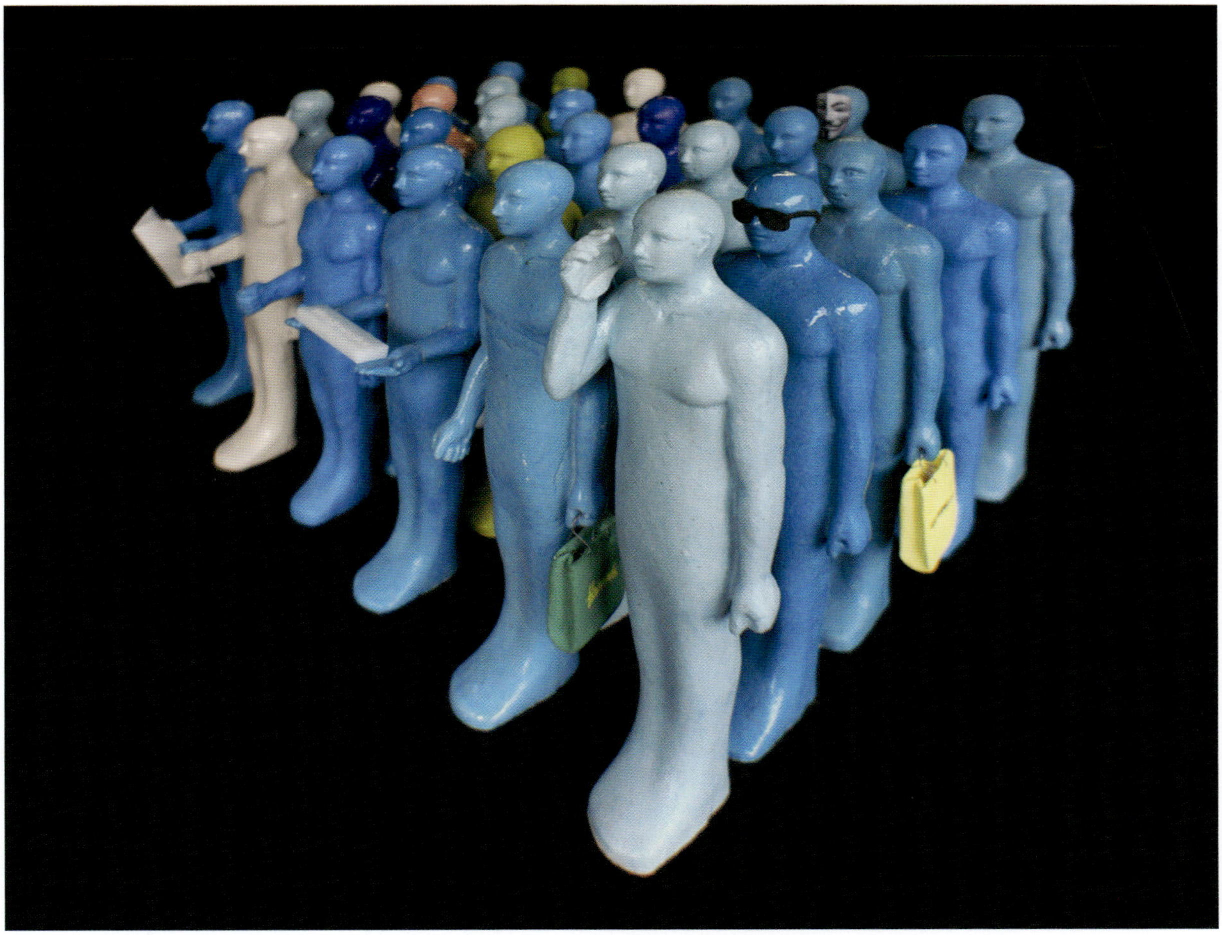

3.27 *Nu-shabtis*, 2014, Zahed Tajeddin, courtesy of the artist

out in entirely new, non-Egyptian colours. There is a rogue pink and a poisonous-looking mustard yellow and green. The Nu-shabtis were exhibited at the Petrie Museum, London, in 2014, placed among the ancient Egyptian archaeological exhibits, in their vitrines. It was an extraordinary conceit, which completely reinvented one of the oldest and most challenging materials and forms known to ceramics and revitalized it with a mix of international politics, revolution, digital technology and social observation.

Conclusion

All of the artists in this chapter have acknowledged traditional or historic forms and materials but have responded by producing entirely new work. These are not pastiches, even where they appear close to an original type. The artists have expanded the conventions of the form or type, liberating the narrative and allowing them to bring a subtlety and delicacy of political analysis to their storytelling. This is particularly apparent in Kate McBride's chess set, which completely rethinks what a chess set might do. The next chapter discusses the work of artists whose practice has been described as 'subversive', mainly because they are using new methods of making. This includes the use of 'ready-mades', where industrially manufactured forms are altered, added to or simply placed in a new context to create new work. In effect, industry enters the studio, releasing studio pottery from its prolonged debt to traditional – or faux traditional – craft practices and fusing industrial craft, technology and design with individual studio practice.

4

Emancipation: New methods of production

Introduction

The most painfully honest pot I have ever encountered is the Indian *kulhar.* It was the handmade, terracotta, single-use cup, thrown by the hundred off a single lump of clay and low-fired by the thousand. They were used daily to serve hot sweet tea to passengers on the Indian National Railway, well into the 1990s, and were immediately discarded once the tea was finished. Embodying consummate skill, made and fired to meet the exact requirements of their use, they were immaculately crafted, produced in industrial quantities and quickly became rubbish. I wanted to keep one, but the low firing makes them easily breakable, so mine, like everyone else's on the train that day, was discarded.

Kjell Rylander's *Street Ware* (2009) (Figure 4.1) is the antithesis of the *kulhar.* He rescues used, discarded paper cups from coffee shops and reinvents them as artefacts, with an added porcelain rim or handle. His vision of ennobling the ubiquitous takeaway cup by turning it into art – or mocking the art world value of porcelain, whichever is preferable – is one of the more iconoclastic examples of the upcycling tendency in contemporary ceramic practice. The porcelain rings attached to his *Untitled* (2007),[1] damaged, mass-produced catering mugs resemble the rings of a planet drifting off into space and evoke the thought of handles but these are handles the wrong way up, too frail to be useful. It is an art object, derived from a combination of industrial design, rubbish and a contrary but inventive mind. Rylander's work might be either holding up a mirror to first-world industrial capitalism to display its disposable and polluting habits or questioning the values attributed to art.

Using ready-mades, new and old; breaking – or otherwise disrupting – existing ceramics and remaking them as something else; using unfired clay or non-ceramic objects associated with clay, such as plaster moulds or paper cups, are now all part of a growing discipline and, in effect, represent the vanguard of the studio pottery movement. Upcycling, taking old objects of little or no value, and reinventing them as art is a close relative of recycling and at least as old. Folk art, since the dawn of time, has relied on turning spent objects to another use, aided by finely honed craft skills. Moreover, as Jorunn Veiteburg observes in *Thing Tang Trash*, the process of

[1] Edmund de Waal, *The Pot Book*, London: Phaidon, 2011, 236.

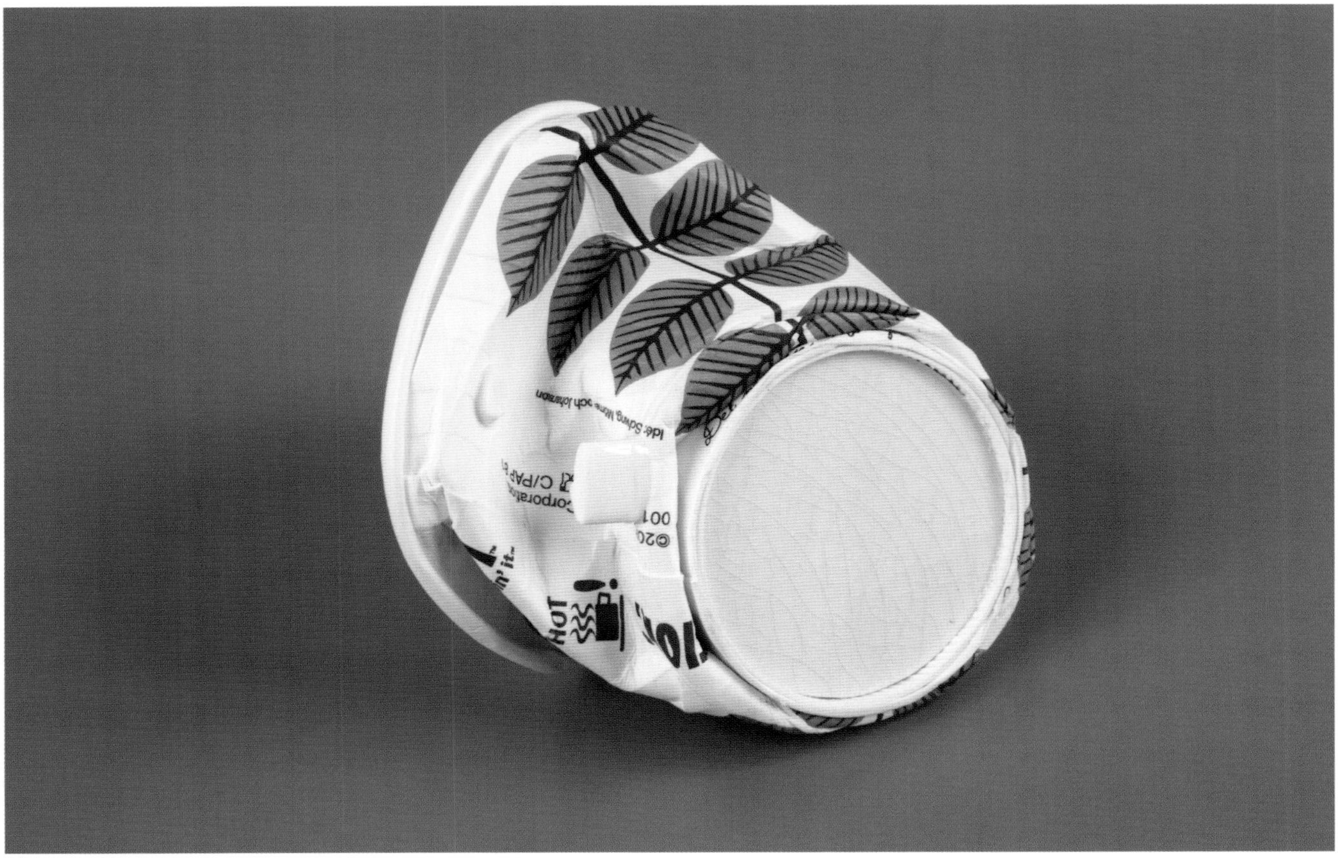

4.1 *Street Ware*, 2009, Kjell Rylander, size 11 x 9 x 7 cm, paper, porcelain, glue, photographer: Ernst Grilnberger

harvesting discarded objects, crafted or industrial, and using them in the making of new work is not new in itself in ceramics.[2] What Kjell Rylander does now is, in spirit, what Carol McNicholl and Richard Slee have been doing since the 1970s. Neither critique nor subversion are inherent in either the methods of production or in the ways the artists think about these ceramics but there is an iconoclastic quality to some of it. Some of the artists work in this way because they want to shake out the more rigid norms of studio pottery, but most do so because it is the best way to advance their craft or articulate a particular narrative. Either way, it is frequently characterized as subversive, so needs to be addressed in these terms.

Willow pattern lost and gained

'Every day was the same, just the sea, the sea. I saw nothing more. The sea and my boat. I had no idea of time, but I know that it was December 21, 2012, when we left. The days at sea and the nights ... they were all one after a while.'[3] Jose Salvador Alvarenga, the Mexican fisherman quoted here, was alone, drifting across the Pacific Ocean for thirteen months. My studio assistant, Hossein, a refugee from Iran, almost lost his life with some three hundred others in an unseaworthy craft built for twenty.

[2] Jorunn Veiteberg, *Thing Tang Trash: Upcycling in Contemporary Ceramics*, Bergen National Academy of the Arts, 2011, 28–36.

[3] Jose Salvador Alvarenga, television news report, 2 February 2014, reported in *The Daily Mail*, 3 February 2014.

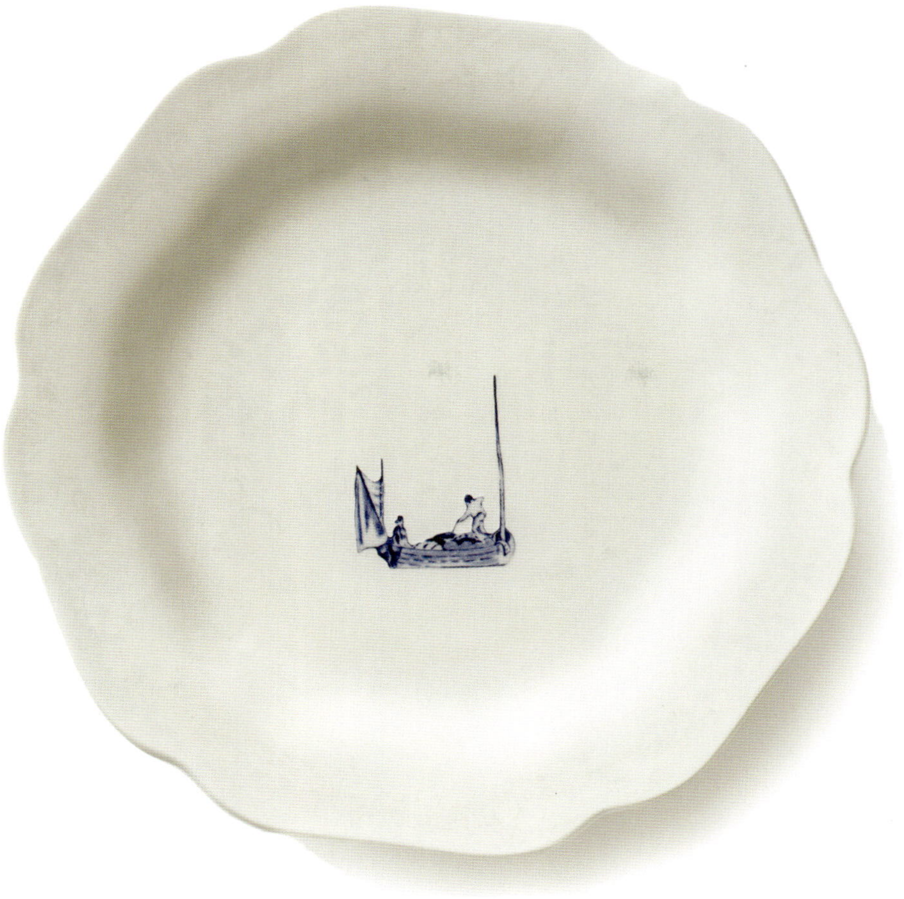

4.2 From the series *Gone Fishing*, 2009, Caroline Slotte, photographer: Oystein Klakegg

Anyone who works at sea, or has had to cross it to effect an escape, knows how threatening its power and vastness can be. Caroline Slotte's epic images of tiny boats alone in a mighty sea of unadorned plate are profoundly affecting, perhaps because the viewer is susceptible, bringing personal experience to the work, or possibly because the busy romantic pattern of the original object, a willow pattern plate, lingers in the memory. That pattern is ordinary to the point of banality but so well known that we inevitably feel its loss and respond to the loneliness of the single, isolated boat.

Slotte breathes life into the most lifeless of objects, transforming old, stained, second-hand plates, complete with limescale rings and stained crackled glaze, into something utterly new and convincing. She cuts and files and sandblasts her way through the layers of glaze and pattern to the bare bones of the plate beneath. Some plates are busier, layered with others of a smaller size, piling up with their centres cut away to reveal some of the image on the plate beneath. The top one has most of the centre removed, cut back to a leafy border, resembling the scenery in a puppet show. Each layer casts a tiny shadow on the one beneath, exaggerating distance and depth (Figure 4.3). It is an astonishingly theatrical production; one half expects the sun to rise and the figures to start ploughing. Slotte's plates are exquisite ruins that embody the spirit of the Romantics. They provoke awe and wonder, such is the power of their rescued, revitalized beauty.

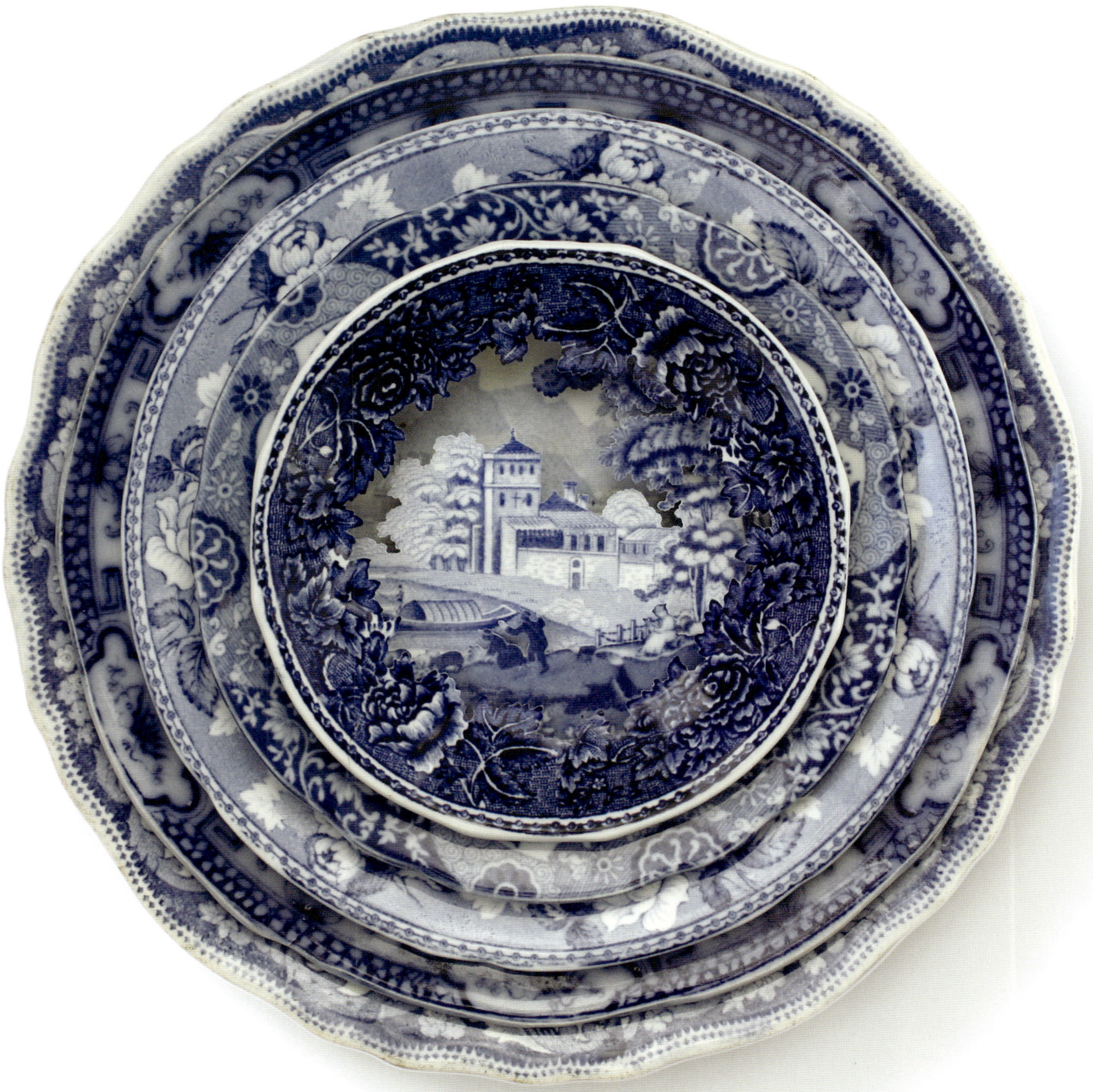

4.3 From the series *Landscape Multiple*, 2012, Caroline Slotte

Paul Scott occupies similar territory, the lyrical strand of the upcycling craft. His most recent work makes use of restoring techniques including kintsugi and stapling, which allow him to use the broken plates in his studio, bought whole from online auction sites but broken by the time they arrive. He is reviving some of the older restoration practices, eschewed by contemporary conservators because they 'interfere with the integrity of the objects'. The conservators are right, they do, but they are perfect for artists creating new works from old.

Alberta No: 5 (2011) is a broken china plate, riveted together with brass staples, with a printed blue image of a house, a lone house on a prairie, near a horizon line half way up the plate, where the break is. The rivets suggest fence posts, one row following the horizon, the other wandering off into the Canadian outback following its own perspective. It is reminiscent of an Andrew Wyeth painting or an old photograph, the sort of image that has no detail but around which one could construct an entire film script. The sense of pathos is overwhelming and hugely appealing. These are contemplative works, as true to their materials, their craft, their manufacture, history

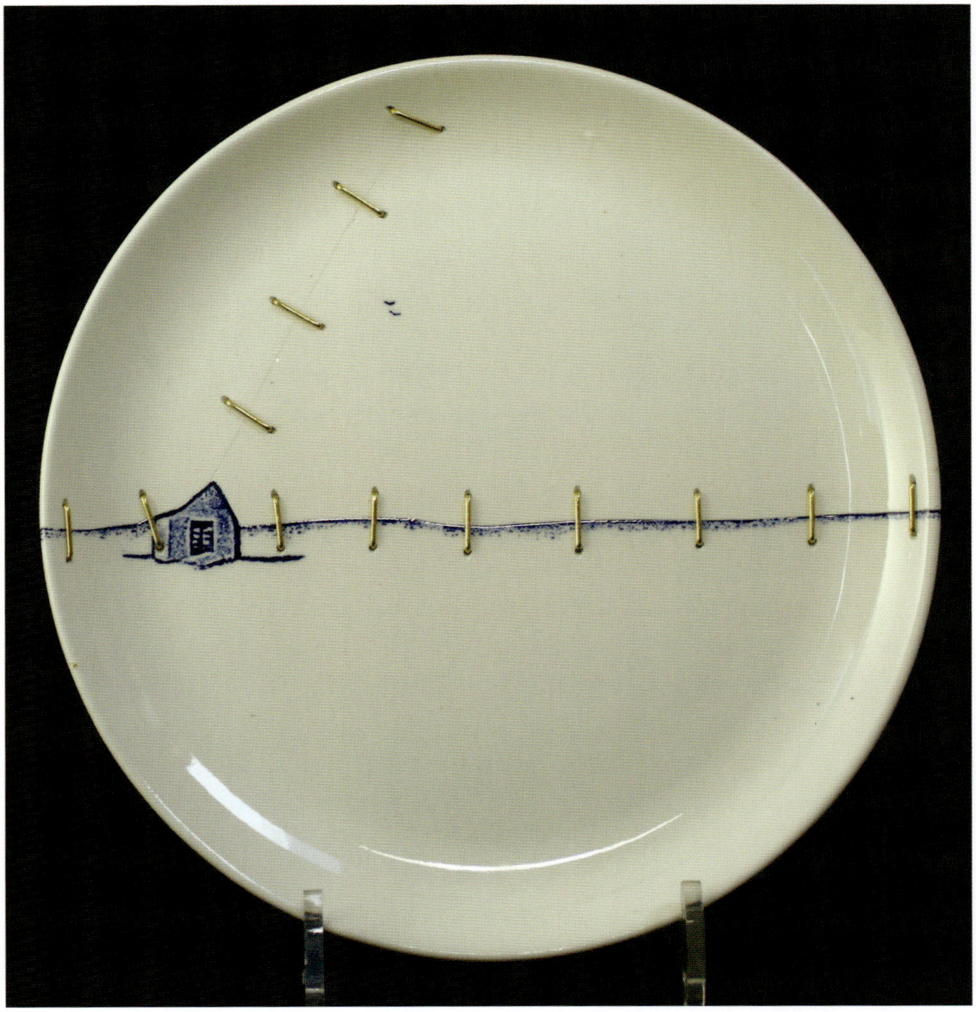

4.4 *Alberta No: 5*, 2011, Paul Scott, Scott's Cumbrian Blue(s), Alberta No: 5. Inglaze decal collage on broken Hycroft china earthenware plate, riveted together with brass staples, diameter 25 cm. Medalta, Medicine Hat, Alberta, Canada and Blencogo, Cumbria, UK

and culture, as any work of art or craft could be. Like it or not, these are profoundly honest pots. If the 'honest pot' is a defining point of studio pottery, nothing proves the point better than the work of Scott, Ryland and Slotte, that the upcyclers are the avant-garde of studio pottery.

Land and sea

A giant, ungainly, barnacled creature has washed up on the sands of Dubai. Resembling a beached whale, this slumped form is crusted in ceramic shards, built up in layers, like the growth of a shell. Bita Fayyazi's concern with discarded things, what counts as disposable and what is valued, is evident in these recent works in *Sculpture on the Beach*, Art Dubai (2013). The pale, almost white form is made up of porcelain shards printed with pink roses, the mass-produced fine china of the tea table. It is one of a group – a shoal, perhaps – of similar works. These objects look and feel as though they may be still alive – just – or have recently died, or perhaps were corpses or wrecks that floated for weeks through the oceans, gathering the discarded flotsam of civilizations that amassed below the sea's surface. They are repellent and fascinating at the same time, which is a familiar and recurring theme in Fayyazi's work, recalling the dead dogs in *Road Kill* and the *Cockroaches* installation. In these works, discarded broken ceramics are not being rehabilitated or remade. They are being upcycled and turned into art, but it is art that represents detritus as the archaeological remains of our various civilizations. *trunKated* (Figure 4.5) refers to the stop–start juddering movement of one civilization breaking and emerging later as another, building up layers of memory beneath and above the ground. It is the stuff of thousands of years amassed from across the globe, presenting itself to the beating heart of international shopping and disposable income as a strange but familiar thing stranded on the beach during the flagship Dubai art fair.

Fayyazi has used a form of allegorical illusion to produce a thoughtful, reflective and politically charged work. She uses industrial process and products as sculptural materials, expanding what ceramics might be, but the potentially subversive – or more accurately, satiric – meaning of the work is produced more by the meeting of narrative with place than by the method of making in itself. The same is true of Israeli artist Shlomit Bauman, whose work is profoundly connected to land, identity and 'locality'. The 'finger' of Galilee, northern Israel, is where Bauman was born and raised on Kibbutz Amir. In 1939 the land alongside the Palestinian village of AlDuwara was drained, initially for farming and to eradicate the malaria-carrying mosquitoes. Nine years later, in May 1948, the village was destroyed and the land became part of the agricultural project of the kibbutz.

Bauman's *Channel AlDuwara* (2007), combining ceramic television monitors, film and sound, uses the 1954 propaganda film celebrating the founding of the kibbutz to begin the re-reading of her own history, a questioning of accepted

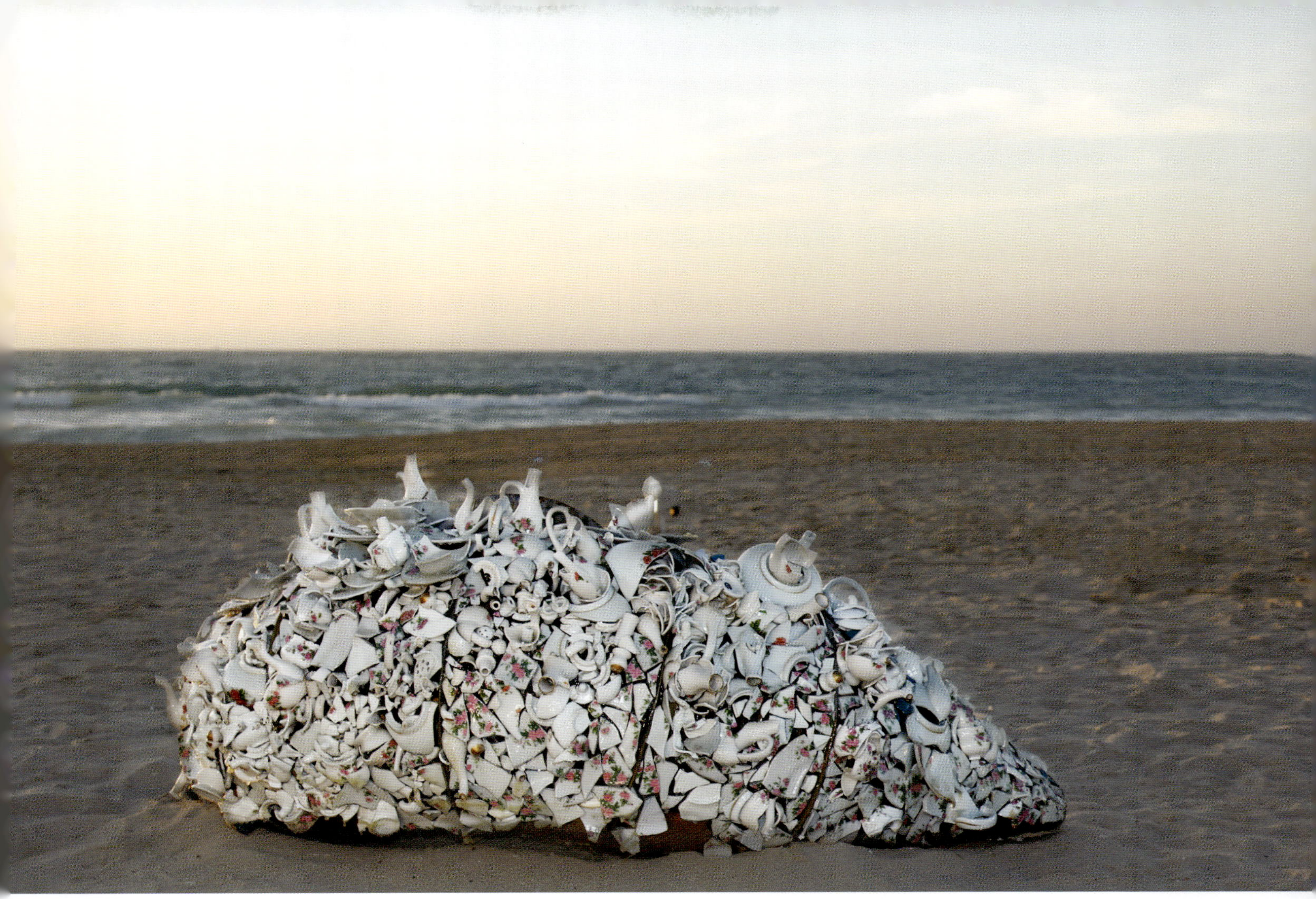

4.5 *trunKated*, 2013, Bita Fayyazi, 2013, photographer: Maziar Sadr

memory. The soundtrack combines the buzzing of mosquitoes with the sound of Bauman's voice repeatedly referring to 'good relations with our neighbours from the village, AlDuwara', alerting the viewer to the untold parts of the kibbutz story. The founding of the egalitarian kibbutzim, which operated along collective, proto-socialist lines, was and is still a central foundation narrative for the state of Israel. Bauman's ceramic televisions, projectors of propaganda, among other things, look bizarre as they assert their material origins, while also emitting moving images. It is an ingenious metaphor which links propaganda and its primary channel, television, to land, or clay in this case.

Channel AlDuwara signalled the beginning of a series of work connected to 'locality', and what it means to be Israeli. Bauman became interested in the Canaanite school of Israeli art which formed in the early to mid-twentieth century with the aim of developing a discrete Israeli identity in art, distinct from Jews in other parts of the world. Connection to land and a concern with archaic forms was an obvious place to start, although it was probably not a coincidence that this linked it with the mainstream of European modernism as well. Craft had also played a significant part in the evolution of these ideas, particularly in the production of judaica, with the founding of the Bezalel School of Art and Crafts in 1906. In the late twentieth century, Israeli artists became increasingly critical of dominant national – and nationalist –

ideology. They questioned the supposed authenticity of the land-based ideas and of the construction of a national memory through art and objects. Many adopted a position of protest against Israeli militarism in their work, and against dominant social and political attitudes towards the Arab–Israeli conflict.

Ran Out (2013) grew out of Bauman's research into 'locality', combined with the news that the earthenware she intended to use for the new work was so drastically depleted that the supply would soon cease. The clay, categorized somewhat prosaically as 'S5', was similar to that used in traditional Palestinian pottery. She immediately ordered the last remaining ton of dry clay and with it produced a collection of extraordinary hybrid works that combine the pale, ochre-tinted terracotta clay, the S5, with porcelain. Her aim was to produce a series of uncanny objects, using the technical and social incompatibility of the two clays as a metaphor for conflict. Porcelain is a high-value, treasured material, loved by collectors and acceptable to the high-end art market, whereas traditionally earthenware is a demotic clay used for low-value, utilitarian objects, and widely understood as the authentic material of ethnic folk craft.

It is not just the materials that are incompatible in *Ran Out*; the objects too are absurdly mismatched. There are ungainly, gleaming white television monitors and keyboard shapes cast from porcelain, lodged in traditional-looking pottery forms, made from the terracotta clay. Something resembling a bizarre relic of either megaphone diplomacy or a noisy demonstration appears, part porcelain, part earthenware. The trumpet-shaped end is supplied by an earthenware bowl with fluted edge, a pot

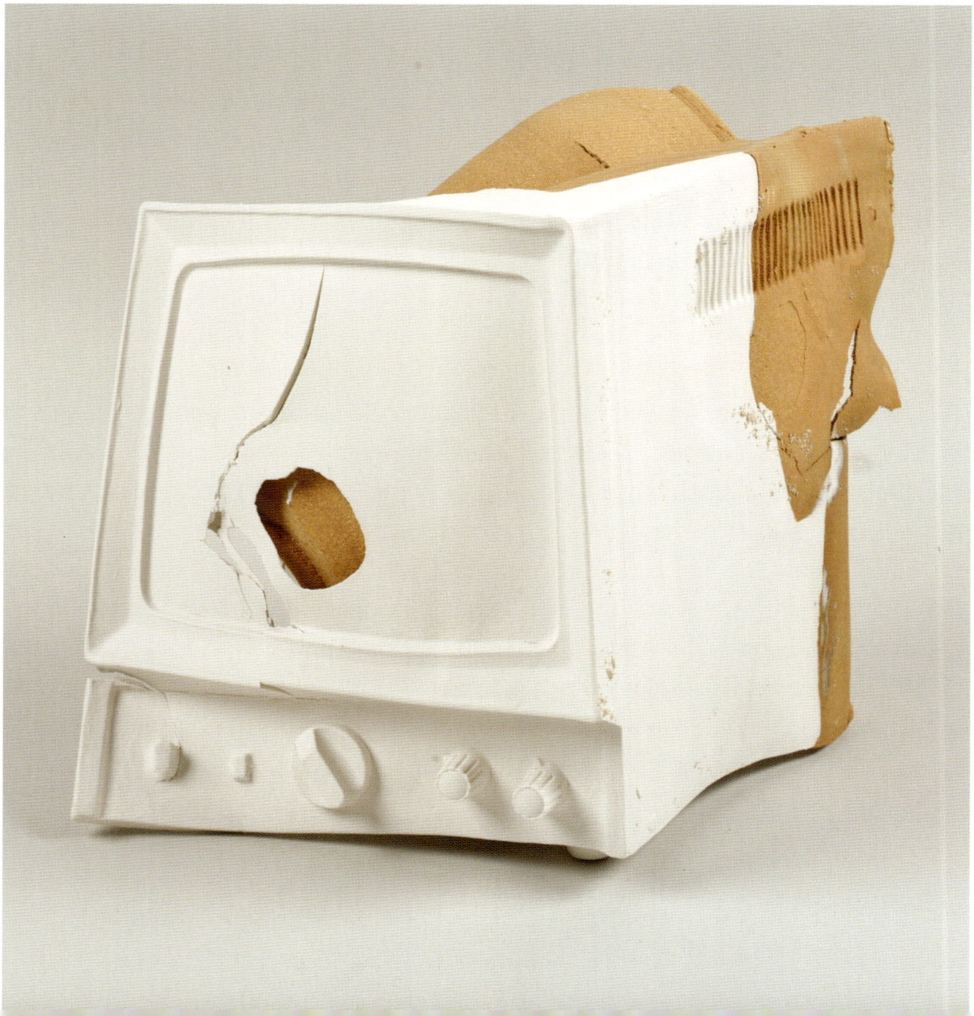

4.6 *Ran Out 11*, 2013, Shlomit Bauman, 2013, photographer: Ilan Amihai. Slip cast, wheel work, local Israeli clay (S5) and porcelain Limoges, height 22 cm

form traditional to Hebron; the handle end, containing the megaphone itself, is cast from porcelain – smooth and satisfyingly perfect. As David Goss commented in his introduction to *Ran Out*, these are 'grotesques',[4] dysfunctional creatures, repellent but fascinating. They mix industrial-style casting methods with handbuilding, and traditional utilitarian forms with smooth, clean, high-tech modernity. The unravelling pot (Figure 4.7) shows the materials pulling apart and causing each other to shatter. This is a craft process, or perhaps anti-craft. It is a wilful act, destined to explode the pot. As a metaphor for conflict, the mutually destructive nature of these works is entirely avoidable; it has been deliberately designed into the process.

Clay is profoundly connected to myths about life as well as to the practical realities of sustenance, survival, community, food and drink. As such it can be a powerfully resonant material and, in the case of *Ran Out*, the depletion of the clay itself suggests a corresponding depletion – or rather exhaustion – of human, social and personal resources, especially in the context of a conflict that shows no sign of resolution and every sign of getting worse. Clay is part of the land, the ground beneath our feet. Conflict in the Middle East is about a great deal more than land alone but, even so, clay, as a medium for expressing some of the relentless pressures of conflict has an unusually powerful presence. As visual and material commentary on the persistence and repetitious nature of conflict, these poetic objects, with no fixed meaning, are not a metaphor for polemic or false hope, rather they are complex, memorable works, which resonate precisely because meaning is not fixed.

[4] David Goss, 'Azal ... Lock, Stock, and Barrel – On Shlomit Bauman's Exhibition', in *Ran Out*, Shlomit Bauman, 2013.

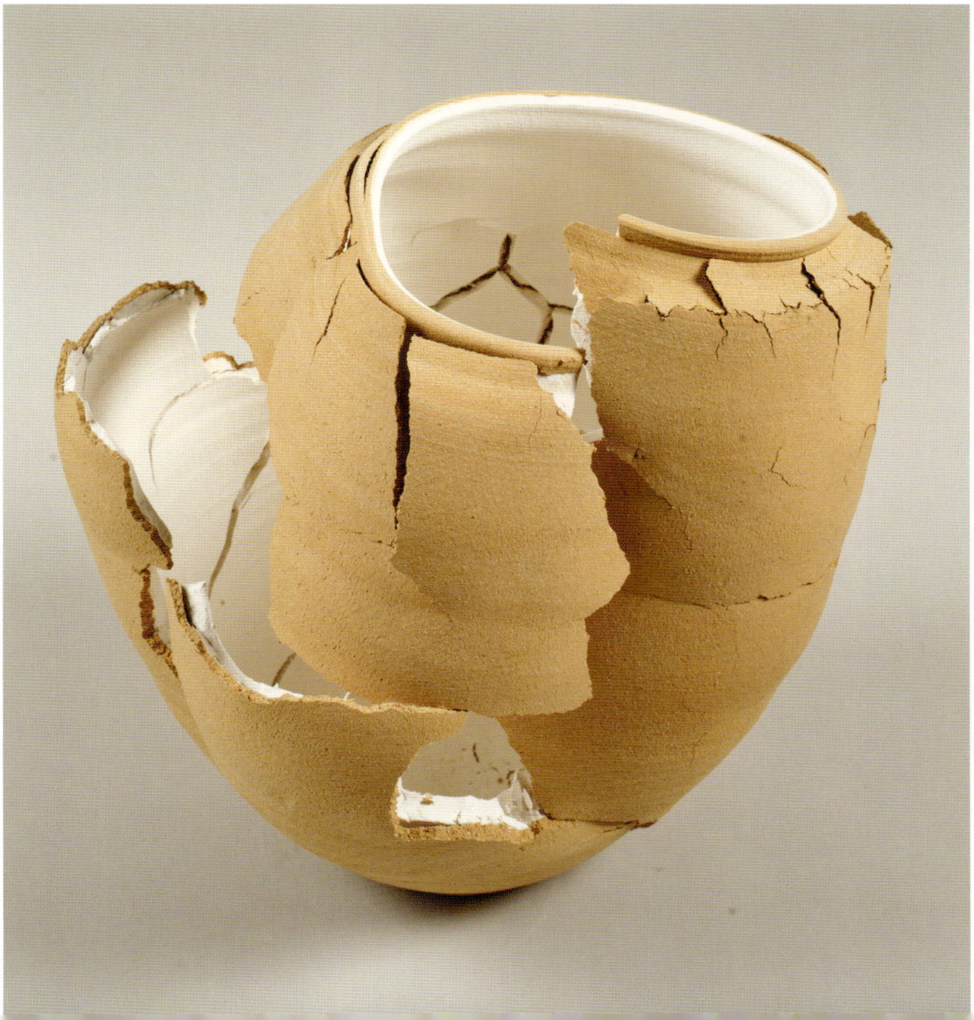

4.7 *Ran Out 03*, 2013, Shlomit Bauman, 2013, photographer: Ilan Amihai. Slip cast, wheel work, local Israeli clay (S5) and porcelain Limoges, height 22 cm

The political life of clay

Vis Unita Fortior was a remaking of the workers' canteen at the now defunct Spode factory in Stoke-on-Trent, formerly the world-renowned centre of the British ceramics industry. The canteen was shifted from its original position at Spode Works, and rearranged in the 'Blue Room', a reception and showroom in the factory for management, dignitaries and visitors, where Spode's trophy pieces were displayed. It contained an exceptionally fine collection, in effect, the history of the factory since 1767. The Blue Room itself was pure parody. It had been designed in mock Tudor style, complete with faux rafters and heavy carved wooden furniture: a ghastly spectacle equating to an English ideal that never existed, and which bore no relation to the ceramics displayed there. With the stark contrast of the formica and steel tables from the workers' canteen and a few personal objects, a tea flask and a newspaper, the restaging, alongside a gigantic photograph of the earlier absurd surroundings, stood in silent rebuke for an abject lack of vision in the local industry and to a failed national economic and industrial policy.

Neil Brownsword trained as a potter, initially through an apprenticeship and work placement in Stoke-on-Trent, where he grew up in the late 1980s. He produced this installation and two others, *Heritage Economy* and *National Treasure*, at the abandoned Spode factory as part of the British Ceramics Biennial, 2013. Brownsword now uses his knowledge of the landscape, the people and the social and economic structures of the ceramics industry as his material, rather than making things with clay. These installations were aspects of the life and death of the industry, which he reconstructed and staged, not as a performance of things past, as in a heritage museum, but as a critique of the process and the impact of that loss. Through these three works he highlighted the profligate waste of one of the most skilled and specialized workforces in the country, built up over two hundred or more years. In the lives of individual workers and the community, the collapse of the industry represented decades of work and experience discarded.

For *National Treasure* (Figure 4.8) Brownsword commissioned a skilled china painter to produce a series of painted plates documenting the closure of the factory and industry. The result was a series of immensely stark images. They parodied eighteenth-century blue and white plates depicting romantic ruins in wild landscapes, but could hardly have been more different. The same skills were used to make them but the plates were upside down: a perfect irony, like holding a magnifying mirror the wrong way to display, in hideous distorted detail, the political vandalism that had laid waste to an entire city. *Heritage Economy* similarly exposed waste, but material waste this time. Brownsword placed pieces of roofing lead, left strewn across the factory grounds after an attempted theft, in a museum-style vitrine. The lead became valuable because the building was being restored as a 'heritage' site rather than a working factory, which, Brownsword argued,[5] would be the only way to preserve it successfully. In the context of the Spode factory, still in an advanced state of decay,

[5] Neil Brownsword, unpublished paper given at British Ceramics Biennial, 2013.

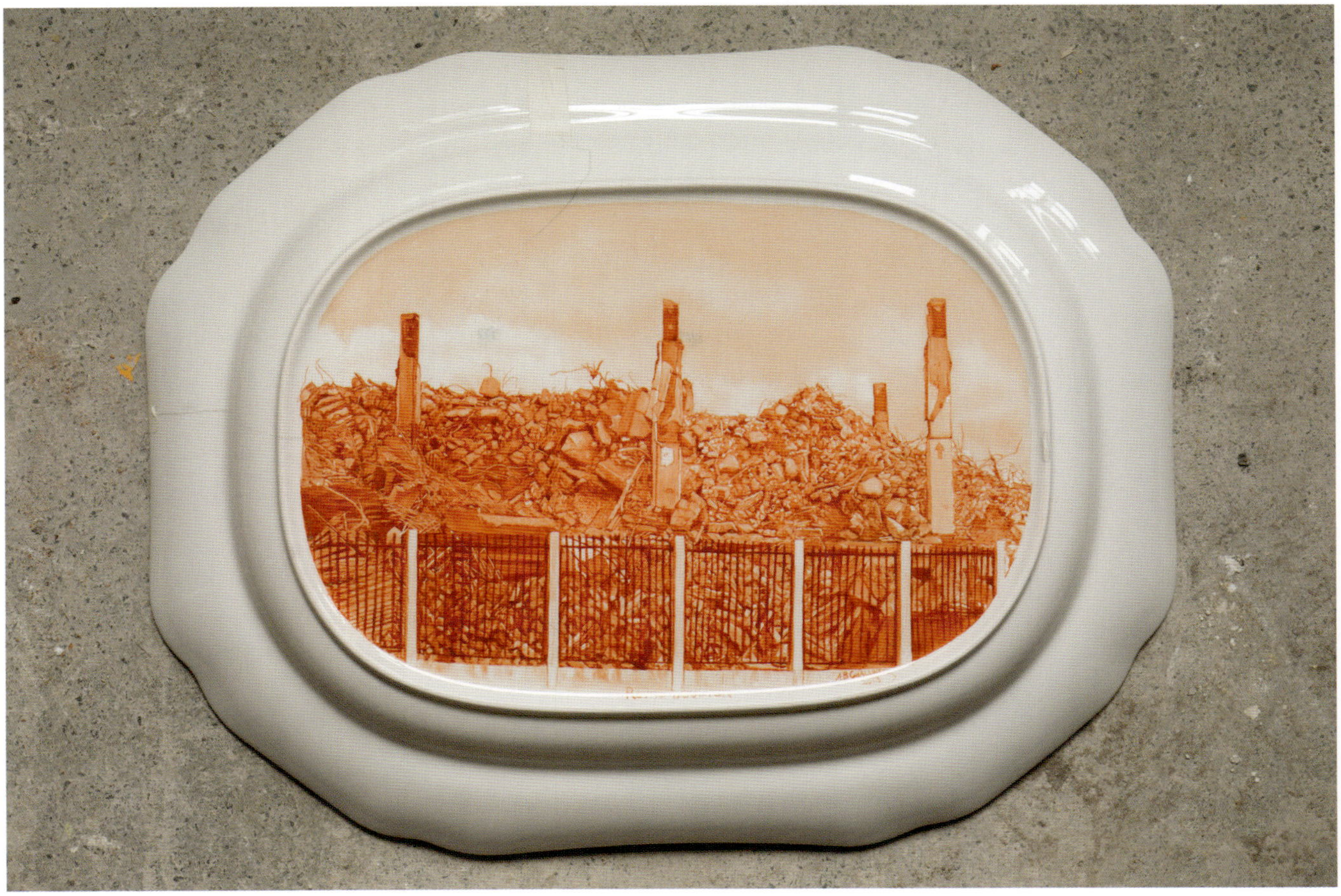

4.8 *National Treasure*, 2013, Neil Brownsword, photographer: Bjarte Biorkum

these were affecting, evocative works. They avoided the sense of precious finds in a reliquary, but only just, in the case of *Heritage Economy*. Site-specific work carried out in places of ruin and destruction often fall prey to a settling haze of pathos and nostalgia which can easily yield to a sense of passive acceptance – exactly what Brownsword would not have wanted. He successfully designed that problem out of these works, chiefly by using 'disjuncture': the works jarred sufficiently with their surroundings that they were noticeable. Once drawn in, the audience was able to connect with and 'read' the images and mini-dramas.

The installations were a small part of *Topographies of the Obsolete* (2012–2015), a gargantuan project involving some forty artists and theoreticians from academic institutions in Norway, England, Denmark and Germany, together with the British Ceramics Biennial, based in Stoke-on-Trent. Brownsword's own work, dating back to 2001, has been connected with the destruction of the ceramics industry. It is an important record of contemporary working-class history, constructed from within, a lingering and serious indictment of successive British governments for their reckless disregard for people, skills and knowledge as well as for industry and the applied arts. It is a significant contribution to the art of dissent as well as being utterly enraging to anyone with the wit to be enraged.

The social and symbolic life of clay

In 2012, Clare Twomey was invited to give one of the keynote speeches at the Australian Triennale conference, entitled 'Subversive Clay'. One of the leading exponents of ceramics as part of our social and symbolic lives, rather than ceramics as a commoditized object, Twomey's work has been characterized as subversive in a number of ways. *Witness*, made for the Jerwood Space in 2008, occupied an entire wall of the gallery space. Twomey painted the wall gold before spraying it with fine porcelain dust. What gallery visitors saw, initially, was an off-white wall, softer looking than a normal painted wall. They were invited to draw and scribble and write messages all over the porcelain screed, which they did, hesitantly at first, then with increasing confidence. As the gold emerged, glimmering faintly through the scratched lines, the surprise and delight in how it looked was entirely at odds with what one might expect from a scratched wall. What should have resembled a long suffering classroom wall at the end of the school year, had streaks of gold rushing across its surface. It still had the look of something partially violated but with a touch of stigmata – wounds that did not bleed.

Amy Dickson, writing about the work, comments on 'the delicious subversion of the properties of that medium',[6] referring to the clay dust. She emphasizes repeatedly the softness of the clay dust, rather than either clay's brittleness when fired, or its solidity when raw; she refers to the light and ephemeral quality of the dust, rather than the permanence of ceramic objects. The subversion of which she speaks is in the supposed expectations of the audience being foiled. The supposition is that the audience expects clay to be hard, heavy, solid and serviceable. It is a valid point to make when discussing ceramics but the Jerwood Space is an art gallery, it is not specifically for ceramics or even for craft in the broader sense. It is debatable whether or not the material qualities of clay are the main concern of the audience in this context, even for an applied arts prize. That the wall delivered a touch of magic – or even a minor miracle – is beyond doubt to anyone who saw it, but the matter of clay behaviour is, perhaps, of greater concern to aficionados than it is to the public.

Twomey sometimes works directly with her audiences in the sense that they become involved in the evolution of the work. A recent work at John Soane's Museum involved male participants emailing her, stating, in a single sentence, how they wished to be remembered. Twomey then printed their wishes onto white china cups. Another work, *The Collection* (Figure 4.9), was hosted at the Victoria and Albert Museum, a three-day event where visitors were given a museum card on which they drew a picture of an object in their own lives that they loved and valued. The card, with the object's portrait drawn on it, was then placed in one of the empty vitrines. *Consciousness/Conscience* was a stretch of unfired clay floor tiles, which required visitors to the exhibition to decide whether or not to walk over them causing them to crumble with every step. She also creates ravishingly pretty spectacles. Three thousand black

[6] Amy Dickson, 'Clare Twomey', in *Jerwood Contemporary Makers*, Jerwood Charitable Foundation, 2008.

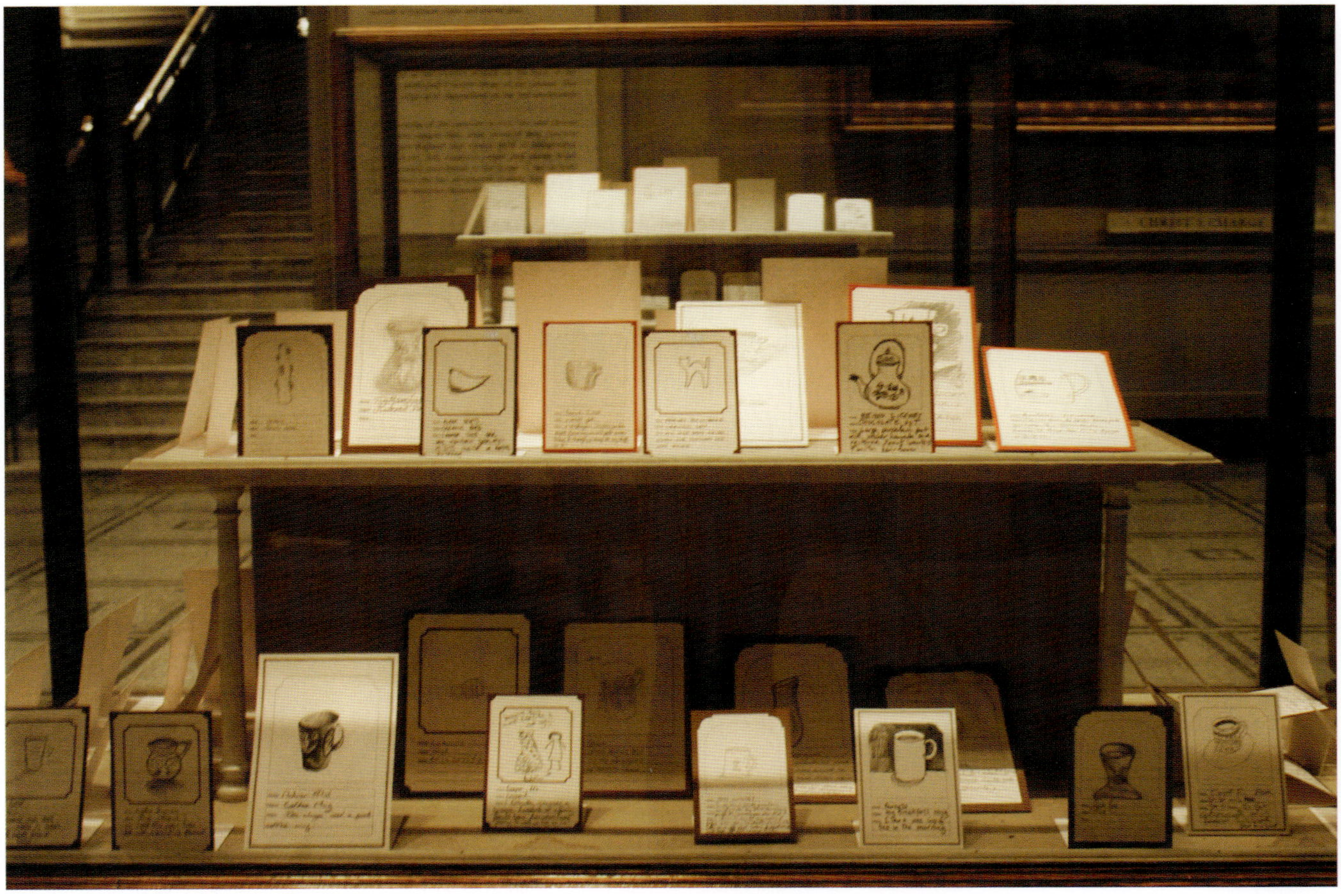

4.9 *The Collection*, 2009, Clare Twomey

glazed ceramic butterflies installed in The Royal Pavilion in Brighton, *A Dark Day in Paradise*, combined opulent surroundings with a swarming mass of butterflies, disturbing at times, but undoubtedly gorgeous.

The academy intervenes

Both Neil Brownsword's and Clare Twomey's work is temporary: it lasts as long as the time-span of the performance, event or exhibition. There is no object to sell so it does not meet the commercial market; its market is the academy. Academic funding comes with a price. To meet its demands, voluminous quantities of published theory must be generated. This might not matter except that, because there is no object in a public or private collection, temporary work cannot, at the moment, be seen again, once its time has passed. Artists producing temporary works may do other similar versions somewhere else, but for now, the only way to remember these works or 'see' them, if not at the original event, is to read the publication, usually available online if not in book form. For this reason, how the work is written about matters far more than it would for materially permanent pieces that can be viewed repeatedly.

Online images are only ever as good as the screen on which they are displayed, and are rarely at high resolution because of copyright issues, so the viewer is compelled to read the text, if only to find a clearer explanation of what happened. Twomey's work *The Collection* states that 'The work forged links between curatorship, collections, and our understanding of what it means to own and display objects.' This is the intention of the work. It has a touch of the wholesome moral project about it but is nonetheless a valid statement of what it means to both artist and institution. It is much more difficult, however, to believe that the two thousand people who took part in this event were thinking about any of the things suggested and no evidence is provided to support the statement. The website features photographs of young people carefully drawing on their cards, the elegant vitrines, the latex gloves, the lofty museum space with its paintings and the cards themselves with their drawings. It has a stagey old-world quality, like a dramatized teaching session, but with no suggestion that any of the participants are indeed pondering 'curatorship, collections or what it means to own and display'. In the absence of evidence, the declaration of purpose appears facile – little more than wishful thinking.

Knowing what audiences think is the implied claim made repeatedly throughout the theoretical writing supporting social, ephemeral or other kinds of temporary ceramic work. Where 'subversive' work is concerned, it is used to justify the stated claim that the work concerned confounds audience expectations. This, we are told, is what makes the work subversive. Amy Dickson, in her seven-hundred-word article on *Witness*, has two references to subversion and two to transgression. Wrong-footing the presumed expectations of the Jerwood's audience is the only reason supplied for the somewhat overstated assertion that the artist is doing anything other than what an artist should be doing, and this is not to devalue the work in any way. What Dickson does is expose what is not there, rather than what is. There is no publicly available evidence that the ceramic art audience or, indeed, any other audience, has been asked what their expectations are, still less had their answers recorded. Audience research is usually empirical but art theory can be rationalized. Even so, it is unusual to find any reference to established learning on the subject. As the reader of the event documentation, I just have to believe what I am told. If audiences really are being challenged in some way, it would be useful to see some evidence and even then, one has to wonder how long audiences will continue, obligingly, to be confounded or have their presumed expectations challenged.

Artists working in an academic context are encumbered with substantial additional work, fundraising, producing publications, and organizing conferences to name but a few of the tasks that go with the funding. These do little or nothing to enhance the art itself, still less the experience for the audience. At worst it uses up time and resources unnecessarily. When a major gallery is able to sell the ideas that produce ephemeral works and when those ideas have a recognized market value and can be reproduced, then we know that ceramics as a discipline can support social, non-material work long term, which would open up the field considerably and, perhaps, dispense with the need for self-justifying explications.

Restoring illusion

The porcelain figurine presents a beautified, idealized image of human life, a fairy tale peopled with characters living a charmed existence. The shepherds are well fed, the sun shines and the sheep never fear the wolf. The boy is a smiling, charming innocent, he's not a syphilitic, rapacious, religious maniac preparing to behead the nearest infidel, or a drunken carouser defecating behind the neighbours' garden wall. The girls – or pretty maids – are similarly well fed and dressed, in spite of being poor shepherdesses. They are not troubled by family honour, oppressed by a paterfamilias, forced into an unwelcome marriage, obliged to work long hours in a factory for little pay or clean other people's houses for even less. In the world of the figurine, zero hours contracts are unheard of and deliverers of takeaway meals and internet shopping are paid a living wage. Visions of health, virtue, charm and happiness, these are blessed creatures whose neat porcelain lives bear no relation to human life in its glory, its squalor, its banality or even its plodding, unexciting, quotidian reality. They also provide artists with a rich seam of satiric possibility.

Bouke de Vries is a ceramic conservator who uses ready-made porcelain figurines, breaks and rearranges them, adding colour with other objects and materials to produce a new work. He stages elaborate crowd scenes from battles to bacchanals, orgiastic displays of lacerated limbs, to which the ready-made porcelain figurines obligingly lend themselves, in deconstructed and reconstructed form. These are virtuoso displays of the conservator's art as well as being highly theatrical and, at times, surreal. He is not alone; there are legions of ceramicists of various provenance, some are studio potters, some designers, some conservators and some are artists in other disciplines entirely. They use the cast and fired figurine to produce a perverse or contrary narrative, often one which superficially, at least, is at odds with the tradition of the figurine as an idealized symbol, a sign for perfect virtuous womanhood or masculine 'honour' and bravery.

War and Pieces (2012, Holburne Museum, Bath) (Figure 4.10) was a porcelain battle scene staged on a full-length state dining table in a gigantic museum vitrine. The 'table' – in reality a series of museum plinths – was set for dinner with Sir William Holburne's Chinese tobacco-leaf-pattern dinner service. The centrepiece was a mushroom cloud explosion of broken porcelain. Fanning out from the explosion were the battle protagonists, all white porcelain, variously shattered and whole, painted and pristine, decked about with plastic toy weapons, gas masks, plastic tubing and mangled cutlery. To the unaccustomed viewer this would probably have been an inspired intervention, greatly enlivening a museum display of cool, tidy, white porcelain. Indicative of immense wealth, these kinds of displays often feel remote and struggle to make meaning to the passing, pram-pushing public, avoiding the rain on the way back from the supermarket. De Vries's mighty ceramic confection would certainly have been a talking point. Looking further into the spectacle, however, revealed little more. It was, just that, a spectacle. Immaculately conceived

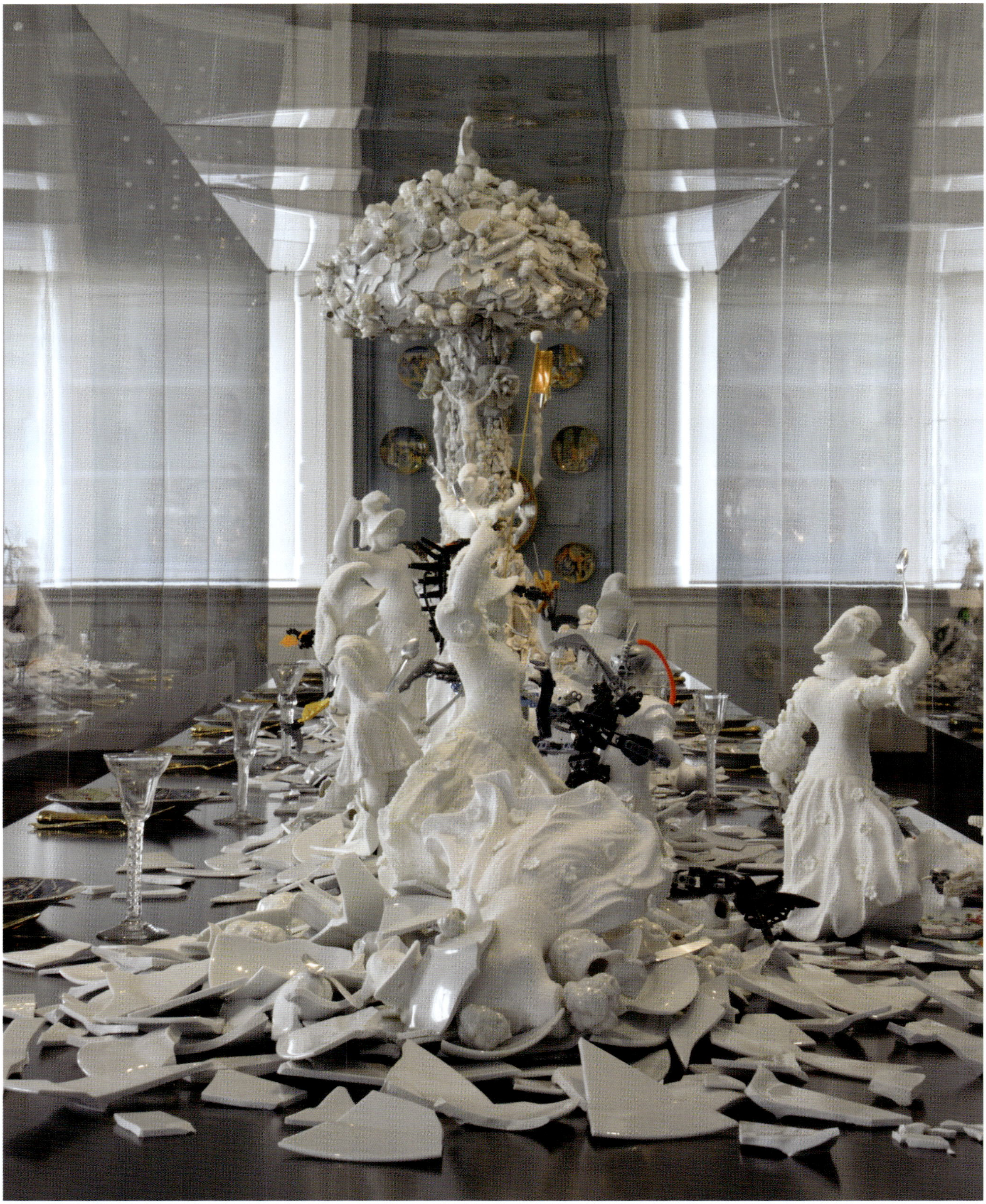

and executed, it was a perfect piece of museum craft and curating: a delicious and extravagant wonder, something that craft, ceramics and, above all, conservators do with considerable flair.

'Subversive Ceramics' was the title of a symposium centred on this piece of work. *War and Pieces* was certainly satiric. In common with all of de Vries's work it deployed a collection of well known satiric tropes: parody, irony, the grotesque and comedy, along with the two that, perhaps, define his work: the burlesque and carnival. Taken formalistically, as a mixture of broken porcelain and plastic in a museum vitrine, it may have operated as an incidental critique of museum exhibits or of the hierarchy of materials. It is difficult to believe that the breaking and rearranging of porcelain in a museum could be regarded as subversive; after all, museums depend on broken pots. They, more than most, know that anything broken can be restored. As a comment on war or conflict, it was entirely vacuous, but it is not clear that the artist intended it to be anything else. He just wanted to create something splendid, which he did.

Leda and the Swan (Figure 4.11) is a tempting subject for any artist. In the seventeenth and eighteenth centuries, particularly among European artists of the baroque and Renaissance, it was a subject much loved by painters and sculptors of rapacious 'love' scenes, painters of 'nudes' and nature, and, above all, painters of covert pornography commissioned by wealthy patrons. De Vries's *Leda and the Swan*, constructed of a broken and elongated porcelain swan, with a plastic doll as Leda, is an image of what appears to be the rape of a very young girl.

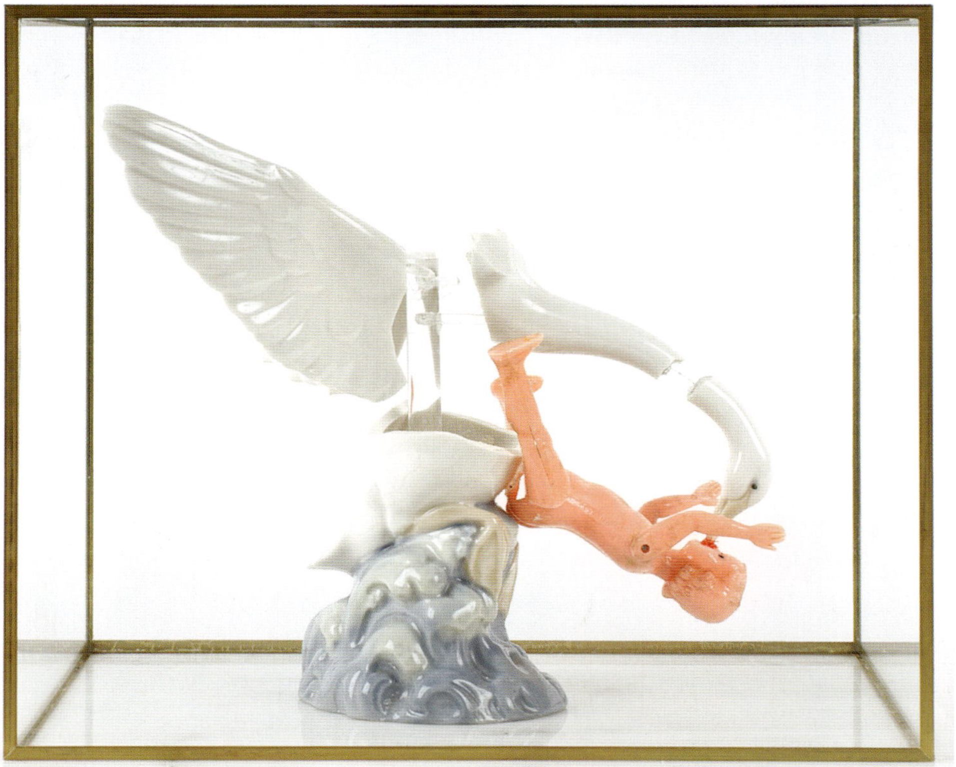

4.10 Opposite: *War and Pieces*, 2012, Bouke de Vries

4.11 *Leda and the Swan*, 2010, Bouke de Vries

As a satire, it could either be ridiculing baroque paintings of classical myths, exposing them as, in essence, fetishistic representations of the rape of girls and young women for the delectation of adult male viewers, or it may be using a grotesque, comic parody to attack the makers, purveyors and consumers of such works. It amounts to much the same thing. Either way, as a satiric attack, it would aim to reflect the image at the consumer and say: 'this is what you are looking at, you are pleasuring yourself with an image of child rape'. I suspect, however that this is an over-optimistic interpretation. De Vries's work as a whole does not suggest an artist motivated by an urgent desire for political change, or one with a heightened awareness of the politics and pitfalls of satire; his work comes across more as the product of playful chance, with a primary interest in the comic and absurd. Moreover, a feminist-inspired attack would likely wish to expose the attitudes and reactions of the artists and consumers since the target should, ideally, be those in positions of power, influence and authority – the instigators and enablers of rape culture and its depictions – rather than those who are oppressed or victimized by it.

In this case, however, our focus is on the abandoned plastic doll. In strictly visual terms, she is the target. She is stiff and un-pretty, disposable and unreal: it is near impossible for the viewer to find any sympathy. The swan, by contrast, is graceful, in spite of being broken, or perhaps because of its elongated, broken state. In reality it is simply a grotesque pairing, and if anything, invites laughter – probably 'stillborn'.[7] It is a comic rendering of the myth, ridiculous as well as grotesque. However, in the context of a society that has been proved, repeatedly, to be unwilling to condemn men who rape and is determined, instead, to blame victims of rape, particularly girls perceived as 'disposable',[8] it comes across as an insidiously nasty example of the masculine rearguard tendency in the contemporary arts, a tendency from which ceramics is not, unfortunately, excluded. De Vries's work has been cited as part of the 'subversive' trend in ceramics but, if the examples shown here are anything to go by, it could all too easily be characterized as part of a fiercely reactionary backlash against feminist progress.

Penny Byrne is a conservator who also trained as a ceramicist. Ready-made figurines are her raw material. She cuts, paints, adds props and variously alters her charges to remake them into protagonists in fields of battle, both civil and military. Her *War on Terror Waltz* (Figure 4.12) at first glance appeared to be an allusion to the admission of gays into the military, since the protagonists look like women. Delightful to find some lesbian action in ceramic form at last, but disappointing that it had to be something as manifestly conservative, nationalistic, anti-feminist and anti-revolutionary as a national army. It turns out, however, that the waltzing couple are a man and woman. It is an excellent example of how gender indeterminate the male figurines are. Their facial and bodily features are highly feminized, assuming we read 'feminine' as the version according to patriarchy – a construction that characterizes the feminine as doe-eyed, submissive and always smiling sweetly. It is, in fact, a satire on the War on Terror, presented as a waltz, a circular dance which has no choreographed finite ending. It stops only when the music stops.

7 Highet, 1962, 21.

8 Maddy Coy, Liz Kelly, Fiona Elvines, Maria Garner, Ava Kanyeredzi, *Sex without Consent*, report, CWASU, 2013; and Liz Kelly, Jo Lovett, CWASU, 2009.

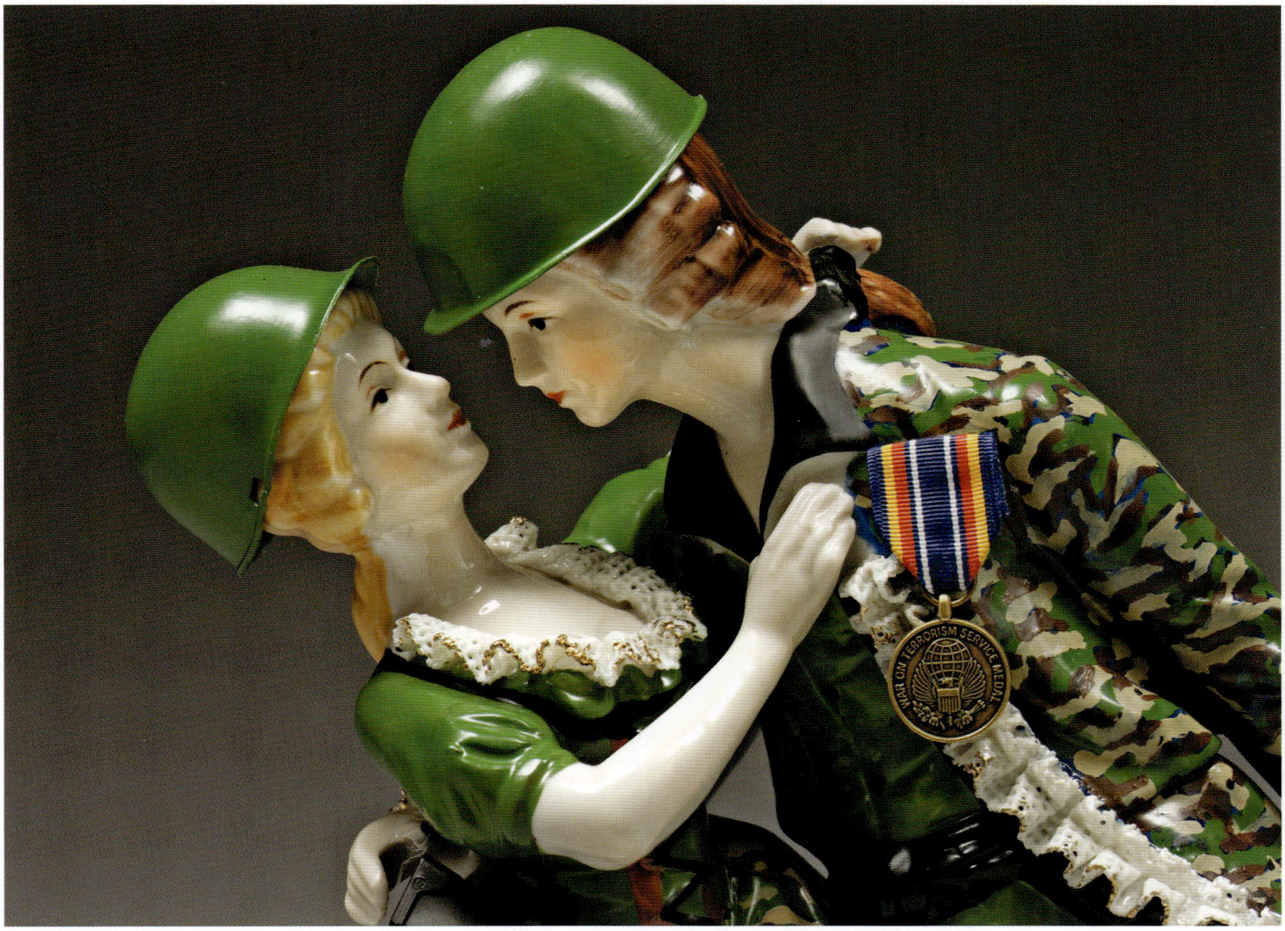

4.12 *War on Terror Waltz*, 2009, Penny Byrne

Byrne works with vintage figures, often damaged or of no particular value, and upcycles them into new art with newly acquired value. The conservator cohort of the upcyclers are particularly well placed to introduce vintage objects as props and to select their raw material taxonomically so it produces additional layers of meaning by itself. Byrne's *War on Terror* pieces, for example, include *Iraq's Most Wanted* playing cards and a vintage toy petrol pump. Byrne says that her work is mostly derived from news coverage and refers to her 'interest in riots and civil unrest'. News coverage, particularly television news, tends to favour the theatrical street dramas of revolutions, riots and demonstrations. Social media is better at revealing more of the human impact and involvement, particularly over time. Byrne's characters are freeze-framed in an unfolding drama. Some of it feels a bit superficial and opportunistic; there is little sense, for example, that she has any serious concern for the people who took part in the 2009 street demonstrations in Iran, but the introduction of some green fabric and a handy title, *Where is my Vote?* does the job – then we can move on to the next street drama. There is a sense of riot mass-production, exacerbated by the use of mass-produced, repetitive raw material, but news coverage can seem like that too, to say nothing of historical process.

Barnaby Barford uses ready-made figurines assembled in groups that resemble scenes from mini-dramas. They capture a single moment in a longer narrative that the audience, to some extent, provides. Barford's figurines retain their wholeness but their context is probably different from that envisaged by the manufacturers. He tweaks them here and there, adding colour and mixing genres of figurine, but alteration is minimal; it is the environment and a few extra props that tell the story. His incomplete dramas are gently satiric social commentary, cast from a distance and quietly amused. *Love Is... I & II* are both 'coming of age stories', in which little boys find out about their sexuality. This is a collection of comic observations that comment on the construction and development of male sexuality. Figurine boys, wreathed in smiles, wide-eyed with painted lashes, sit in a sea of pornography, or masturbate quietly in a darkened environment under a single lamp. The boys are simultaneously funny, absurd and immensely unappealing. A particularly nasty scene is a boy trying to pressure his girlfriend figurine into anal sex – a grotesque, if honest, exposure of the sense of male entitlement that pornography endorses and the normalizing of a coercive male sexual attitude. Two more figurine boys learn about sex through voyeurism, seeking out places where they can watch a copulating couple or masturbate secretly while watching a naked woman sunbathe. The figurines grow up and marry, as all good social conservatives should, and slowly become deceitful, unfaithful and probably miserable. It is a comic litany of despair in figurine form. The comedy is in the grotesque mismatch of the cute figurine with the tawdry nature of the story but, again, the laughter is 'stillborn'.[9]

In the other *Love Is...* group, figurine boys are watching a naked doll woman in a peep-show type performance. It is a two-way mirror – a light switched on behind the mirror reveals what is actually going on. These boys are finding out about sex through watching the sexual antics of the pumped-up, exaggerated prototype 'woman'. There are two scenes showing adult male figurines, one negotiating a price for additional services, the other either the pimp or a regular customer. There is also one girl, perhaps being advised that being prostituted is a lucrative occupation or frightfully good fun: 'the sky's the limit', says the caption, jauntily. While the first series of *Love Is...* is nastily comic, the second evokes an air of suppurating pathos. Neither are works of biting satire, but certainly not the second. Comedy is present throughout but the overriding feel is one of self-pity. Barford's work is acquiescent in spirit, more of a resigned sigh than a fierce critique: 'This is how things are. We are destined to tread the road to inevitable failure, having been led astray by wilful women and deceived by pornography.'

It is the prettiness of the second *Love Is...*, its bijou scale and charming little antique, peep-show look, combined with soft, low lighting, that makes it appear nostalgic. This, of course, is part of the irony. Nostalgia is one of satire's tropes but also one of its Achilles' heels. It has the faux innocence of Edwardian pornography – also part of the conceit. These qualities are emphasized by the old-world figurines and by the doll-like proto-woman. We don't believe in her any more than we believe the figurines. This is equal opportunities nastiness. Barford chooses to mock or ridicule the

9 Highet, 1962, 21.

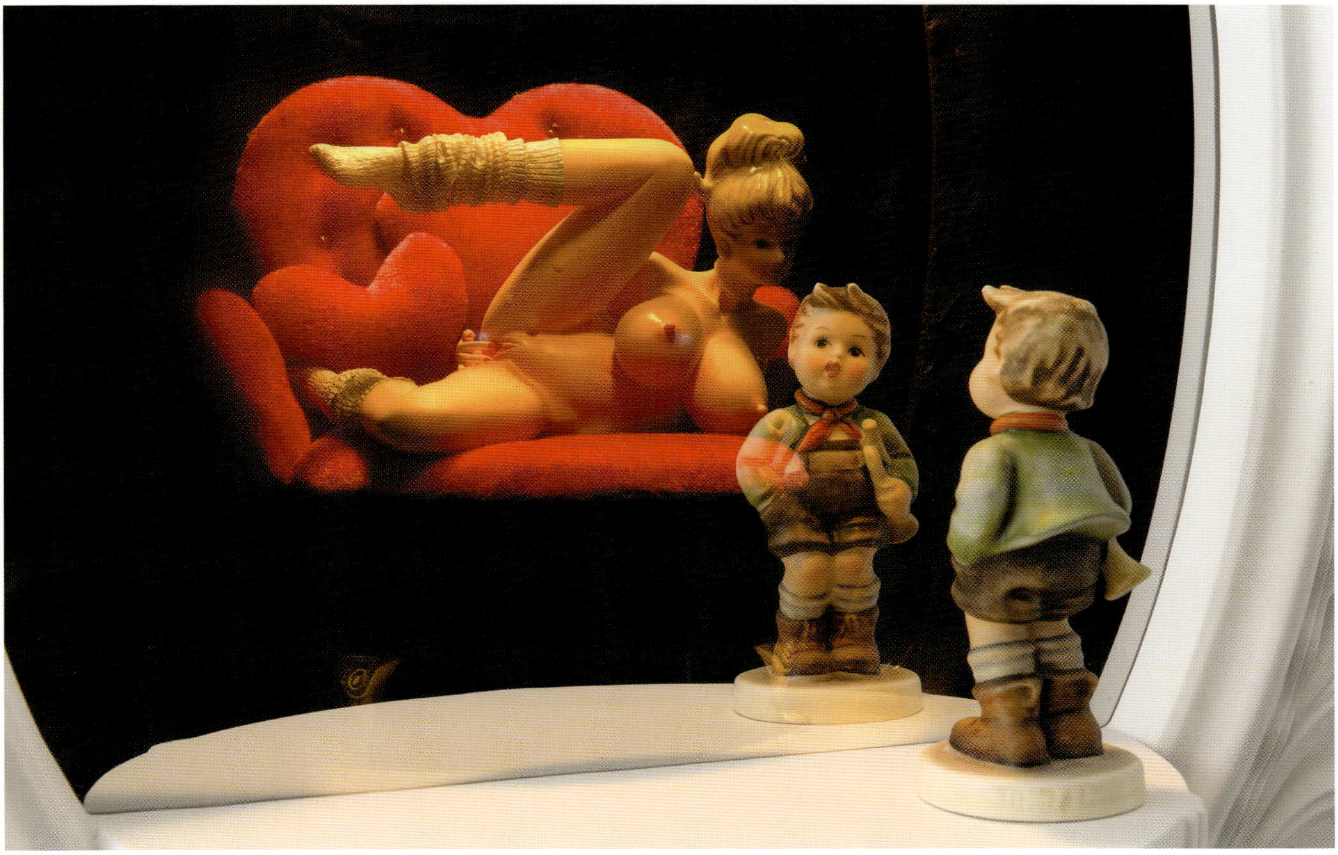

4.13 *Lezioni de Tromba* (mirror detail), 2011, Barnaby Barford, photographer: Noah da Costa, courtesy of David Gill Galleries

growing pains of little boys and the corresponding disappointed expectations of adult men. It is a mild but affectionate critique of masculinity, not one that demands change. He is colluding with the happy state of deluded man and proto-woman – his males are the beneficiaries, suffer little and provide fodder for good jokes and wordplay, so why change? His girl and lady-figures are all playing their properly appointed roles of either conniving 'other' or virtuous maid. They, too, are smiling cheerily, happy with their lot. It leaves the viewer unable to identify with any of the characters in his dramas so we have no choice but to identify with the artist – hence the irritation. I have no wish to identify with self-pitying, colluding males, not even good-natured ones.

Were I to mobilize a harsher analysis, one more consistent with a feminist demand for change, I would have to say that Barford's little dramas consistently project the woman as the enabler, or agent, of oppressive systems and structures, and the boy or man as the victim of an unjust and unforgiving system. At his best, Barford produces socially acute observations, which are entertaining into the bargain: *Damaged Goods* is a fine example. At worst, his work comes across as a colossal, bed-wetting whinge. He presumably had no intention of making a pro-feminist statement or one that might emancipate the male from the relentless thud of masculine stereotyping but even so, even cute jokes can be insidious. What adds to the problem is the infestation of extraordinarily vapid curatorial comment – even by craft standards – that has built up around it. Simon Martin establishes his position in his first paragraph introducing *Love Is...* 2011:

> In the not-so-distant past access to sexual imagery for men involved furtive activity: the purchase of Playboy, Razzle, Readers' Wives or any number of similar titles from the top shelf of a newsagent, or videos from a Soho sex shop.[10]

At no point, during his entire description and analysis of Barford's work is there any mention of female desire or sexuality, and certainly no feminist reading of the work. This is strictly a boy's club. Nothing wrong with discussing male sexuality and the social construction thereof, but Martin is generalizing throughout – in other words his normative position is male. While there is no specific denunciation of feminism, Martin is, not so subtly, presenting Barford as a valiant soldier attacking its vicious, man-harming forces. This is exactly the kind of snivelling, runny-nosed anti-feminism we thought had been shown the door decades ago. 'There is no room for prudery', he warns, for Barford-the-Brave explores 'the margins of what is socially acceptable', boldly opposing the middle-class hand-wringing of the 'broadsheets and Radio 4', as they lament the sexualization of society as a whole and youth in particular.[11]

How a relatively young, twenty-first century art professional can generate such drivel without even the slightest hint of irony is impossible to discern. Easy though it is to be facetious about this kind of writing, it is ultimately damaging to artists' work precisely because it inflates it to an absurd degree, which makes it immensely difficult for any viewer, never mind a sceptic, to take it seriously. Suffice to say, there is nothing out of the ordinary in Barford's work, which is precisely the point; it is a study of the everyday. His is both a tabloid and a broadsheet vision, inherently socially conservative, insipid but funny, and mildly moralistic. He 'exposes' social ills but does not offer any analysis of or opposition to the underlying causes and certainly shows no interest in change, still less revolution. Martin likens Barford's work to Hogarth's, but while Hogarth could be vehemently moralistic, Barford's response is more of an indulgent chuckle. Martin's assertion that 'Barford's work derives much of its power from subverting the image and social expectation of such pieces',[12] is little more than wishful thinking.

Ready-mades are inherently parodic. They tend to reproduce the sexist vernacular of which they are a part. While de Vries's vision helps sustain rape culture, whether or not that is his intention, Barford's is, in essence an anti-feminist, moralistic, tabloid vision: 'I'm doing fine, let's just have a joke about it and keep things as they are.' Compare this to Jo Pipkin's work: she does the same thing when she upends her fairy tales, marshals a tabloid vision to show their reality when applied to contemporary lives and produces a searing critique. No one is spared, and certainly not the audience. A similar comparison can be made between Rose Wallace's invitation to laugh with her *Three Graces* and de Vries's *Binge Drinker* (2009) (Figure 4.14), par excellence a tabloid vision offering us no choice but to judge.

4.14 Opposite: *Binge Drinker*, 2009, Bouke de Vries

[10] Simon Martin, *Love Is*... 2011, *Continued*, 2011, available at http://www.barnabybarford.co.uk/image_gallery/node/128 accessed 29 October 2014.

[11, 12] Martin, 2011.

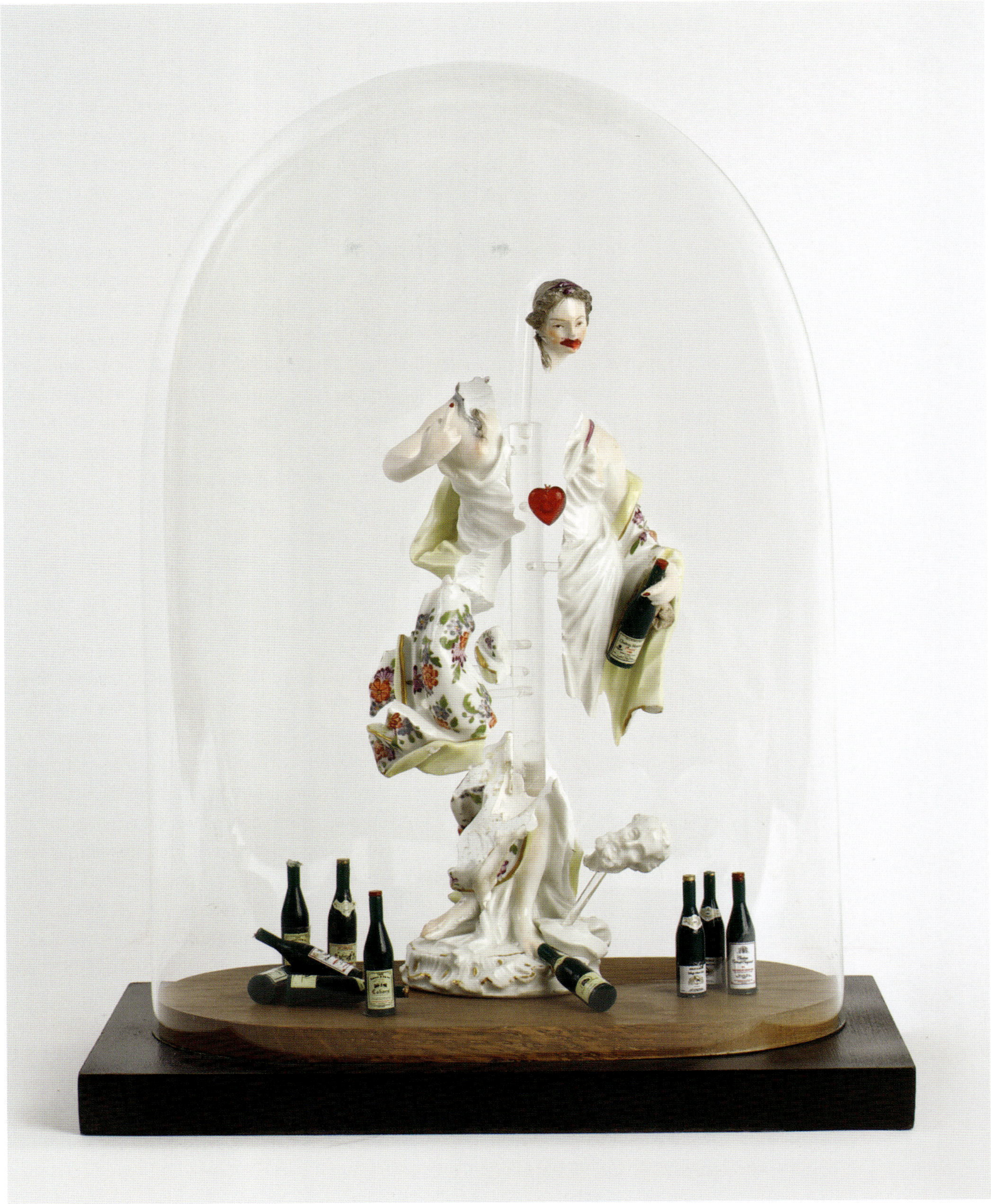

Conclusion

This chapter discussed the work of artists characterized as 'subversive' mainly because of their working method, and illustrates the problems that result from the promiscuous use of this term. We have here a collection of artists whose work does not easily co-habit. While it is true that all the artists have used industrial mass production – either its process or products – in their work, this has not produced work that is inherently subversive – in some cases quite the opposite – and whether or not it has 'subverted' industrial process itself depends very much on the political positioning of the audience. It could be argued that co-opting mass production and turning it into individual studio art for the delight of wealthy patrons or the art market is, politically, counter-subversive, or reactionary: something of an academic nicety, perhaps, but arguable nonetheless. Ephemeral work is certainly not inherently subversive, except where the artist designs it so, and site-specific work produces its own problems, particularly when carried out in sites of ruin and destruction. The next chapter discusses protest ceramics and the work of artists who use ceramics specifically to 'rewrite' or re-imagine established political narratives.

5

The Campaigning Trail

Introduction

Cast in the most idealized terms, the honest pot was a protest. Its makers railed against the dull conformity of the industrial product and against the gendered divisions of labour and exploitation of industrial workers. The handmade mug, wholly produced by one potter in a studio, was, in effect, a domestic anti-globalization protest. By the mid-1980s, the industrial product in Britain was largely outsourced to Third World countries where, for pitiably low wages and often with no rights or organized labour to protest their situation, impoverished and grossly exploited workers supplied industrial 'blanks' to the British ceramics industry, which marketed the end product as domestically produced. Conversely, handmade mugs are expensive compared to the industrial product and the British public are, in the main, no more willing to pay the price of crockery than they are the price of food, books, journalism, drama, music or dance. As a result, the handmade mug becomes either an *objet d'art* or a museum piece, or else it must join the 'luxury goods' class, with or without the bling.

The industrial mug, an object reeking almost certainly as much of exploitative labour relations as Columbian roses or sweatshop clothing, may well be dishonest about its origins but it certainly does not qualify as 'pretentious', that quality so derided by studio potters whose mugs are at least as pretentious as those they condemn. The industrial mug, therefore, must be a paradox along with its studio pottery counterpart. Studio mugs are certainly 'display' kitchen-ware, if not art objects. Visiting friends who know their cost usually refuse to use them. While mugs made by studio potters only rarely carry verbal or pictorial messages of protest, industrial blanks are manufactured by the tens of thousands, in atrocious conditions, and are then embellished with anti-globalization slogans and other, similarly antithetical protests from anti-war and anti-nuclear to atheist and feminist slogans.

Campaigning craft and industry

The internet-based company Zazzle buys in blank mugs and enables its customers to assemble their own surface design, using images uploaded from their own desktops with the website tools provided by the company. Alternatively, designers and artists registered with the company have created hundreds of proto-protest mugs which can be bought via the site. One of the best known feminist protests in recent times has been the 'this is what a feminist looks like' campaign. Campaign supporters uploaded a photograph of themselves holding a placard carrying the slogan to a social networking site. The campaign aimed to debunk outmoded stereotypes about who can and cannot be a feminist and demonstrate the extent of the movement and its sympathizers. It was very much of its time, dependent on social networking and the instant upload facilities provided by smartphones. The images were often selfies and almost always phone photographs, which were then shared on social networking sites. It has been remarkably effective in popularizing feminism and in encouraging young men, in particular, to be part of the movement. As a campaign and as an idea, there are doubtless numerous critiques, but it marked a moment in grass roots feminism and the mugs are there to prove it.[1]

Yellow and blue 'boob prints' are the trademark symbol of Femen, internationally known and, in some circles, among the most notorious feminist groups of the early twenty-first century. The group, which formed in 2008 with four young Ukrainian women, initially protested against the trafficking of women from Ukraine to supply the burgeoning sex industries of Western Europe. Their bare-breasted protests were condemned as 'hooliganism' in Ukraine, resulting in weekly arrests with one of the group serving a short prison sentence. The yellow and blue symbol was made when they painted their breasts in the blue and yellow of the Ukrainian flag and printed them on paper. The resulting design was printed on mugs and T-shirts and sold to raise funds for further actions.

Femen are still operating in 2015 and have received some degree of respect, recognition and validation, partly for their fearlessness and persistence, but mostly because of their vehement and sustained campaigns against trafficking for prostitution and pornography and against the grotesque misogyny of religions, particularly Islam, Orthodox Christianity and Catholicism.[2] The bare-breasted street actions, symbolized on the mugs, challenged the double standards of Ukraine where police and, by implication, government, colluded with traffickers while simultaneously arresting and condemning women who took off their T-shirts. They also confronted the Orthodox Church and its support for the Russian and Ukrainian governments, which trample on women's human rights. In effect, they also challenged feminist allies in Western Europe, many of whom were sceptical of the value of naked protest. In the face of colossal organized opposition from Ukrainian, Russian, Belarusian, Turkish, Tunisian, Iranian and French judiciary and, in some cases, governments, Femen have stood their ground, attesting to the strength of their naked vulnerability. Press TV, the English-language branch of Iranian state television, devoted an entire forty-five minute programme to denouncing them, the first time they have ever thought to mention, never mind oppose, a feminist group of any sort anywhere in the world.[3] Like them or not, the designs on the mugs, which represent that central point about the force of naked flesh against the might of military police and religious fanaticism, mark their presence, which is now unlikely to be forgotten.

---

1 Ben Ellery, '62p An Hour', *Mail Online*, 1 November 2014. The leaders of the three main British political parties were photographed wearing T-shirts emblazoned with the slogan, made by women in Mauritius earning 62p per hour, according to *The Daily Mail*. The claim was refuted but it underscores the problems of mass-produced protest.

2 Inna Shevchenko was a speaker at the Secular Conference, London, 11–12 October 2014.

3 Tariq Ramadan presents 'Islam and Life: Can Islam Defeat Femen?' Press TV, 9 May 2013.

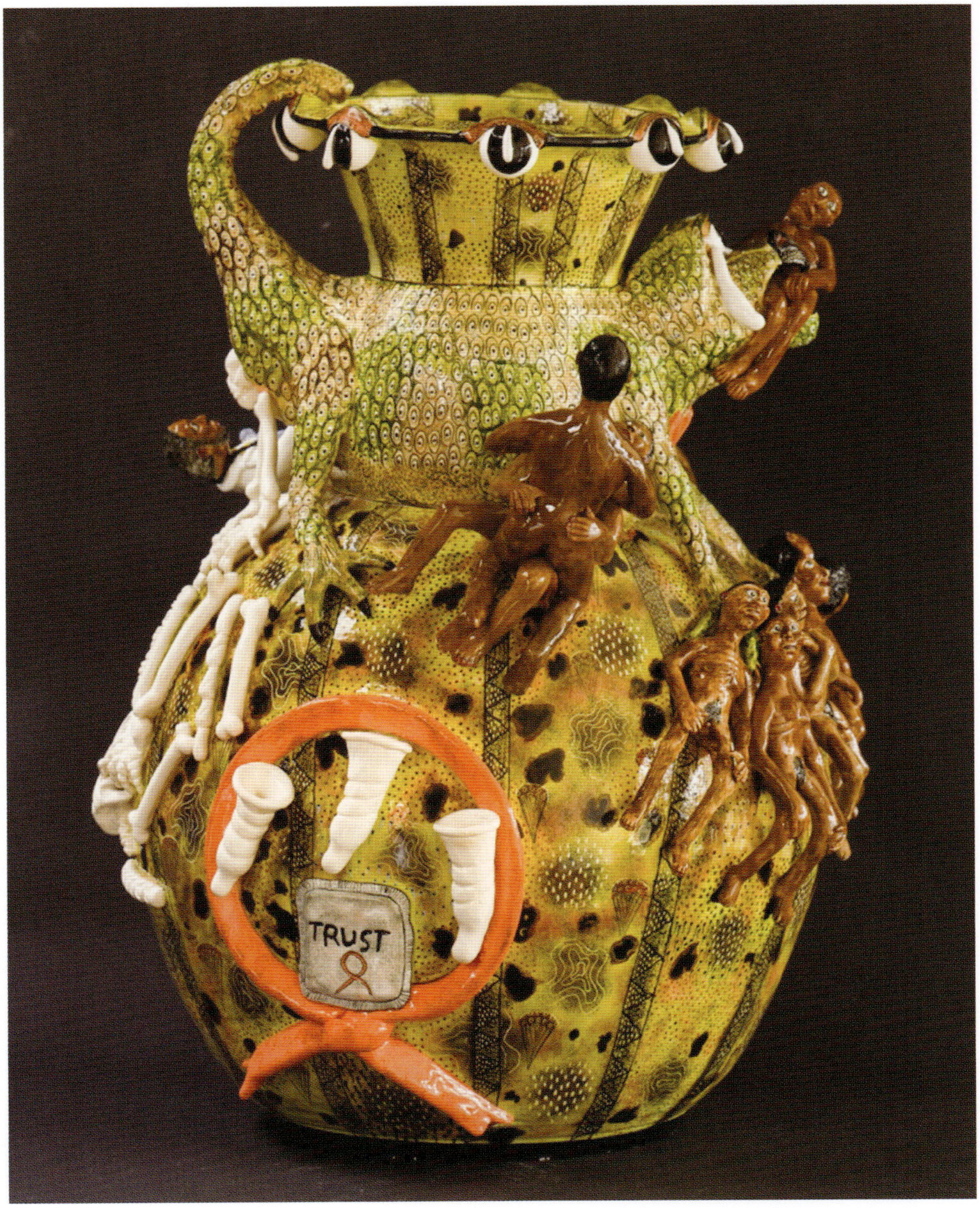

5.1 Monster Aids Vase, c. 2008, Roux Gwala, Ardmore Ceramic Art

The South African company Ardmore, based in Kwa-Zulu Natal, have excelled in the art of campaigning ware since they first set up in the 1990s. The Ardmore studio trains artists and provides them with studio, materials and a guaranteed market. The artists then create their own distinctive styles and narrative. Some produce elegant tableware, others giant vases or tureens with bold, vigorous modelling, others concentrate exclusively on finely detailed animal and plant sculptures or painting, some specialize in urban narrative scenes, others in portraiture. What unifies this highly diverse group of makers, apart from the shared studio and the name, is the extraordinarily complex animated surface design and painting, whether it is painted flatware or involves extensive three-dimensional modelling. The relationship between

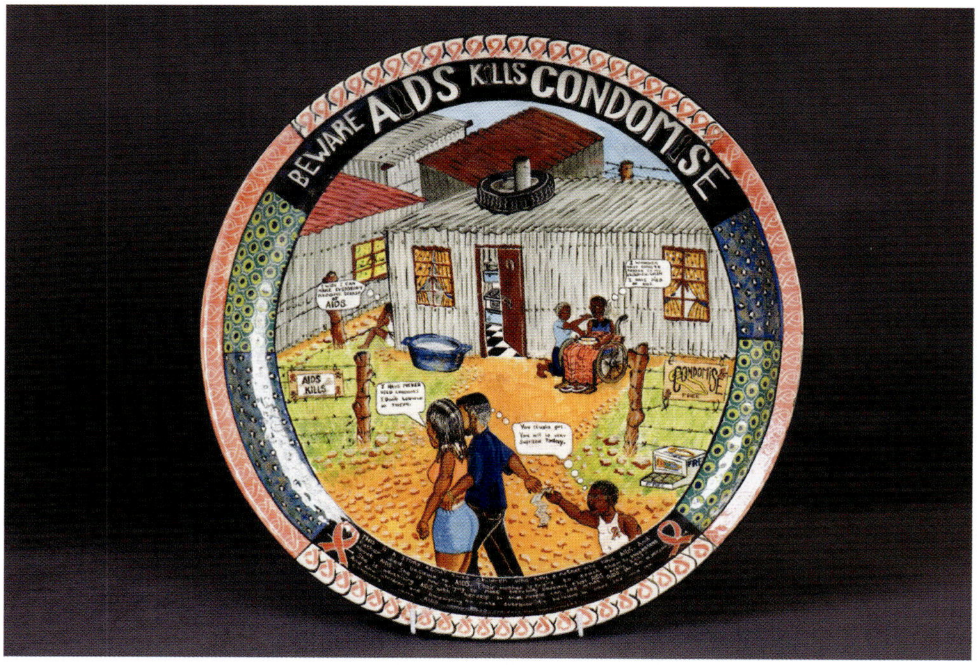

5.2 *Beware, Aids Kills, Condomise*, c. 2001, Andrew Sokhela, Ardmore Ceramic Art

two- and three-dimensional imagery in a single piece is a defining feature of Ardmore ceramics and is always executed with considerable flair and skill no matter which artist is the maker and no matter how different they may be.

Tatham Aids Vase, also known at the 'Monster Jug' (Figure 5.1) and *Beware, Aids Kills, Condomise* (Figure 5.2) could hardly be more different. *Tatham Aids Vase* has a folkloric quality to it, with its patterned surface and scaley beast, whose tail serves as a handle. The eyes around the opening watch beadily, as emaciated figures slide down the outer wall of the pot, clinging on to life. On the other side the gleaming white bones of the dead are piling up, a threat and a warning. This is what happens if the Aids Monster devours you. Inside the embrace of the Aids Awareness red ribbon are three condoms, and 'trust'. It mobilizes a magical, allegorical approach for a campaign that carries a rational message: use a condom. It is profoundly human, appealing to the senses and imagination as well as providing simple information that appeals to the practical need for self-protection. Its mythical quality makes it both compelling and memorable, which is exactly how consciousness-raising needs to be if it is to convince.

Beware, Aids Kills, Condomise uses an explanatory approach mapped out within a domestic and community scene on a plate. This is the ceramic pamphleteering as opposed to the mystery play of the jug. Its pictorial, cartoon-like style, addresses people's fears, assumptions and prejudices, which are aired in speech bubbles, aiming to break down the barriers of silence and invite disclosure, mutual support and responsible sexual conduct. The messages are varied, targeting people with Aids, their families, partners, friends and children to discuss and respond to the reality of the situation and, above all, to take precautions. The Ardmore Aids collection has been exhibited worldwide and is an outstanding educational tool as well as a document of a time and place. The campaigns of the 1990s and early 2000s had to overcome a huge barrier of suspicion, ignorance and government inertia, coupled with religious interference, and patriarchal male pride and entitlement which dictated that using a condom was a form of emasculation. Ardmore artists have produced, arguably, the finest campaigning ceramics of our time. They will certainly be a hard act to follow.

Flight suspended

'Regardless of age and achievement, when it comes to travel, all these women are treated like a flock of suspended doves.' These are the words of the Saudi Arabian artist Manal Al Dowayan, whose ceramic and fibreglass doves are printed with the permission documents of some two hundred women and girls. When Saudi women travel, they must have written permission from their male guardian, whether they are sixty years or six months old. Many of the women whose travel permissions are printed onto the doves are professionals with an international reputation, research scientists, journalists, engineers, artists and teachers. The restraint on women's movement is government policy: this is not the individual choice of families or specific men, it is embedded in the political structure of the country. When something is 'normal' in a society it can be

5.3 *Suspended Together*, 2012, Manal Al Dowayan

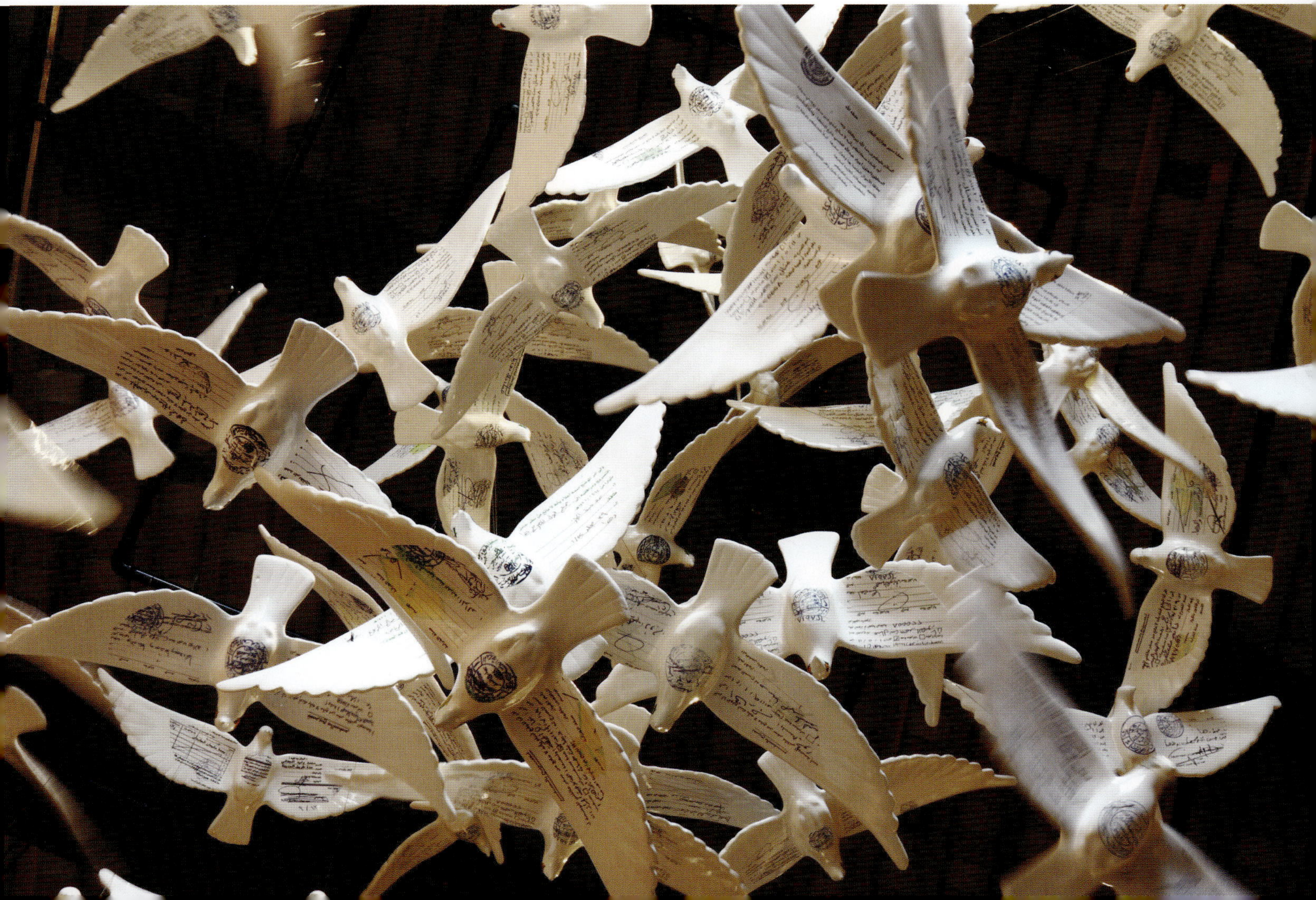

extremely difficult to present the situation as oppressive to those within that society who are accustomed to it. Al Dowayan's installation is beautiful and telling. It expresses 'suspended' flight or arrested movement perfectly. The industrially produced ceramic birds are frozen in space, an enforced immobilization repeated endlessly through the ceramic multiples. It is a very public challenge to Saudi patriarchal norms and authority, beautiful but unequivocal. The work has variable readings but they do not stray far from the central narrative which is a clear, if polite, rebuke.

Shattered

The five pots in *Shattered* are a response to women's accounts of surviving sexual violence. The survival story is key to this work. Women, in the main, do not die from rape but live with it, either the impact of the experience or the fear of it. Some women do die and *Shattered* is a memorial to them as much as it is a call for action to the living. I had been listening to these accounts for the preceding three years and, in reality, for the fifteen years before that. I had worked for Rape Crisis in the 1980s, and since then had listened to many more women, mainly because they needed to talk and I was a willing and practised listener. 'I was shattered. Now I'm starting to piece myself back together', was an expression I had heard in numerous variations from women who had survived rape and sexual abuse. The pots were broken before the

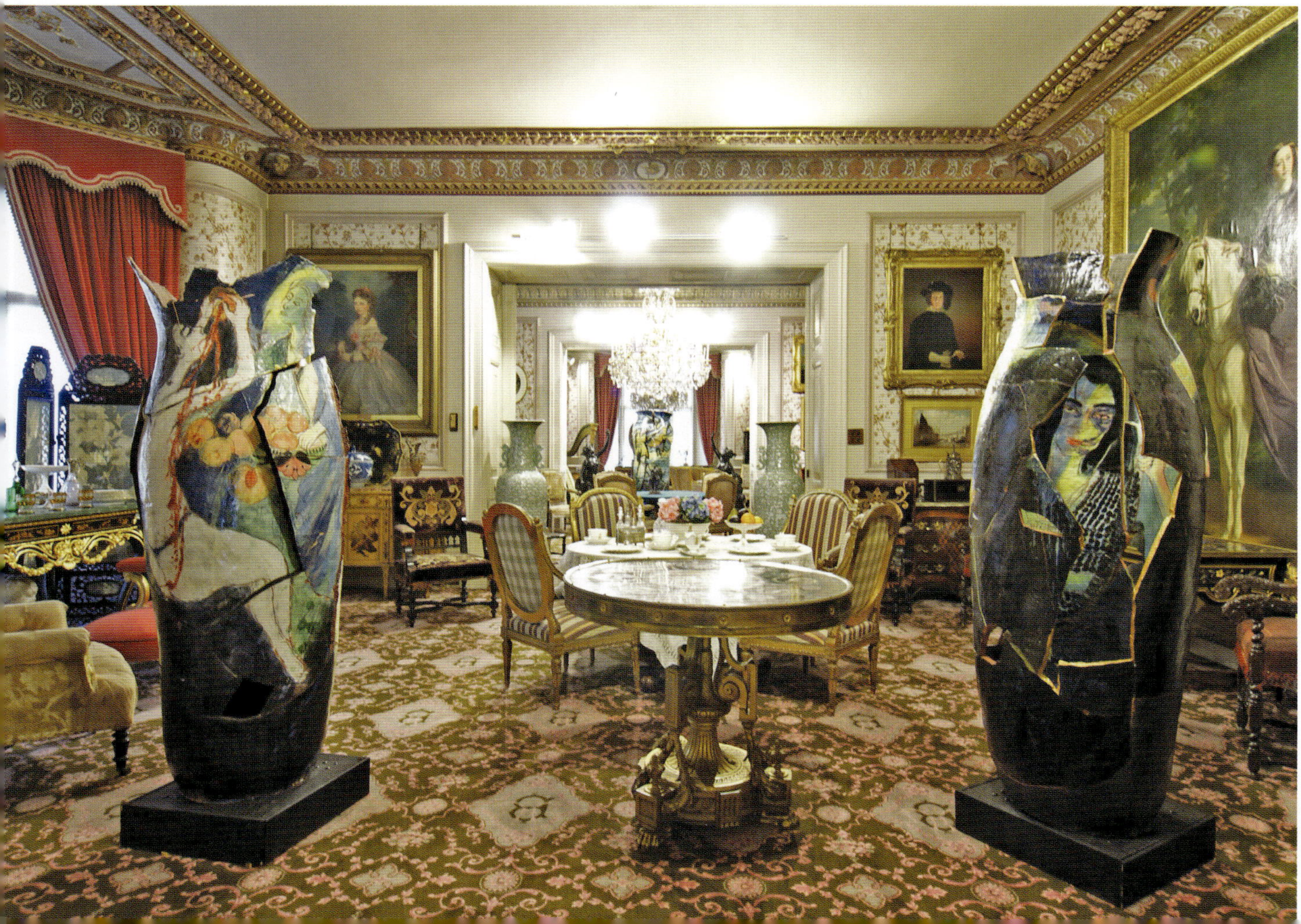

5.4 Three Pots from *Shattered*, 2007, exhibition at Cliffe Castle, 2010, Claudia Clare, photography: Bradford Metropolitan District Council

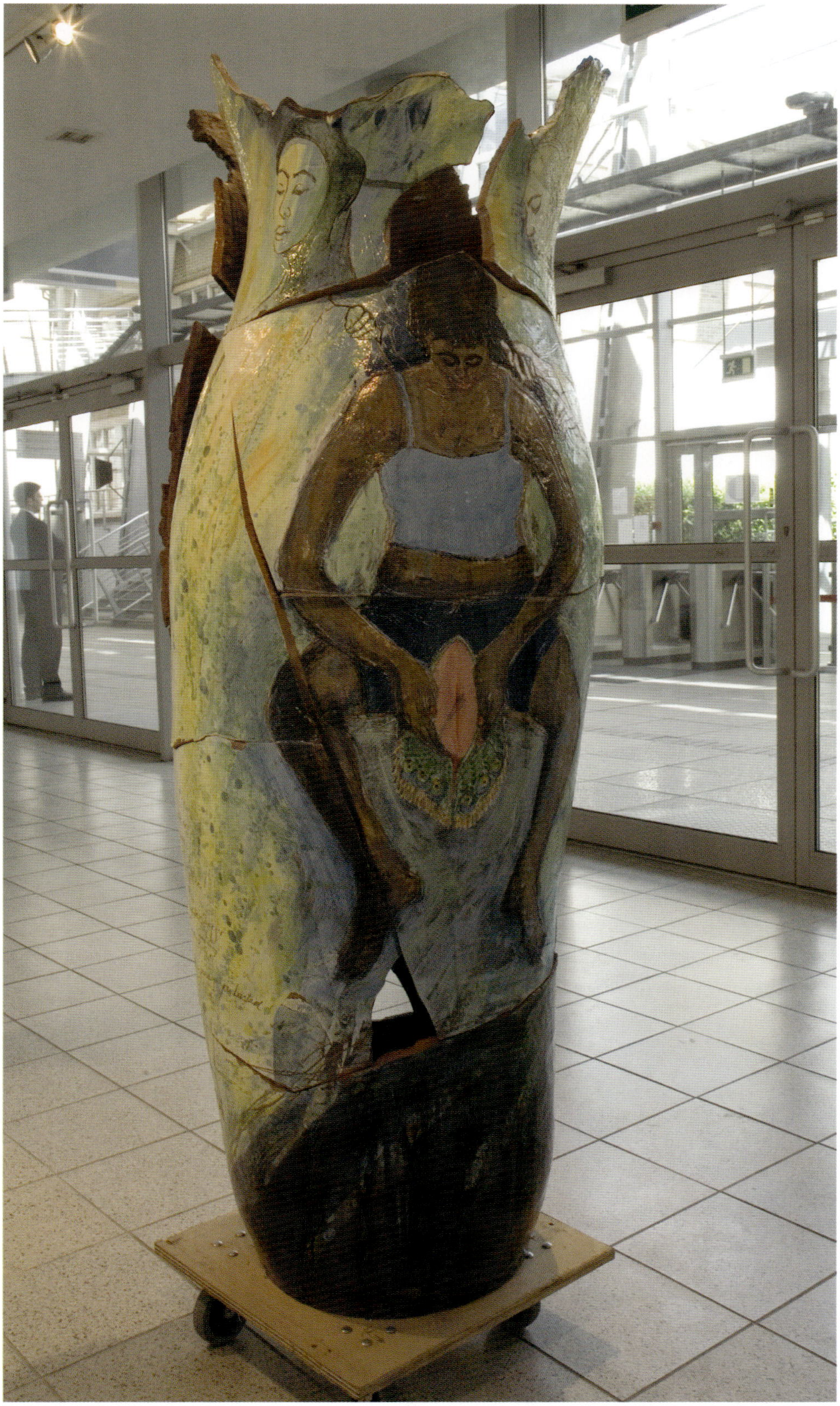

5.5 *Princess Hymen*, 2007, Claudia Clare, photographer: David Freeman

first firing and the shards fired separately, which resulted in each piece being slightly distorted. These pieces could not then be reformed such that the pot regained its original shape. That they could be mended but not precisely restored and, in certain circumstances, could break again, if subject to intense pressure, struck me as a compelling parallel to the kind of trauma that survivors of sexual violence experience: life continues, but slightly differently.

The stories that inspired *Princess Hymen* (Figure 5.5 and Figure 5.4, left-hand side) came from women of Middle Eastern and East African origin, but almost all living in London, in my neighbourhood. Some were about hymen reconstruction and the pressures of living in a culture where virginity is tested and insisted upon as a requirement of marriage. Others were about genital mutilation, forced marriage and violence in the name of family honour. All of these things were happening – or were instigated – in London,[4] but covertly; it was not in the main, public knowledge. The pot depicts a group of women in a bathhouse, also in London. Some are from drawings of real women done from memory, others adapted from Ingres' *Le Bain Turc* (Paris, Louvre). The white woman eating the pomegranate has echoes of Ingres' *Odalisques*, the black woman's make-up bag is based on the peacock-feather fans in the same group of paintings. The choice of imagery was high-risk; these paintings were quasi-pornographic productions destined for wealthy male patrons. The aim was to hold up a mirror and reflect the way that women in both the Middle East and the West are distorted and fetishized in equal measure by both sets of dominant patriarchal social values. The script down the side of the pot refers to hymen reconstruction, genital mutilation and lists some of the numerous terms used for the vagina, some slang, some pejorative, some pornographic.

The other four pots in the group responded to different groups of stories, notably rape as a war weapon,[5] domestic violence and trafficking – also known as 'grooming'. *Traffic* (Figure 5.4, right-hand side) was based on stories from women who lived locally who had been trafficked and prostituted. The women are pictured inside the pot. The exterior shows an urban night-time scene. It contrasts – counterintuitively, perhaps – the relative freedoms and safety of the exterior, public space, with the danger and suffocation of the interior space, one that was difficult to escape. *Shattered* was an emancipatory work; the aim was to raise awareness and to call for action and change. In London the show ran in conjunction with the United Nations' sixteen days of action against violence against women, and was part of Haringey's annual campaign to publicize their domestic violence services and ensure that local women know where to go for help. It was reviewed in English, Turkish, Greek and Farsi, and one of the London shows was extended for a week because it was so popular. It is a curatorial nightmare, however, being so large and fragile. My second attempt working with a different but related narrative is certainly easier to place.

Remembering Atefeh (Figure 5.6) was a smaller version of a similar idea. This time the pot was broken after the first firing so it has retained its shape. The breakage occurred as part of a demonstration with a group of eighteen Iranian refugees outside

5.6 Opposite: *Remembering Atefeh*, 2013, Claudia Clare, photographer: Sylvain Deleu

4 Mark Bentham, 'Met Will Prosecute Parents Who Send their Girls Abroad to be "Cut"', *London Evening Standard*, 18 February 2013.

5 Seada Vranic, *Breaking the Wall of Silence: The Voices of Raped Bosnia*, Izdanja Antibarbarus, Zagreb, 1996.

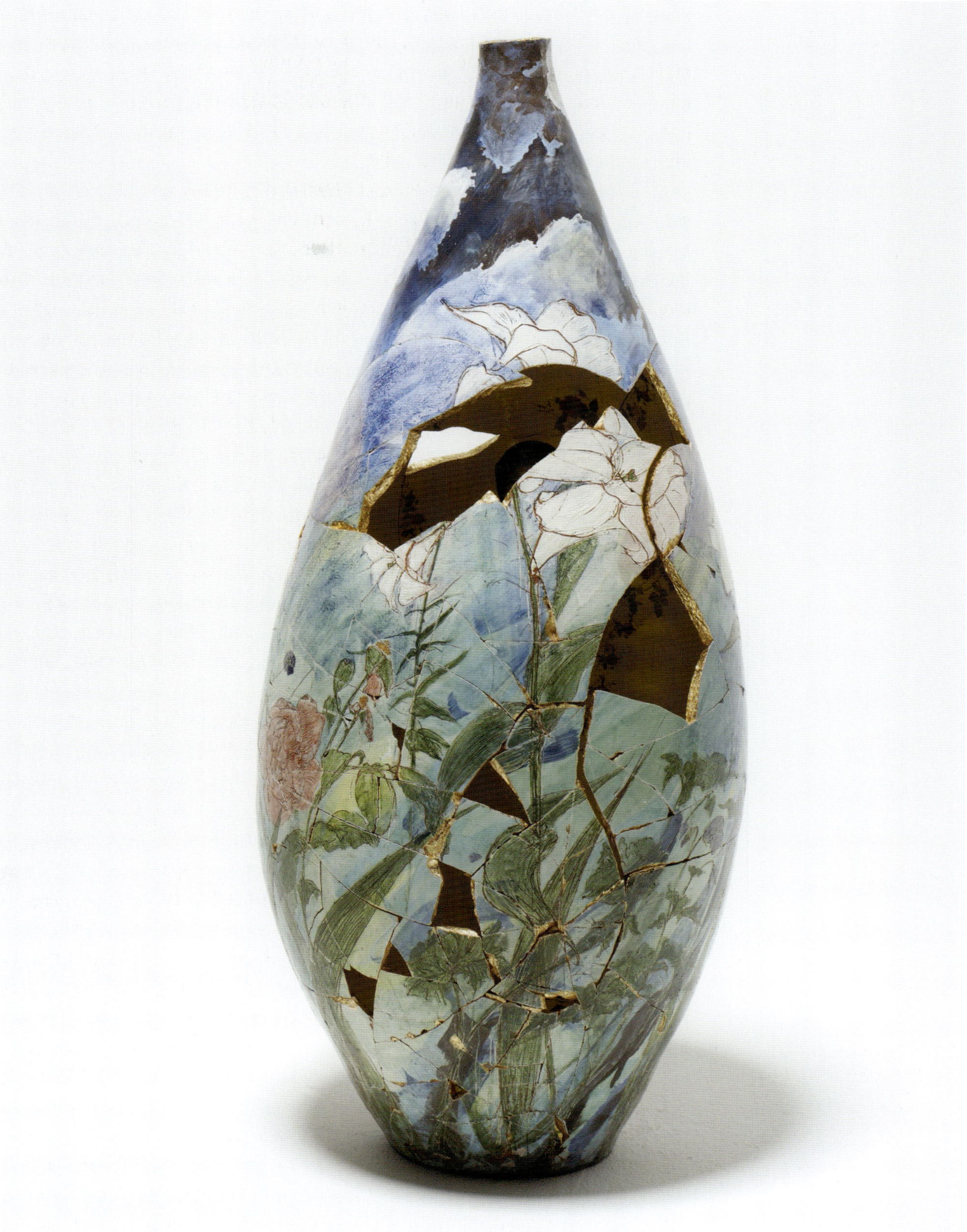

the Iranian Embassy in London, on 15th August 2011, the seventh anniversary of the execution in Iran of Atefeh Rajabi Sahaale, aged sixteen, for 'crimes against chastity'. The purpose was to remember Atefeh, and also to remember all the girls and women imprisoned in Iran and around the world for 'honour' based crimes. In Iran, it is the national 'honour' that is offended; women and girls are expected to embody, sustain and reflect the virtue of the nation. Atefeh's 'crime' was being repeatedly raped over a period of four years by a fifty-seven-year-old taxi driver, a former member of the Revolutionary Guard. *Remembering Atefeh* was exhibited at 'In the Name of Honour', a fundraising exhibition for a domestic violence charity also supporting victims of 'honour' based violence. It was also shown as part of the British Ceramics Biennale, and in a London gallery for six months. Although there is strength enough in the material making of the work this time, it bears a similarity to martyr imagery with the gold leaf framing the internal imagery. This was intentional, but the nature of the internal images may need adjustment if a religious iconographic quality is to be successfully circumvented.

Retrieving histories

Artists of every sort turn to ceramics to make work that contests established histories or comments on contemporary events. Yinka Shonibare's *Upstairs Downstairs*,[6] shown at the Birmingham Icon in 1997, was an elegant porcelain dinner service in a vitrine backed with a photograph of an eighteenth-century stately home. The dinner service was consistent with the aristocratic house but was inscribed with the names of estate workers. Carrie Mae Weems produced a series of plain white porcelain plates inscribed with a short memorial text recalling the lives of black people lived against the odds. 'Commemorating Harriet Tubman for being willing to take even her husband's woman to freedom' (1992, private collection), remembers one among many extraordinary women in the vanguard of the black civil rights movements. Another, 'Commemorating every black man who lives to see twenty-one' (1992, private collection), is a reflection and indictment of the death rate among young black men in America today.

Lubaina Himid, a painter whose work has been a process of retrieving hidden histories and invoking the biographies of people obliterated from historical records, even while they were alive, has connected her painting to ceramics at least as far back as 1992. Her work is first and foremost about people, black African people. The memorial she imagined in a painted sketch on canvas, *Study for a Fountain* (1992),[7] depicted a cascade of plates falling from a tabletop and spilling across the gallery floor. As the drops of water in the painting met the gallery floor they became real plates, made of tin and painted. 'Each real plate [was] hand painted as an icon to a Black person; the plates, like the jugs in the studies, are people.'[8] *Memorial to Zong* (1991),[9] a painting in the same exhibition, depicts a jug on a classical white column. Painted with the portrait head and shoulders of an unknown black man, the jug is a

[6] Moira Vincentelli, 'The Politics of Print', in *Ceramic Review*, 183, 30.

[7] Jill Morgan, 'Women Artists and Modernism', catalogue essay in *Revenge*, Rochdale Art Gallery, 1992, 19.

[8] Morgan, 19.

[9] Morgan, 12.

proto-bust, in effect, quietly satirizing the bust tradition. Water pouring from the jug down the column suggests the waste of human lives – discarded for want of water. Approximately one hundred and thirty captured African men and women were pushed overboard to save drinking water for the Zong's crew and the remaining 'cargo'; surely the most vindictive example of cost–benefit analysis in the entire history of trade. This was not an uncommon practice; only the numbers involved were exceptional. The lawsuit that followed was an insurance dispute rather than a murder trial but the publicity it gained became a major spur in the formation of the abolition movement.

A similar shaped jug appears in another painting, *Venetian Maps, Ceramicists* (1997),[10] an exploration of hidden African lives in Renaissance Venice, and ten working potters feature in *Naming the Money* (2004),[11] a collection of one hundred life-size, portrait cut-outs, transforming forgotten and invisible slave-servants into lively portrait images. The cut-outs occupied first the Hatton Gallery, Newcastle, and then the V&A, a demonstration against banking and money long before any Occupy demonstration filled public spaces in cities across the world after the banking crisis of 2008. They were also a demonstration of the immense social, political, economic and cultural contribution Africans have made to Europe and the Americas.

Ceramics – especially container or vessel forms – water, and money are key symbolic images in the work of Lubaina Himid. She has produced two bodies of work in which she paints over the patterns of old, industrially produced plates, jugs and bowls. Ceramics suggest human life: sustenance, sharing and sociability, but the growth of the ceramics industry in Britain was based on the trade in commodities: sugar, coffee, tea and chocolate, all trades dependent on colonization, slavery and murder, and all inscribed with associations of class and money. Ceramics are long lasting, they are our museum pieces, they resonate with the values of human life. In Himid's work their social and utilitarian associations remind us that slaves were human and her overpainting provides another layer of detail, comment and insight. Her painted ceramics imagine the trades, occupations, community and family relationships of the slave-servants they recall, thus transforming them from anonymous units, traded and commoditized, to portraits of people: providers, makers and consumers.

Swallow Hard: The Lancaster Dinner Service (2007) was commissioned by Lancashire Museums for the Judges Lodging and Gillow Museum in Lancaster. It temporarily displaced the one that would usually have graced the splendid, eighteenth-century mahogany dinner table made by the craftsmen of the world-renowned Gillow furniture-making company. While the skill of Robert Gillow undoubtedly played its part, it was the mahogany, harvested in the West Indies and prepared for export by slave labour, which accounted for his colossal success. Himid's work is always more than an exercise in revealing unacknowledged historical substrata of economics or demographics, important though that is. In the absence of personal records left by slave-servants, aside from the sales receipts and shipping records, she creates a fictionalized counter-narrative of the people captured from West Africa – Ghana, Nigeria, Mali and all along the West coast. These are 'biographies' of people who had everything taken from

[10] Lubaina Himid, *Venetian Maps*, 1997, Harris Museum and Art Gallery.

[11] Lubaina Himid, *Naming the Money*, 2004, Hatton Gallery, University of Newcastle upon Tyne, 16.

them including their names: 'It is an attempt to get to the bottom of the dilemma of losing your name, being relieved of your real identity, being saddled with another more convenient or less embarrassing identity and how you then have to invent something else equally real simply to survive, to make sense of being alive.'[12]

The Lancaster Dinner Service depicts, in bright primary colours, the hidden history of slavery – the labour that created the wealth that, in turn, paid for the stately homes and their fine furnishings. It reveals the social, economic and political context of the trade that made Lancaster a prosperous town. The plates provide the canvases for painted representations of the trading ports, their buildings and bridges, ships, maps and plants, and of the many fine homes of plantation and slave owners. They depict, in cartoon stereotypes, the lawyers who served them, the bankers and businessmen, their accountants and families, the clergy and the abolitionists. It illustrates the trajectory of the slave-trading business, including the collapse of the trade and fortunes made and lost. The slave-trading beneficiaries are represented at work and play, buying and selling shares, riding horses and vomiting copiously at the prospect of abolition. The jugs and tureens show the slave-servants portrayed upright, standing out from the horizontal plane, more visible than the characters painted across the plates. These are portrait-style paintings of men and women with expressions and features, their painted, shaded and textured brown skins standing proud against the smooth, white and patterned ceramic background of the object. They appear isolated and, in part because of that, we start to wonder who they were. Placed on the dining table, *The Lancaster Dinner Service* is a salutary reminder of the origins and human cost of the delicious puddings, rich tobacco and mahogany that embellished the lives of a prosperous new social class. More important, however, is the life-enhancing dramatization that re-imagines vast numbers of otherwise vanished lives, dreams and achievements.

Jellymould Pavilions is also a kind of memorial but is about finding an architecture of pleasure, one which could be shared. It brought the different African nations together via painted images of patterns and people. Jellymoulds are an elaborate, architectural ceramic form. They indicate luxury, pleasure and partying along with sugar, vanilla and cardamom. Painted with patterns from the West coast of Africa, and with portraits of unknown but knowable people, they imagine a huge open space, a public, urban park, dotted with brightly painted pavilions. It is a public holiday and tiny plastic people are out enjoying the park in twos and threes, running, in conversation, or playing among the slightly bigger plastic trees. The *Jellymould Pavilions* are an architect's model. Alongside the people and trees, the jellymoulds become giant, architectural wonders, landscaped inside, needing to be explored. It takes nerve as well as knowledge and wit to create a landscape of pleasure from the historical context of slavery. In doing so, Himid has strengthened her project to show African slave-servants and, perhaps by implication, any enslaved people, past or present, as fully human, with the capacity for inventiveness, pleasure and human connection.

5.7, 5.8 Opposite: *The Lancaster Dinner Service*, 2007, (details), Lubaina Himid, courtesy of the artist

[12] Lubaina Himid, 2004, 3.

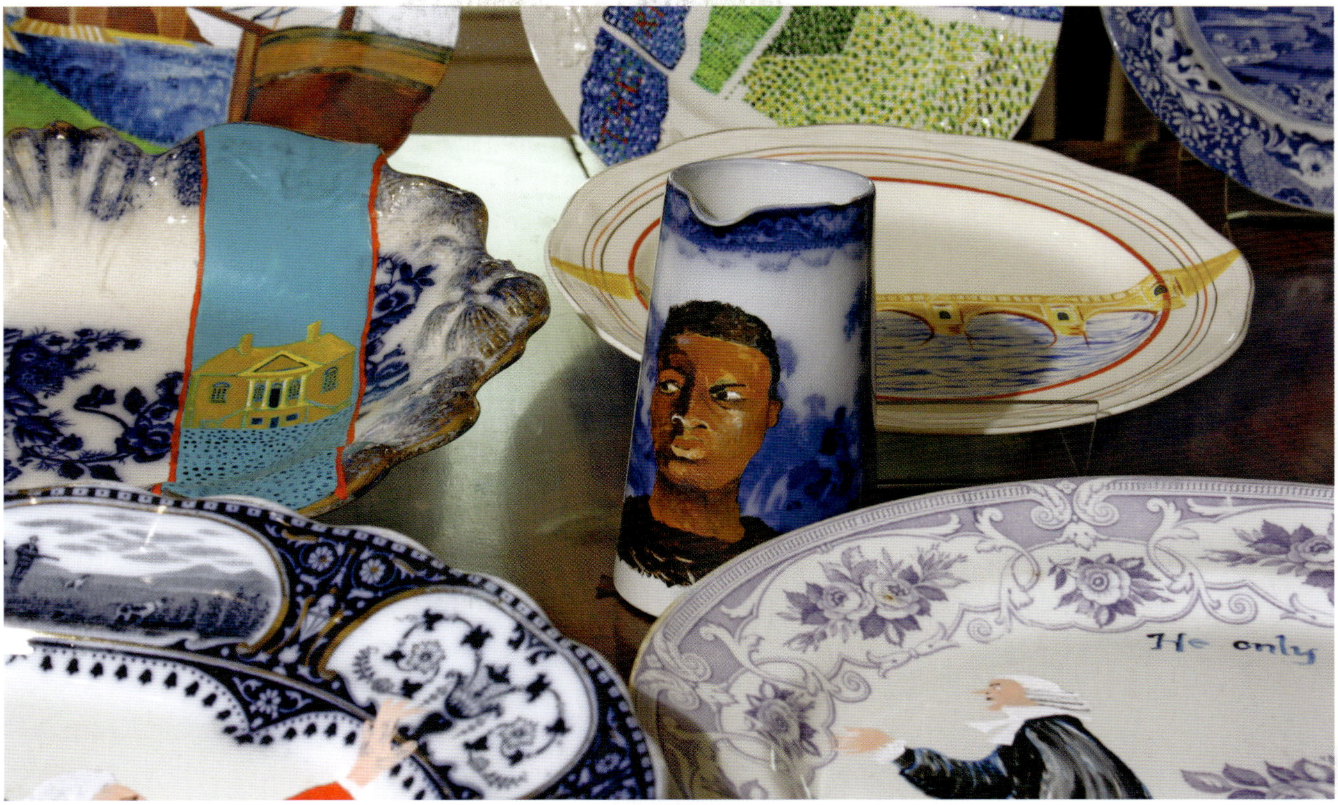
He only

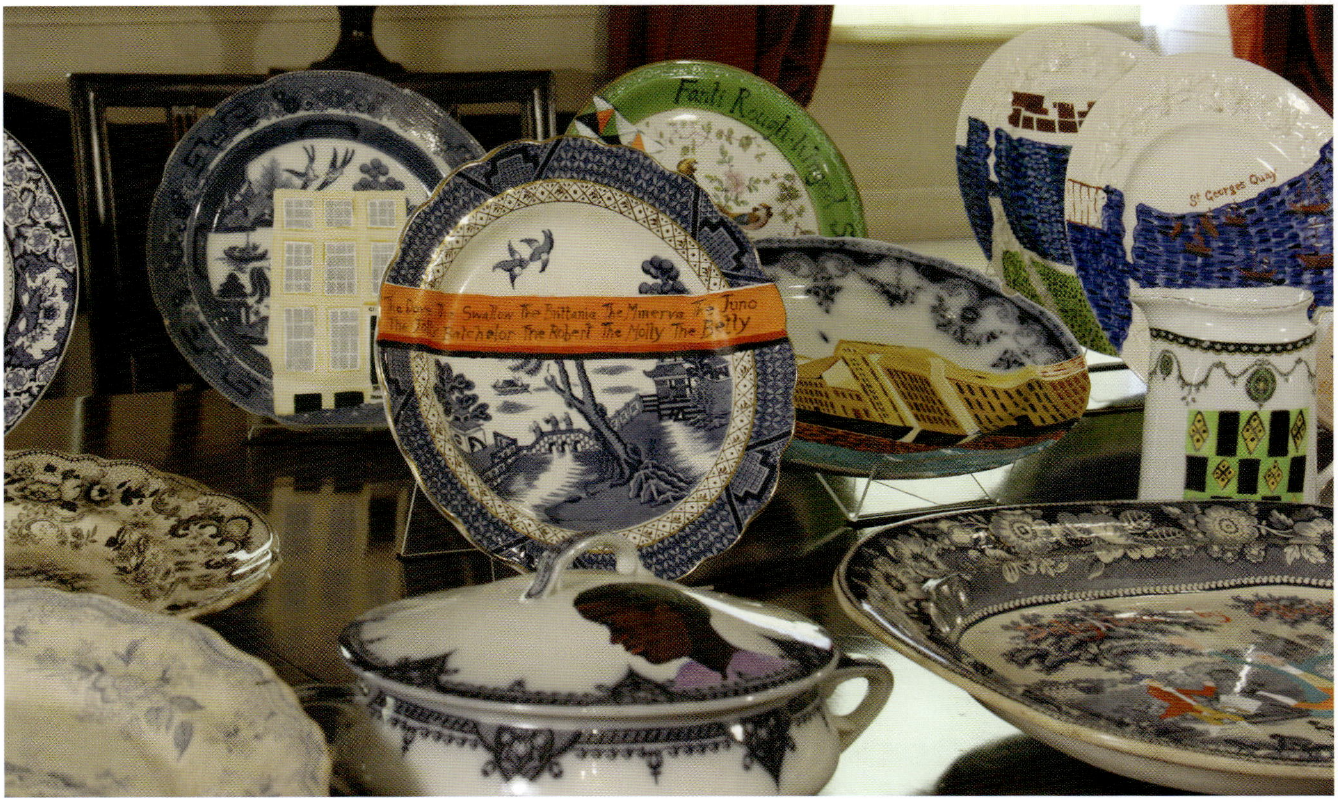
Fanti Rough-winged
Swallow The Brittania The Minerva The Juno
Batchelor The Robert The Molly The Betty
St Georges Quay

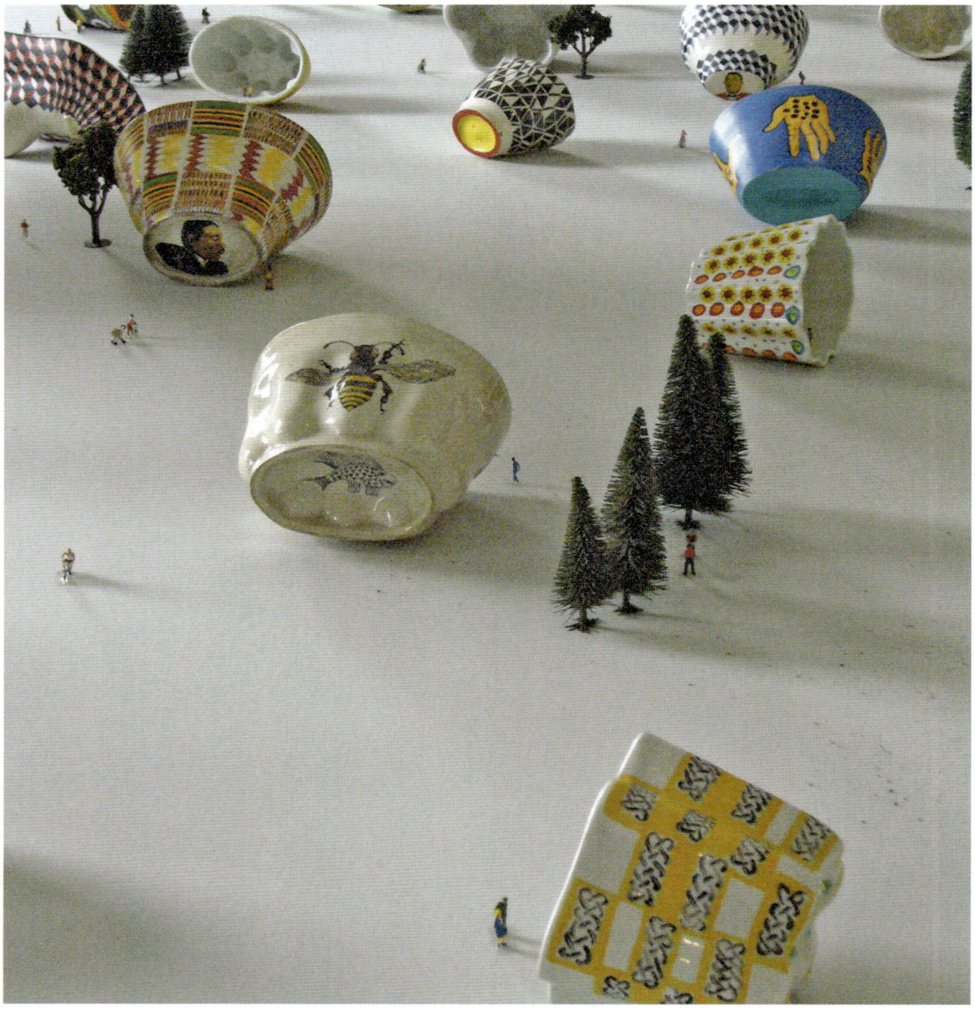

5.9 *Jellymould Pavilions*, 2010, Lubaina Himid, courtesy of the artist

Also reflecting on colonial and contested histories, Stephen Dixon produced *Clocking On* (2012–2013) (Figure 5.10) as part of the 'Cotton Exchange' exhibition, an art exchange project between Manchester and Ahmedabad. Artistically, the aim of the project was to explore the links between the two cities, based on their common industrial heritage of the cotton industry and by reference to their corresponding rise and fall in economic power. *Clocking On* was one of a number of artworks exhibited in the now abandoned Rajnager Textile Mill, Ahmedabad, in 2013. A collection of a hundred slip cast tiffins and billy cans formed two concentric circles on the factory floor of the former weaving room, tracing the pattern of the giant clocking-on machine at the factory entrance. The clock contained a mechanism for punching holes in a card recording the entry and exit times of an individual worker, so the factory manager knew how much to pay them. The system was often grossly abused, however. It could be easily 'adjusted' if a manager wanted workers to put in extra time without the discrepancy showing on the clock, and by implication on their card. The lives of entire communities were dictated and often tyrannized by factory hours, recorded by the clock.

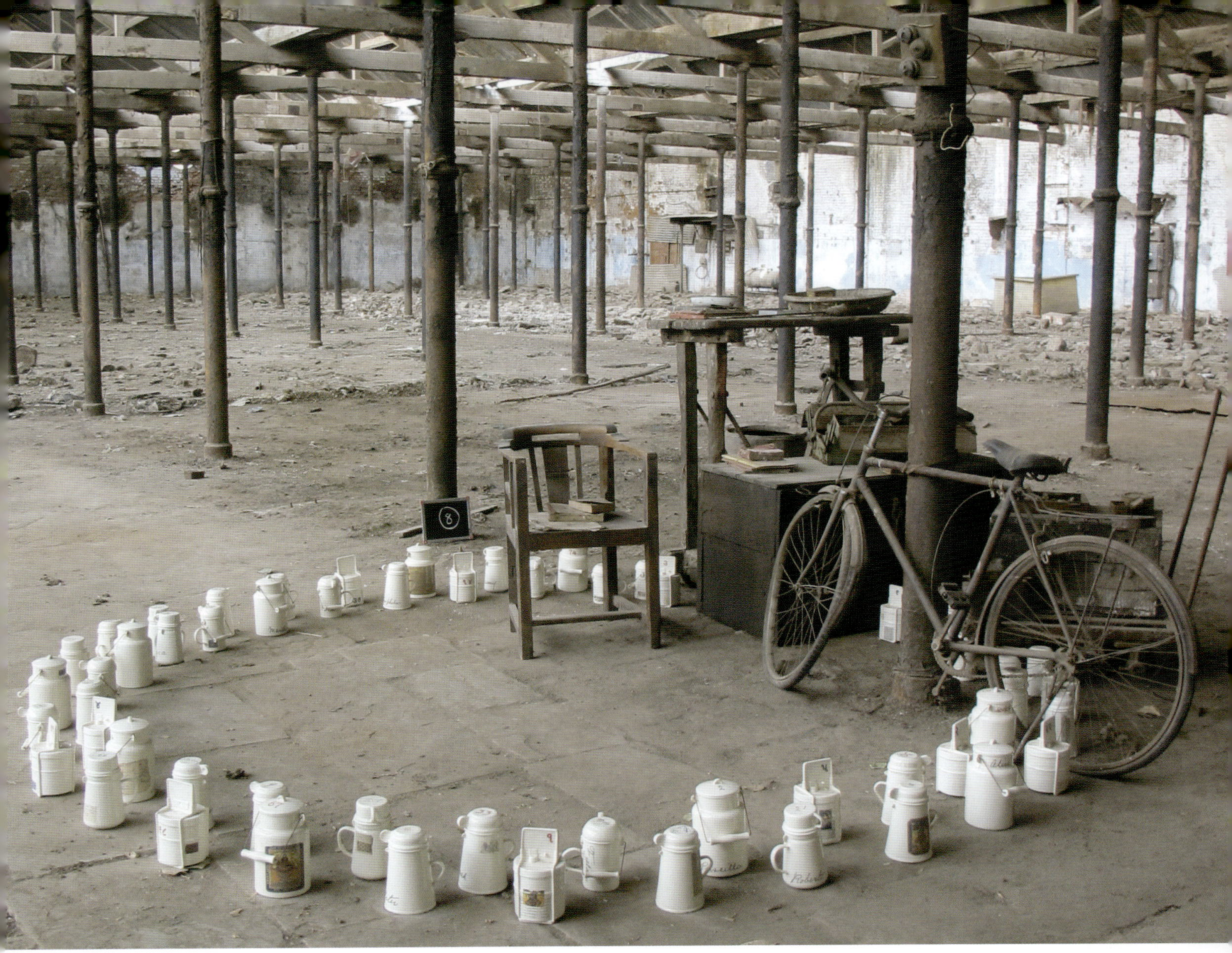

5.10 *Clocking On*, 2012/13, Stephen Dixon, photographer Tony Richards

Dixon's delicate porcelain cans, printed with the name of a worker, a statement of accounts or a payslip, and on all of them a number, are at once profoundly personal and entirely impersonal. Tiffins were the food containers used by the Ahmedabad workers and billy cans were used by the Manchester workers for brewing tea. Now objects of 'retro' curiosity, they were, at that time, utterly utilitarian, ubiquitous and unremarkable. Turned into artefacts they either embody and remember the individual worker with a name and a life, or, because of the sense that they could be repeated a thousand times more, they project the industrial ideal that workers are anonymous units that exist solely to maximize production, mechanistic and unmemorable.

An ageing bicycle – an earlier work but also related to the project – its front wheel and seat encrusted in bone china flowers, was shown in various locations in Dahl Ni Pol, in the old walled city in Ahmedabad as part of the International Arts Festival in 2010. Dixon found fifty thousand of the china flowers in the old Spode factory in Stoke-on-Trent, and used them for the Dahl Ni Pol residency. Its title,

Hero (2010) (Figure 5.11), has a strongly nostalgic flavour, suggesting that the bicycle is a relic rather than a useful means of transport. Liz Mitchell comments on the 'humanity conjured up by a battered second-hand bike garlanded with flowers',[13] but, in conjunction with what is, in effect, a regeneration project aiming to capture the interests of tourists, it has a slightly cloying, sentimental feel. *Clocking On* is a tougher work that was also shown in the old weaving shed in the Queen Street Mill Textile Museum, Burnley, in Lancashire. There, however, it was part of a well maintained, industrial 'heritage' museum, rather than the dilapidated or 'distressed' environment of the Ahmedabad exhibition, which presented the work itself with a different set of problems.

Romanticized tourism is the spectre that haunts these post-industrial, artistic commentaries, whether in abandoned mills in northern India or in prettied-up museums in borthern England. It threatens to reduce the work to an exercise in nostalgic contemplation. Dia Da Costa, a scholar in global development studies, remarked about the Ahmedabad version of this exhibition: 'in remaking place, art mobilizes sentiments – here, nostalgia and hope – while erasing violence and inequality'.[14] In the Ahmedabad environment, this was certainly not helped by the photographic record. The dilapidation is real, the result of economic depression, but the wistfulness of the photographs resemble the faux 'distressed' look of an interior design shoot. This is further enhanced by Dixon's highly crafted, slip cast, retro-looking porcelain cans, objects easily linked to the domestic interior. The other artists in the show were also using craft forms, particularly textiles. It is likely that the 'interior design' quality comes across much more strongly in the photographic record than it did in real life but Da Costa was clearly not convinced: 'in Ahmedabad today, art is being mobilized to obscure dispossession and exploitation in the name of urban revitalization and heritage production'. Warming to her theme, she goes on to quote her own conversation with the curator, 'It does not seem to connect the heritage of the textile mills in this city, to this city. To unemployment, or communal violence, or anything else.'[15] It is a harsh assessment, perhaps one to be expected from a development scholar, but she has a point. By itself, *Clocking On* is a very finely calibrated work, both elegant and eloquent. Immaculately made, as Dixon's works always are, it may be a little too beautiful to be able to comment forcefully on the grotesque abuses of the colonial relationship; the degradation of cities and their populations in the process of industrial decline and the continuing appalling conditions of labour from which the former colonial power, Britain, still benefits. Beauty, like humour, can be complicit when it comes to the production of critical or anxious objects. That said, politically committed artists cannot afford to alienate audiences by hitting them over the head. The work has to appeal enough to bring the viewer in, allow them to absorb the meaning of the work and consider it. The vexed question between the intention of the artist, the appeal of the work and the ways the audiences may or may not understand the work will probably never be fully resolved.

5.11 Opposite: *Hero*, 2010, Stephen Dixon, courtesy of the artist

[13] Liz Mitchell, 'Material Memory', in *Ceramic Review* 257, 47.

[14] Dia Da Costa, 'Sentimental Capitalism in Contemporary India: Art, Heritage and Development in Ahmedabad, Gujarat', abstract, Antipode, 2014, DOI: 10.1111/anti.12103.

[15] Dia Da Costa, 2014, 1.

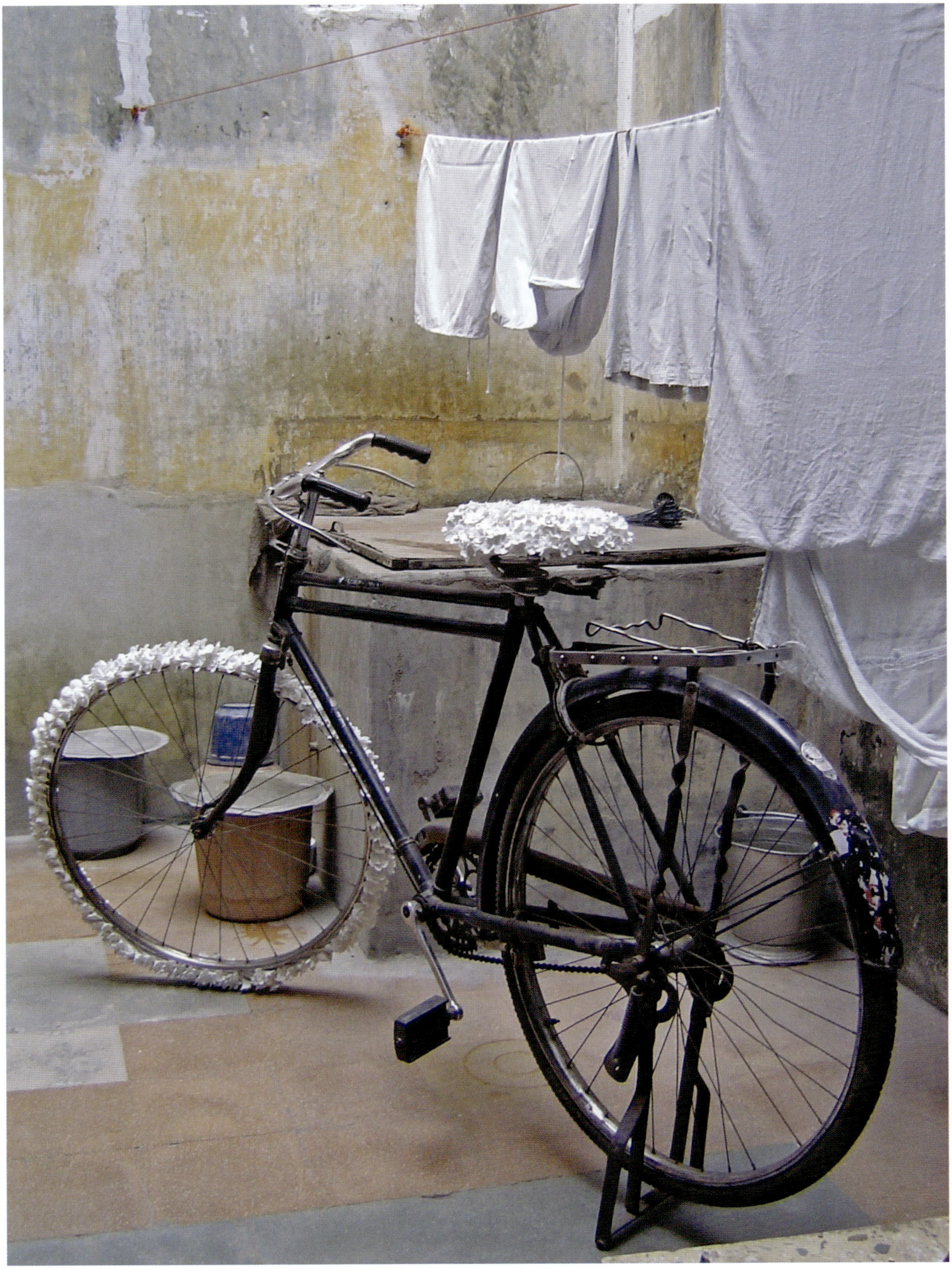

War and peace

Angola's bloody civil war and its equally brutal history of colonization and slavery are embedded in the material, forms, colours, techniques and imagery that define Helga Gamboa's pots. They are both a document of present fracture and a memorial to a devastated past. In their very existence and particularly in their recognition of traditional, pre-colonial forms and material, they are also an expression of hope and continuity. Helga Gamboa grew up in Luanda, Angola's capital city, during the colonial period, knowing nothing of the languages or traditions of her country and certainly not its pots. Colonization and wars have left Angola with a disastrous legacy. Much of the land is unusable, being littered with landmines, which kill and maim almost daily, as well as erasing much of the indigenous material culture. While Gamboa was living in England, her pots were formed from industrially prepared clays, cleaned and processed for immediate use by the studio potter. Her shapes, textures and making methods, however, drew on those of the Kwanyama pottery, one of the original Angolan pottery types which she studied in England in a collection assembled by Antoinette and Diana Powell-Cotton in the 1930s; a rare moment when a woman of a colonized nation was able to make good use of the activities of the colonizer. She was able to build up her ceramic vocabulary through studying the collection and combining this learning with her knowledge of blue and white, tin-glazed Portuguese ceramics that were part of the colonial culture which surrounded her in the urban environment of her upbringing. Gamboa's relatively small, beautifully fashioned and proportioned pots resonate with the many voices of a vast, epic and inglorious history while being, in themselves, extraordinarily original artefacts and testifying to survival and self-determination.

Aftermath (2003)[16] is a hand-coiled pot, burnished according to the Kwanyama tradition, white tin-glazed at the neck and printed with three rows of documentary or photojournalistic-style imagery. One row shows repeated images of a woman going about her life, with one leg and two crutches, the result of a landmine injury; the row above shows a boy with a similar injury. Another pot, *Lost Childhood* (2004) (Figure 5.13), made the same way, shows photographs of children's faces staring out of the neck of the pot, framed by the black and white of the vase. The black and white photographic images are perfectly calibrated to work with the burnished black pot, which, at first glance, seems wholly unsurprising. It is, however, almost unheard of to use a European tin glaze, recalling the European Renaissance, with a handbuilt, burnished southern African pot form, and add printed contemporary, photojournalistic imagery. It is also the antithesis of the child-photograph. We do not know if these children are dead or orphaned, either way it is an intensely shocking object, but one with a 'slow burn'.

Madonna and Child (2005)[17] shows a photograph of a mother hugging her sick baby, printed in cobalt blue on a white tin-glazed ground. The rim and the tabs on the outer wall are coloured with silver lustre, usually made from platinum, redolent of the aggressive competition among global mining corporations for the rights and access to valuable resources, diamonds in the case of Angola. The use of lustres is also perhaps

5.12 Opposite: Earthenware Vessel, 2005, Helga Gamboa Ceramics Collection and Archive, Aberystwyth University

[16] Helga Gamboa, 'An Angolan Heritage: The Ceramics of Helga Gamboa', in *Interpreting Ceramics*, issue 10, 2008, online: http://www.interpretingceramics.com/issue010/conf_contents.htm [accessed 2 February 2015].

[17] Gamboa, 2008.

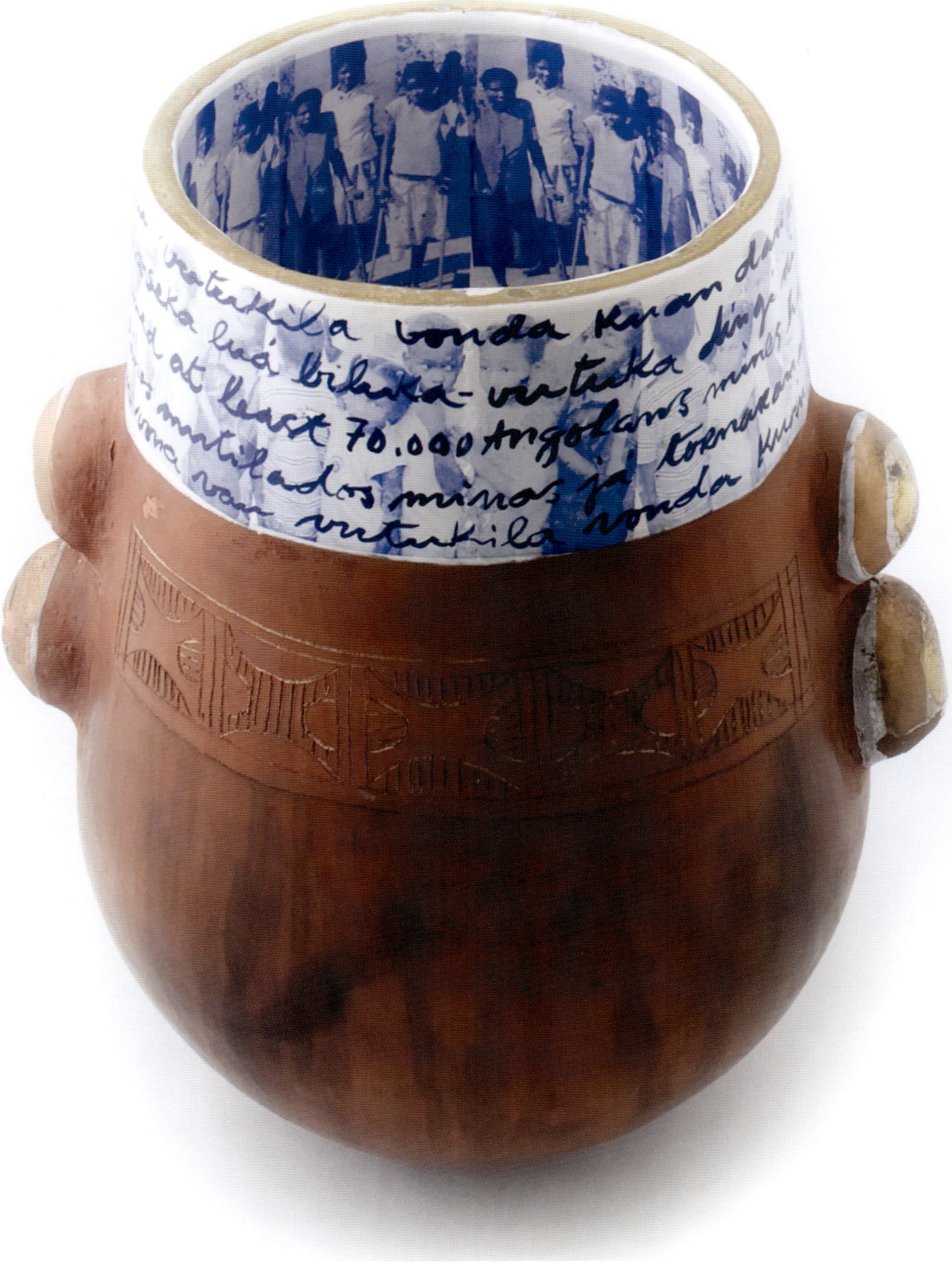
vonda
at least 70.000 Angolans
mutilados minas já
vutukila vonda

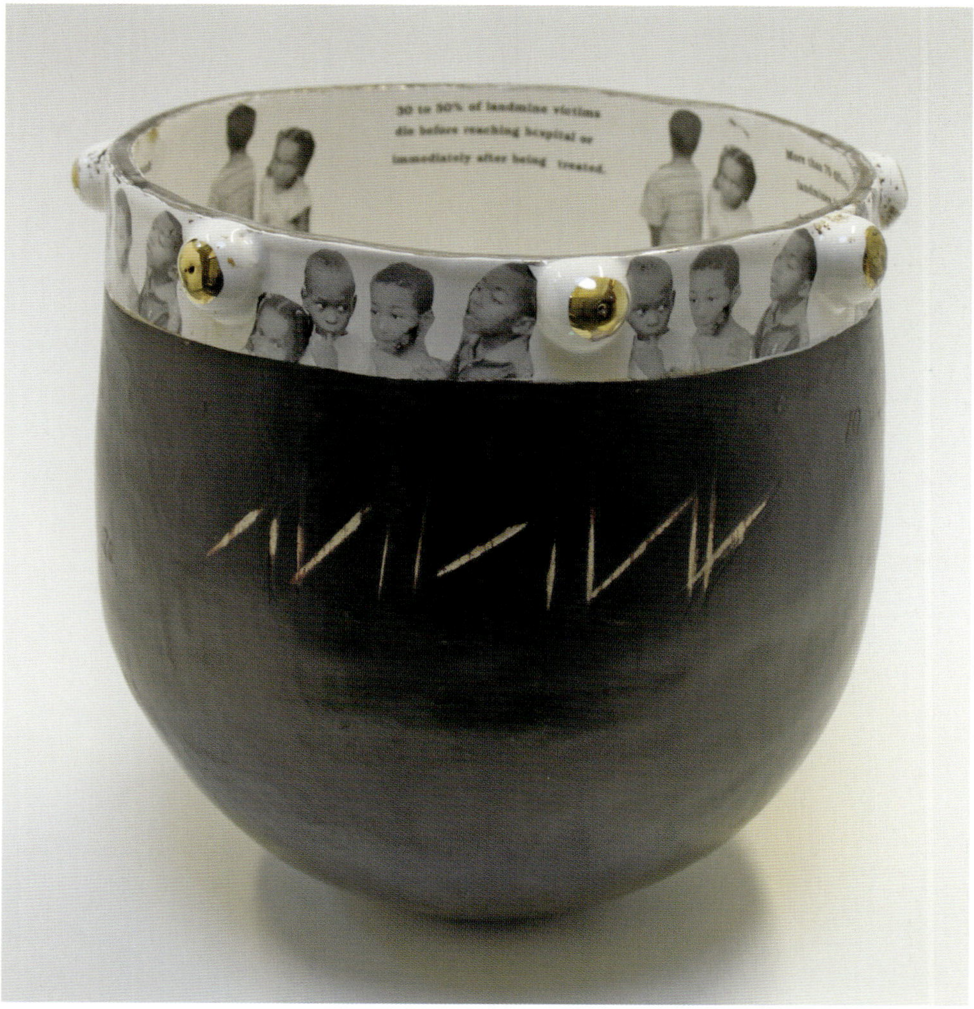

5.13 *Lost Childhood*, 2004, Helga Gamboa Perlman Center for Learning and Teaching, Carleton College

a material reminder of the fortunes made from the trade in Africans for slave labour. The title refers to the colonial religion, Catholicism, as does the use of blue and white, but the form is traditionally Angolan. Similarly, *Servitude II* (Figure 5.14) is a burnished terracotta pot, with the tin glaze addition round the top and the rim picked out in platinum silver. Printed in black, direct onto the red clay body, are images of the slaving ships, showing the hold where the people were packed as close as possible for maximum profit. The interior of the pot has the 'danger' sign indicating the presence of landmines – as well as being a chilling understatement when associated with the images of the middle passage – while the tin-glazed collar is printed with images of women going to and from the market, all affected by the memory of mines, civil war and slavery. These are ominous, uncomfortable images to use with a pot that speaks of tradition, food and comfort. The pots themselves are intensely absorbing and demonstrate the power of even the most traditional of materials and methods to produce work that is hard-hitting politically, while also operating as contemplative memorials. A sense of future and continuing life is also suggested in her choice

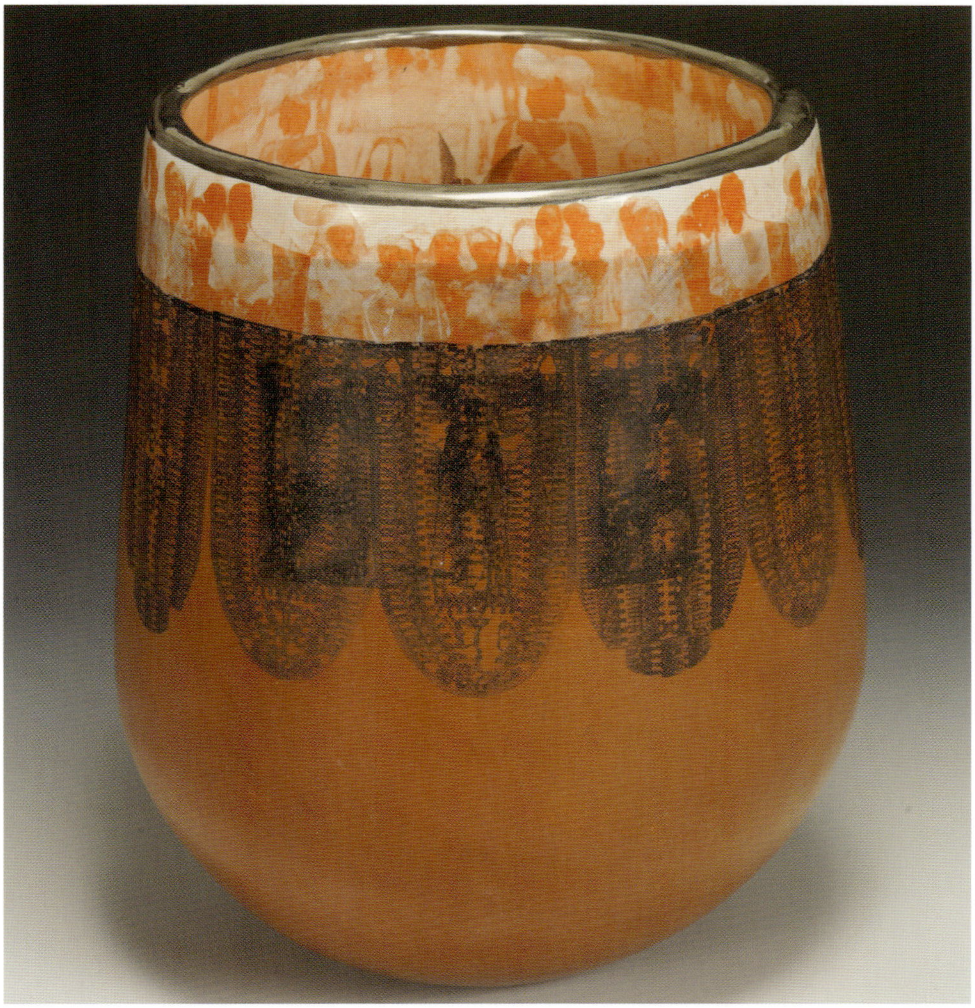

5.14 *Servitude II*, 2008, Helga Gamboa, Ceramics Collection and Archive, Aberystwyth University

of imagery: Gamboa always includes images of women, children and young people, busy, and on the move. The inclusion of a visual perspective, suggesting the direction of moment, gives these works an edge that deftly steers them away from anything that might privilege loss over survival.

A harsh, metallic, silver ovoid, bristling with bullets inside and out, Peter Lewis's *Olive 1* (2009) (Figure 5.15) is a vicious-looking object. This is ceramics at its least domestic. Executed with neat precision, Lewis is fearless when it comes to producing ceramic objects that cannot and should not please. The *Olive* series came from his month-long residency in the Palestinian city of Ramallah, in the West Bank, one of a series of visits between 2003–2005. *Olive 1* is a military object that demonstrates clay's chameleon qualities: it can shine as menacingly as any newly minted bomb or rocket. The series contrasts images of what should be rural, agricultural life in the West Bank with the militarization of the entire region, in the form of Israeli air strikes, and the destruction of the olive groves to make way for new Israeli settlements. The olives themselves have correspondingly contrasting surfaces, some busy with

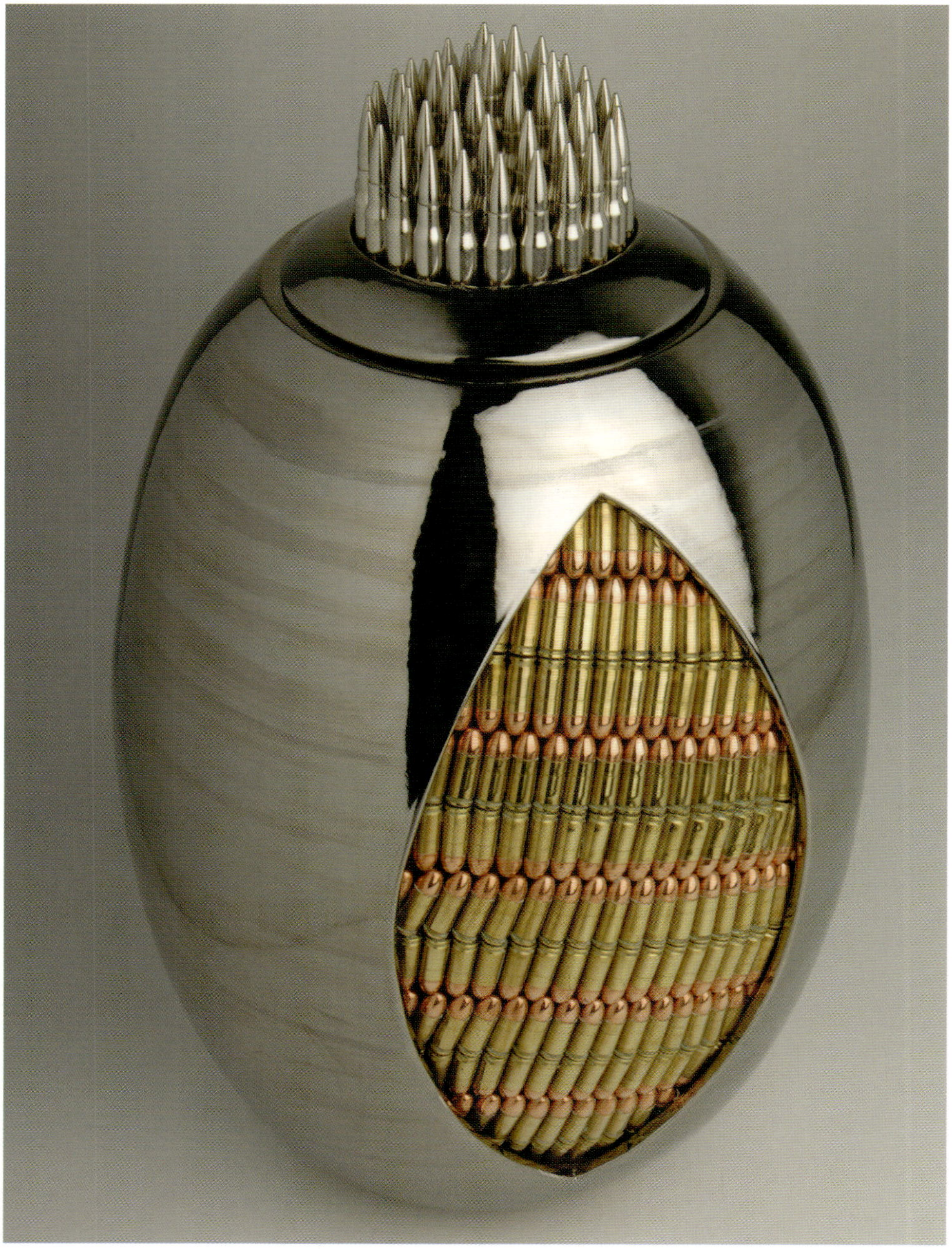

5.15 *Olive I*, 2007, Peter Lewis, courtesy of the artist

5.16 Opposite: *155H*, 2010, Peter Lewis, courtesy of the artist

maps and Boy's Own imagery, others with sprigged motifs, almost looking like 'proper pots', and others with a fiercely industrial shine. *155H* (Figure 5.16) is a group of three bombshells, the sort fired from tanks and rockets, painted with cartoon images, lyrical landscapes and bomb-making diagrams. With their metallic tips they are simultaneously threatening and absurd, resembling everyday domestic objects, toys or souvenirs, while yielding not one jot to the temptation to make something beautiful or affecting. On the contrary, they are grossly symbolic of the normalizing of militarized violence in areas of conflict.

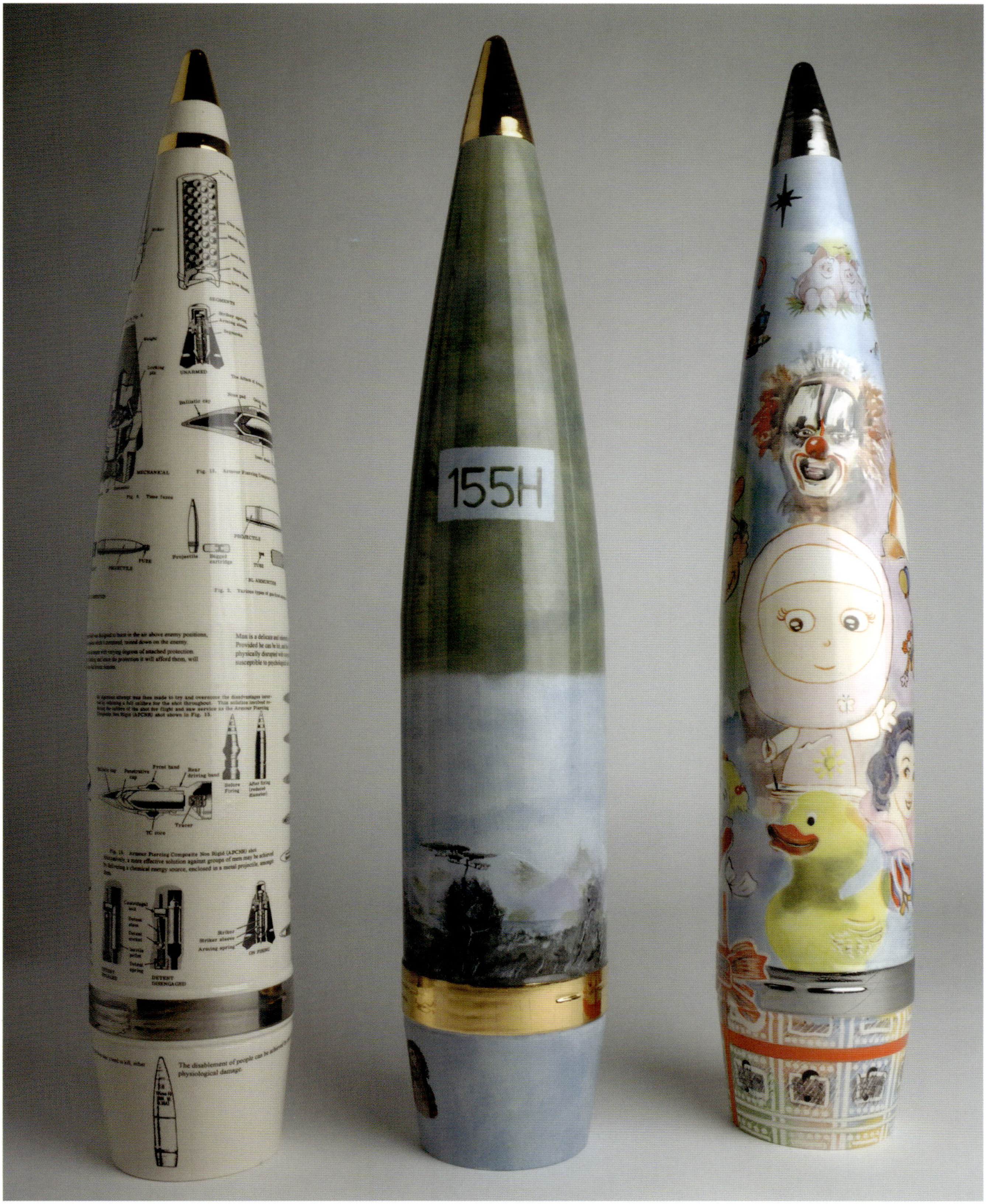
155H

Paul Scott's *Gaza Airport 2014*, a response to the Israeli military pounding of Gaza in summer 2014, is collaged from a lyrically beautiful, orientalist plate, overprinted with the ruins of the airport, now no more than a pile of rubble. The blue and white Adams earthenware dessert plate, c. 1840, features an assortment of palm trees, minarets, domes, a pagoda, tents and horses. It is a feast of 'exotic of the east' madness. The distinctive Chinese mountains of the Pearl River mix with delicate, feathery date palms along with Ottoman mosques in the distance. What is now Gaza was part of the Ottoman Empire, but under Egyptian rule at the time the plate was made, so, although the Chinese influence is stretching it a bit, it is less mad than it seems. Dessert plates were not, of course, intended to meet the requirement of geopolitical accuracy, they were the stuff of fantasy and, overprinted with the grainy newsprint image of the remains of the airport, with a plane flying overhead, the dreamworld charm of the original is grossly interrupted. It is a classic 'collector's' piece, with a 'Palestine' stamp on the back to which Scott has added his various insignia. The taxonomic approach adds layers of narrative, the more so considering Gaza was hosting a battle for supremacy between British-backed Ottoman forces and Egyptian troops in 1839–1840, as well as being laid waste to by the bubonic plague and a couple of earthquakes.[18]

Khosrow Hassanzadeh's *Dome* (2010) is a representation of the *zurkhaneh* which, translated literally, means 'house of strength'. It is a building for sport but the *zurkhaneh* is also a uniquely Iranian institution, profoundly embedded in Shia Islam and the Iranian concept of masculinity, ancient and still very much alive in contemporary Iran. In the *zurkhaneh*, the model Iranian male develops his strength using bodybuilding techniques, but this is no ordinary gymnasium; the sport, as it is practised, is highly ritualized, involving drumming, chanting and prayer. The names of the Shia imams are invoked, and the displays of masculine virility in the form of wrestling, weightlifting, martial arts and strongman displays with chains and batons, are performed in the name of God and of Shi'ism. It is an intensely romantic vision of manhood and of masculine beauty, valorizing honour, piety, sacrifice and martyrdom. It is also central to the construction of a romantic Iranian nationalism, mediated through socio-religious ritual and through the actual bodies of its people.

In principle, this work may have no place in this book, as its narrative is religiously charismatic and patriarchal. Hassanzadeh has made a contemplative rather than an explicitly subversive work, but his European and American galleries and curators package his work as 'controversial'. Much of the writing on his work focuses on two earlier screen-printed and painted series: *Prostitutes* (2002) and *Terrorist* (2004). We are being invited to consider this artist as 'edgy and a bit dangerous'. The *Terrorist* series, in which his mother and sister are photographed and labelled 'Terrorist', was meant to be a critical parody of what Hassanzadeh considered was the 'West's' inclination to classify all Muslims as terrorists. The work was marketed by European galleries to appeal to the *bien pensant* of the left, which presented itself as even more critical of the belief that 'Muslims are terrorists' than the 'East'. The whole idea falls

5.17 Opposite: *Gaza Airport 2014*, Paul Scott, Scott's Cumbrian Blue(s), Palestine, Gaza (airport) 2014. In-glaze decal collage and gold lustre on partially erased Adams earthenware dessert plate, c. 1840, diameter 22 cm

[18] Gudrun Kramer, *A History of Palestine: From Ottoman Conquest to the Founding of the State of Israel*, Princeton University Press, 2011, 69–70.

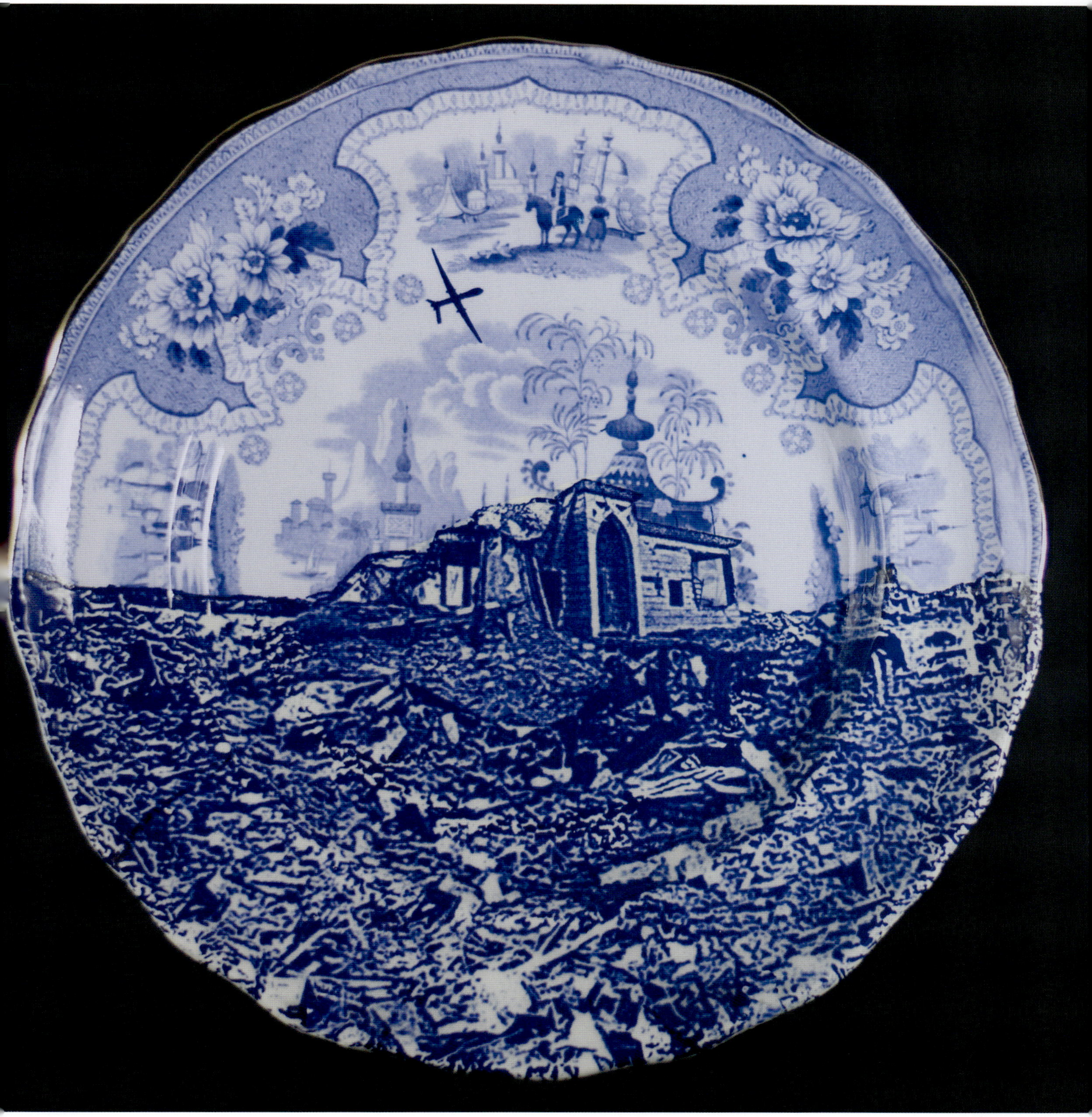

apart when set in the context of Iran itself where the regime delights in telling its benighted citizens that the 'West' considers them all terrorists, a label it wears like a badge of honour. It falls apart still further in the context of the European art world, which is inclined to forget that their 'West', has a great many Iranian refugees living in it, who tend to look at such images, nod sagely, and mutter, 'Yes. They are.' As the hailstorm of inverted commas in previous sentences indicate, the works themselves are inescapably trapped in an absurd East–West binary that descended into farce some years ago, so one has to ask why this artist's European dealers still concentrate on his past works when his more recent ceramic works are so much richer and more complex. *Dome* was not intended to be a satire but it cannot help but expose the cynicism of Western European art professionals and the credulousness of both the art market and the cognoscenti.

The beautiful, clean-shaven, pink-lipped young man in the foreground of the *Dome* image is Ghalamreza Takhti, an Iranian, gold-medal winning, Olympic wrestler and leading exponent of the ancient ritualized sport of the *zurkhane*. Takhti is still a national hero in Iran and, inevitably, both his life and death have been subject to the process of political myth-making and claimed by all interested factions. Surrounding Takhti inside the *Dome* are more '*pahlavan*': these are the heroes of the ritualized sport of which weightlifting and wrestling are a part. To the left, for example is the Daf player who sounds the rhythm of the chanting. The Persian text is from a part of Ferdowsi's epic poem, the *Shahnameh*, or *The Book of Kings*. It is from a part called '*Haft Kahne-e-Rostam*', *The Seven Labours of Rostam*, which tells of the trials and travails of Rostam on his journey to manhood. Also accompanying Takhti in his quest for a virtuous manhood is a warrior figure with the horse. He is from the *Ta'zieh*, a Shia passion play, performed annually to remember the life and death of Imam Hossein, the third Shia Imam. A giant copper bell hangs down from the middle of the dome in the completed work which features as part of the religious ritual, along with the drumming and chanting.

To reach Hassanzadeh's work it is necessary to understand some of the underlying complexity of Iran's socio-political and religious environment. Khosrow Hassanzadeh is an Azerbaijani Iranian, who has chosen to live and work as an artist in Iran rather than, as many of his compatriots have done, leave to work in Dubai, Western Europe, America or Canada. All artists working in Iran must have their work approved by the *Ershad*, the Council of Islamic Guidance, so to choose to stay in Iran is to abide by the highly restrictive codes of censorship, not an easy choice for any artist to make. There is some flexibility if artists do not show their work inside Iran but the risk is still there. Hassanzadeh fought in the Iran–Iraq war, was a member of the Basij, is a committed Shia Muslim and comes from a working-class background – his family are fruit-sellers. He is not 'Western orientated', but nor is he of the regime and nor is he of the opposition elite. In principle, he should be loved by the regime: his work sells well abroad, which is good 'soft power' for Iran, but he elected to leave the institutions of government, which indicates at least a degree of dissatisfaction.

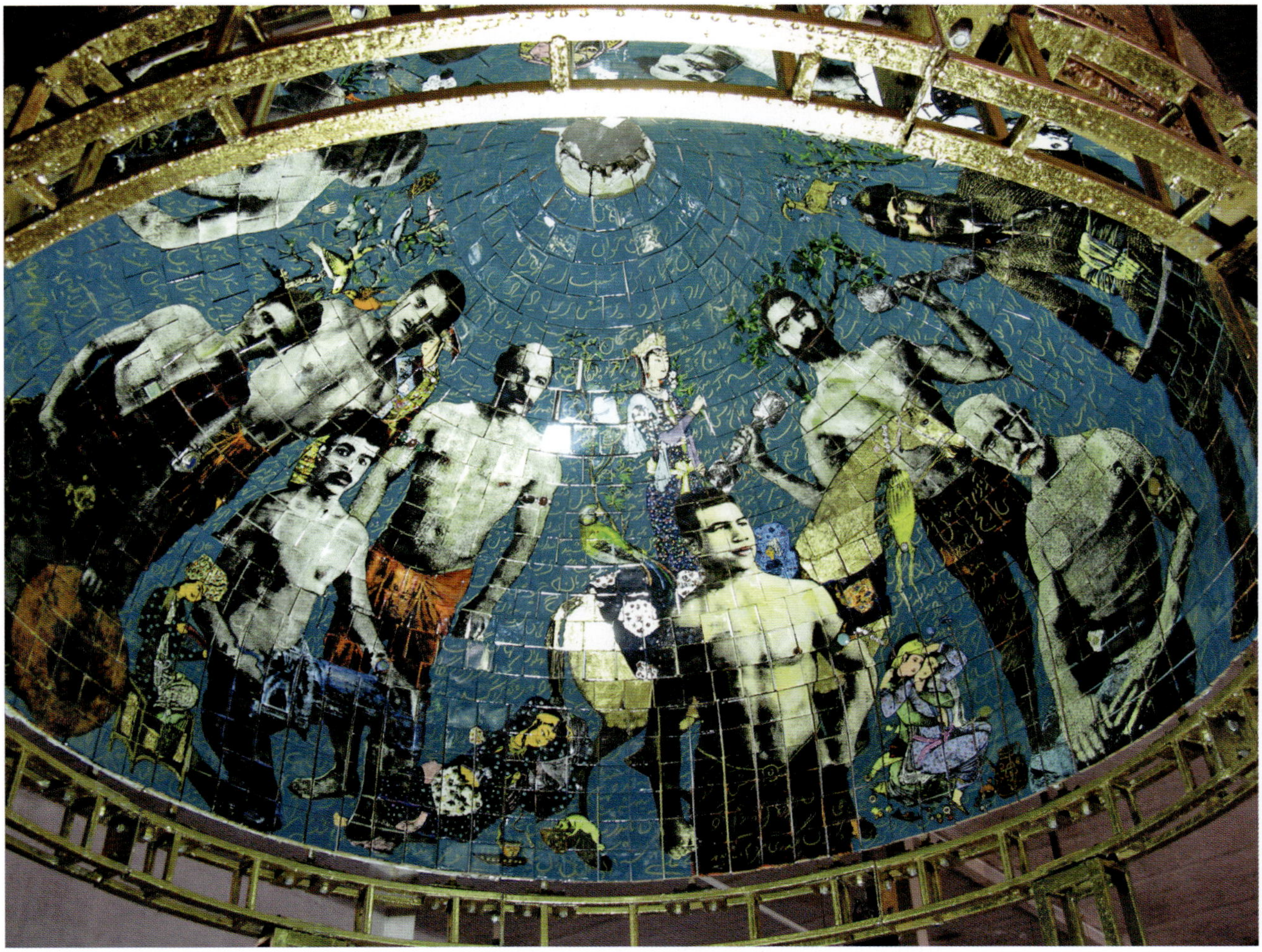

5.18 *Dome*, 2010, Khosrow Hassanzadeh, courtesy of the artist

The political narrative of his work, particularly this one, treads a finely balanced line between dissident and regime art. His clear statements of faith doubtless charm the Ershad. His reference to pre-revolutionary heroes and culture will charm the dissidents. His chosen heroes are all lionized by the regime, however, so the ground is still safe. It is only his apparent desire to reclaim masculinity that implies that it needs to be reclaimed and poses the question, 'From who or what?'

Hassanzadeh's *Dome* is a meditation on Iranian masculinity and, perhaps, an attempt to retrieve it from the more toxic layers of political narrative that have coalesced around it and, to some extent, shaped the consciousness of the younger generations of Iranian men. It is intended to be a positive depiction of manhood, where honour is rehabilitated from the crimes of murder and violence committed in its name, sometimes by individuals in the name of family honour, but more often by the Iranian regime, in the name of national and religious honour. The beauty of the male is retrieved from the conformity of a fixed range of politicized depictions: regime males sport a short beard and, stereotypically at least, grim features; opposition males, especially of the upper middle class and intellectual elite, often keep the beard but wear their hair long, tied in a ponytail, frown earnestly and recite poetry, or try to. Regime supporters are understood to be poor and traditional, the opposition, rich, Western-orientated and 'modern'. As ludicrous as they are, these stereotypes are pernicious and remarkably persistent and, regrettably, expatriate Iranians are inclined to perpetuate and reproduce them as much as any westerner.

Dome looks both ways. Its political resonance depends on who you are. It is drenched in religious idiom and reference but, simultaneously, delivers a dignified but stern rebuke to the theocratic dictatorship, censuring its belligerence and presenting an alternative manifesto for a more peaceful, productive existence. It is an idealistic if appealing attempt to re-imagine patriarchy as a set of power relations solely concerned with power within rather than power over. From the point of view of a sceptical feminist writer, it offers a rare and fascinating insight into the fanciful but also compelling dreams of an exponent of masculine chivalry.

Conclusion

How ceramic objects are interpreted as visual images is not well understood. The work featured in this chapter is at least as much visual art as tactile or utilitarian. Moreover, much of it uses figurative or representational imagery either as surface design, or in its form. Ceramics that set out to project a readable narrative carry their own dangers as far as the curator is concerned, particularly in times of heightened anxieties about 'causing offence'. The anodyne abstract and match-the-curtains modernism is so well loved and understood partly because it is safe as houses, by contrast. Not only will it not offend anyone and therefore not attract the unwelcome attention of censors, it has an established following and body of literature ready prepared to instruct the audience how to think. Part of the process of reaching a better understanding of both satire and subversion and how they operate, succeed and fail will require a better understanding of ceramics as a visual medium.

Conclusion: Observations and recommendations

On subversion

It is high time we dropped the use of the term 'subversive' to describe anything that looks a bit unfamiliar. As Bonnie Kemske observed, 'Once subversion has been accepted into the "institution", it can no longer be subversion; it becomes the next thing to be subverted.'[1] A genuinely subversive artwork, of any sort, will continue to resonate politically, even if the authority it challenges has been overturned. The sheer power and audacity of David Drake's pots, with their boldly inscribed surfaces, continue to amaze those who see them, particularly for the first time. Bita Fayyazi's work changes its meaning slightly with each decade but its power persists: it continues to challenge religious authority and associated social norms. Al Dowayan's doves seem to be increasingly subversive, acquiring more traction as women's freedom of movement is increasingly restricted across the Middle East by ever more authoritarian de facto states and the social mores fostered within them.[2] From the 1970s, Marisa Rueda's tortured forms continue to have meaning. The generals of Argentina may have departed but there are plenty more taking up positions of power all over the world. These are all fired ceramic works, so all have material longevity. Even if the names of their makers are forgotten, or the history to which they refer is buried, they will still be there and their meaning can be excavated, as Drake's pots so eloquently attest.

Conor Wilson's question: 'Can an artist be subversive in a democracy?' has been left hanging throughout this book, but I will hazard a 'yes' in reply, with the caveat that it depends on the democracy. Shlomit Bauman's work certainly questions some of the foundation narratives of Israel but it also appeals to an established dissident Israeli position, one that is tolerated within Israel. She goes further than reproducing simple protest, however; her work has considerable emotional impact – it reaches into the heart of the relationship between nationalism and land. This is dicey territory because it challenges not only Israeli nationalism but all nationalisms, including Arab. *Channel AlDuwara* and *Ran Out*, between them, unsettle the certainties of almost every audience she might encounter in her context.

1 Kemske, 2012.

2 Quilliam Foundation: *Women of the Islamic State: A Manifesto on Women by the Al-Khanssaa Brigade*, translation: Charlie Winter, February 2015.

Challenging social mores and religious authority are the more likely routes to subversive work in a democracy, unless the artist considers overturning democracy itself a productive course of action. I would defend their right to express the opinion as long as I have equal right to expose their idiocy. Matt Smith has satirized Catholicism on numerous occasions, particularly in a group of work from 2008, featuring *Papal Surprise* and *Bullhead Madonna*, among others. It has to be said, however, that satirizing Christianity has not, in recent decades in the UK, brought censure and certainly has not resulted in threats to life. Grayson Perry, who has also satirized Catholicism, scandalized London's cultural elite when he casually observed: 'I've censored myself ... The reason I haven't gone all out attacking Islamism in my art is because I feel real fear that someone will slit my throat.'[3] Until January 2015, visual artists in Western Europe may have believed they were not a target for Islamists. The murder of five cartoonists including the editor of the satirical magazine *Charlie Hebdo*, by Islamists, has clarified the matter beyond doubt. Perry's fear was well founded but it is something of a bitter irony that the only artists challenging Islamism in this book are those who are in the most danger from it, namely Bita Fayyazi, Khosrow Hassanzadeh and, although her emphasis is perhaps more on governance, Manal Al Dowayan.

On satire

Much is demanded of the visual satirist, assuming there is no explanatory text. Jonathan Swift's *A Modest Proposal* (1729) is no gently mocking satire; on the contrary, it is vicious, but the target of its critique is also abundantly clear. The written word can provide a clarity that the visual image rarely does; imagery is almost always open to interpretation and variable interpretation can be a political minefield, as some of the examples in this book have shown. In contemporary, pluralistic democracies, there is not always agreement about who is in a position of power, and in visual satire it is not always obvious who or what is the target. In Britain and America, the *Charlie Hebdo* murders prompted an unedifying and highly polarized debate that revealed the ignorance of visual satire among writers, artists and academics. The arguments foundered on precisely this problem: the magazine's detractors claimed that the target was not clear and that the imagery was racist; its supporters claimed the detractors were wilfully stupid, implying that satire was infallible. The questions that now need to be asked and deserve serious attention are: can satire serve liberation or emancipation movements? Can it speak on behalf of, or be used by marginalized or oppressed people or will it always be co-opted by the majority culture and reproduce oppressive stereotypes in the name of parody, the grotesque, comic burlesque and so forth? Can satire fail and, if so, how?

[3] Ben Hoyle, 'Artists Too Frightened to Tackle Radical Islam', *The Times*, 19 November 2007.

On feminism

Feminism is a persistent presence in this book and in ceramics, and has been since the 1970s. I included work from new and established makers whose narrative is wholly or partly shaped by feminism, including those who are challenging the norms of masculinity. The feminist makers, perhaps, produced the work that was most clearly subversive within the democratic context. Jo Pipkin's *Red Riding Hood* stands out as an exceptionally courageous challenge to male sexual entitlement as well as being, by implication, an attack on state and legal inertia, and Louise Hindsgavl's *FGM project* is a fierce rebuke to the pernicious influence of cultural relativism. There are and probably always will be artists in other media who turn to ceramics specifically to express emancipatory narratives, often feminist ones yet, to date, there are no books on feminism and ceramics, no conference or symposium has been convened on the subject, nor has any exhibition been curated. To end where I began, Holburne Museum, Bath, hosted another ceramics symposium, Ceramics and Politics, in November 2014. The speakers' abstracts were more varied than they were in the 2012 symposium, but conspicuous by its absence was feminism. Perhaps, in the world of craft ceramics, feminism is the real subversion.

Bibliography

Ahmed, Samira. 'Widespread Sexual Abuse in Rotherham has Caused Outrage – But Little Action', *The Guardian*, 6 October 2014.

Alvarenga, Jose Salvador. Television news report, reported in *The Daily Mail*, 3 February 2014.

Beighton, James. 'A Matter of Manners: Subversion in the Ceramics Field', unpublished paper, Subversive Ceramics symposium, 2012.

Bentham, Mark. 'Met Will Prosecute Parents Who Send their Girls Abroad to be "Cut"', *London Evening Standard*, 18 February 2013.

Bindel, Julie. *Straight Expectations*, Guardian Books, 2014.

Bindel, Julie. 'The Ordeal of Muslim Women: No More Excuses', in *Standpoint*, March 2014.

Bindel, Julie. 'Mothers of Prevention', *The Sunday Times*, 30 September 2007.

Bindel, Julie. 'The Victims of Sex Gangs are Never Heard', *The Guardian*, 9 May 2012.

Biswas, Sutapa, Sarah Edge and Clare Slattery. *Along the Lines of Resistance: An Exhibition of Contemporary Feminist Art*, Cooper Gallery, Barnsley, 1988.

Brownsword, Neil. Unpublished paper, British Ceramics Biennial, 2013.

Buncombe, Andrew. 'Rise and Fall of the Indian Rope Trick', *The Independent*, 19 November 2009.

Buncombe, Andrew. 'Letter from Asia', *The Independent*, 18 February 2014.

Clare, Claudia. 'Constructive Dialogue', in *Ceramic Review*, 208.

Clare, Claudia. 'Woman, Mysterious and Eternal', in *Ceramic Review*, 214, 2005.

Cohen, Nick. *You Can't Read This Book*, Fourth Estate, 2012.

Corsiglia, Christina. 'Victor Schrekengost: Evolution of a Cleveland Ceramist', in *Cleveland as a Center of Regional American Art, Symposium*, Cleveland Artists Foundation, 1993.

Coy, Maddy with Liz Kelly, Fiona Elvines, Maria Garner, Ava Kanyeredzi. *Sex without Consent*, report, CWASU, 2013.

Da Costa, Dia. 'Sentimental Capitalism in Contemporary India: Art, Heritage and Development in Ahmedabad, Gujarat', abstract, Antipode, 2014, DOI: 10.1111/anti.12103.

Dahn, Johanna. Introductory address to Subversive Ceramics symposium, 2012.

Davies, Norman. *Europe: A History*, Oxford University Press, 1996.

Dickson, Amy. 'Clare Twomey', in *Jerwood Contemporary Makers*, Jerwood Charitable Foundation, 2008.

Edge, Nina. Contribution to the article 'Along the Lines of Resistance', in Feminist Art News, vol. 2, no. 9.

Edge, Nina. 'Nina Edge' in *Artists' Stories*, Anna Douglas and Nicholas Wegner, AN Publications, 1996.

Ellery, Ben. '62p An Hour', *Mail Online*, 1 November 2014.

Gamboa, Helga. 'An Angolan Heritage: The Ceramics of Helga Gamboa', in *Interpreting Ceramics*, issue 10, 2008, online: http://www.interpretingceramics.com/issue010/conf_contents.htm [accessed 2 February 2015].

Goss, David. 'Azal ... Lock, Stock, and Barrel – On Shlomit Bauman's Exhibition', in *Ran Out*, Shlomit Bauman, 2013.

Griffin, Dustin. *Satire: A Critical Reintroduction*, University Press of Kentucky, 1994.

Hall, Anna. *Edge of the City*, 2003–2004, Channel 4.

Hammond, David. 'Pottery Packs a Powerful Punch', *The Huddersfield Daily Examiner*, 27 September 1996.

Harpham, Geoffrey Galt. *Introduction to the Grotesque*, Princeton University Press, 1982.

Highet, Gilbert. *The Anatomy of Satire*, Princeton University Press, 1962.

Himid, Lubaina. *Venetian Maps*, Harris Museum and Art Gallery, 1997.

Himid, Lubaina. *Naming the Money*, Hatton Gallery, University of Newcastle upon Tyne, 2004.

Hockaday, Mary. *The World Service*, exhibition catalogue, 1996.

Hoyle, Ben. 'Artists Too Frightened to Tackle Radical Islam', *The Times*, 19 November 2007.

Jardine, Lisa. *Worldly Goods*, Macmillan, 1997.

Javadi, Hasan. *Satire in Persian Literature*, Fairleigh Dickinson University Press, London, Associated University Presses, 1998.

Johnson, Pamela. 'Subversive Ceramics', in *Crafts* magazine, no. 95, 1988.

Jury, Louise. 'Huhne's A Smashing Subject for Grayson', *Evening Standard*, 21 October 2014.

Kelly, Liz with Sheila Burton and Linda Regan. 'Researching Women's Lives or Studying Women's Oppression? Reflections on What Constitutes Feminist Research', in *Researching Women's Lives from a Feminist Perspective*, Mary Maynard and June Purvis, London: Taylor & Francis, 1994.

Kelly, Liz and Jo Lovett. Report, CWASU, 2009.

Kemske, Bonnie. 'When Subversion becomes the Norm', unpublished paper, Subversive Ceramics symposium, 2012.

Kettering, Karen. 'Domesticating the Uzbeks: Central Asians in Soviet Decorative Art of the Twenties and Thirties', in *Colonialism and the Object: Empire, Material Culture and the Museum*, Tim Barringer and Tom Flynn (eds), Routledge, 1998.

Keuls, Eva C. *The Painter and Poet in Ancient Greece: Iconography and the Literary Arts*, Stuttgart: Teubner, 1997.

Kramer, Gudrun. *A History of Palestine: From Ottoman Conquest to the Founding of the State of Israel*, Princeton University Press, 2011.

Kramer, Hilton. 'Judy Chicago's The Dinner Party Comes to Brooklyn Museum', *The New York Times*, 17 October 1980.

Leach, Bernard. *A Potter's Book*, Faber & Faber, 1940.

Lobanov-Rostovsky, Nina. *Revolutionary Ceramics: Soviet Porcelain 1917–1927*, New York: Rizzoli, 1990.

Mannoni, Edith. *Les Faiences Revolutionnaires*, Massin, 1989.

Margolin, Sam. '"And Freedom to the Slave": Antislavery Ceramics 1787–1865' in *Ceramics in America*, Chipstone Foundation, Milwaukee, 2002.

Martin, Simon. *Love Is... 2011, Continued*, 2011, available at http://www.barnabybarford.co.uk/image_gallery/node/128 accessed 29 October 2014.

Midgley, Clare. *Women Against Slavery: The British Campaigns 1780–1870*, Taylor & Francis, 1995.

Mitchell, Liz. 'Material Memory', in *Ceramic Review*, 257.

Morgan, Jill. 'Women Artists and Modernism', catalogue essay in *Revenge*, Rochdale Art Gallery, 1992.

Novak, Justin. 'Freeze Frame: A Moment in Narrative', Storytelling and Poetry seminar, Guldagergaard, International Ceramic Research Centre, Denmark, 2005.

Oldfield, John. *Popular Politics and British Anti-slavery: The Mobilisation of Public Opinion against the Slave Trade 1787–1807*, Psychology Press, 1998.

Papet, Edouard. 'Daumier: Sculpture and Lithography, Return Journeys', in *Daumier: Visions of Paris*, Royal Academy of Arts, London, 2014.

Perry, Grayson. *Guerrilla Tactics*, Stedelijk Museum, Amsterdam, 2000.

Perry, Grayson. *Midweek*, BBC Radio 4, 9 February 2005.

Pollock, Griselda. *Avant Garde Gambits, 1883–1893*, Thames & Hudson, 1992.

Quilliam Foundation. *Women of the Islamic State: A Manifesto on Women by the Al-Khanssaa Brigade*, translation by Charlie Winter, February 2015.

Ramadan, Tariq. 'Islam and Life: Can Islam defeat Femen?' Press TV, 9 May 2013.

Reichardt, Rolf and Hubertus Kohle. *Visualising the Revolution: Politics and the Pictorial Arts in late Eighteenth-Century France*, Reaktion Books, 2008.

Reilly, James. *Casual Influences*, Oriel Mostyn, 2000.

Rueda, Marisa. *Artist's Statement*, archived in the Women's Art Library, Goldsmiths, University of London, 1978.

Sani, Elisa P. *Italian Renaissance Maiolica*, V&A publishing, 2012.

Spivey, Nigel. 'Greek Vases in Etruria', in *Looking at Greek Vases*, Tom Rasmussen and Nigel Spivey (eds), Cambridge University Press, 1991.

Sulter, Maud. *Passion: Discourses on Black Women's Creativity,* Urban Fox Press, 1990.

Todd, Leonard. *Carolina Clay: The Life and Legend of the Slave Potter, Dave*, Norton, 2008.

Veiteberg, Jorunn. *Thing Tang Trash: Upcycling in Contemporary Ceramics*, Bergen National Academy of the Arts, 2011.

Veiteberg, Jorunn. *Craft in Transition*, Bergen National Academy of the Arts, 2005.

Vincentelli, Moira. 'The Politics of Print', in *Ceramic Review*, 183.

Vranic, Seada. *Breaking the Wall of Silence: The Voices of Raped Bosnia*, Izdanja Antibarbarus, Zagreb, 1996.

de Waal, Edmund. *The Pot Book*, London: Phaidon, 2011.

Wilson, Timothy. 'Le Maioliche', in *Il Rinascimento Itlaiano e l'Europa, IV, Commercio e Culture Mercantile*, F. Franceschi, R. Goldthwaite and R. Mueller (eds), available online in translation: http://www.ashmolean.org/documents/Staff/WilsonTim/CassamarcaEssay.pdf [accessed 16 February 2015].

Winch, Dinah and Peter Lewis. *Fired Up, Ceramics and Meaning*, Gallery Oldham, 2010.

Index

155H (Lewis) 144, 145

A Dark Day in Paradise (Twomey) 110–11
academy, the 111–12
Acknowledged Sources (Chowdhary) 28, 29
Aesop 39–40
African people 132–3
Aftermath (Gamboa) 140
Aids awareness 125–7
Alberta No: 5 (Scott) 103–4
allegory 24–8, 86
Almagest (The Great Book) 78
'Along the Lines of Resistance' exhibition 26
American twentieth century 60–3
And as for our dead, how will they be heard? (Rueda) 21–2
Andreoli, G. 40–1
anti-imperialist/anti-racist works 18
anti-slavery ware 51–6
anti-war ceramics 93–6
Apocalypse '42 (Schreckengost) 63
Ardmore 125–7
Aristophanes 35
Athens 35–7
Attic red ware 35–7

Baps and Buns (Pipkin) 90–1
Barford, B. 118–20
Barthe, F. 48, 50
Bastille Plate 47
Bauman, S. 104–7
beauty industry 90–1
Beighton, J. 16
Beware, Aids Kills, Condomise 126–7
Bindel, J. 92–3
Binge Drinker (de Vries) 120–1
Bingeing Britain (Wallace) 70
Biswas, S. 24–6
black rights movement 60–2, 132–4
Bloomfield, L. 68–9
Brownsword, N. 108–9, 111
Buncombe, A. 24, 26
Burton, S. 18
Byrne, P. 116–17

campaigning 15, 123–50
'Catherine Lelar Bone, Citoyenne' plate design 46
Cawsey, J. 29, 31–3
Centaur (Ortiz) 95–6
Channel AlDuwara (Bauman) 104–6
chess sets 57, 93–5
Chicago, J. 19–20
children, sexual exploitation 88–90, 115–16
Chowdhary, L. 28, 29
civil rights movement 60–2, 132–4
Clare, C. 13–14, 15, 128–32
clay 48–50, 106–11
Clay Canteen with Leather Strap (Ortiz) 81–2
Clocking On (Dixon) 136–8
Cockroaches (Fayyazi) 104
Consciousness/Conscience (Twomey) 110
Corsiglia, C. 63
'cottaging' 73
Cry Baby (Folwell) 80–1
Curtis, E. 78, 80–1

Da Costa, D. 138
Dahn, J. 19
Damaged Goods (Barford) 119–20
Danko sisters 57–60
Davies, N. 45–6
Democracy in Action (Gregory) 60, 61
Dickson, A. 112
Disfigurines (Novak) 29–31
Dixon, S. 136–9
Dome (Hassanzadeh) 148–50
Double Spouted Teapot 73–4
Dowayan, Manal Al 126–7
Drake, D. 54–6

Edge, N. & S. 24–6
emancipation 99–122
Etrog 1 pots (Sheffer) 78, 79

Factory Farm Worker (Gregory) 60
faience 42–7
Falling General (Rueda) 23
Fanfare design 43–4
fasces lictoriae 44–5
Fayyazi, B. 24, 26–8, 104, 105
female genital mutilation 92–3
Femen 124
feminism 17–18, 19–20, 24–6, 57
  anti-stereotype campaigns 123–4
  FGM 92–3
  male sexuality 118–20
  tableware 68–70
  vases 74–81
working-classes 70–2
Fishing (Slotte) 101
fleur de lys 43–6
folk art 99–100
Folwell, S. 78, 80–1
Free Kiranjit Ahluwalia! Resistance No Crime! (Clare) 13–14, 15
French Revolution 42–7
From Latin America with Hate (Rueda) 21–2
Fugitifs (Daumier) 50

Gamboa, H. 140–3
gay movement 17–18, 73–4, 84

Gaza Airport (Scott) 146, 147
genital mutilation 92–3
Gregory, W. 60, 61
Griffin, D. 19
'grooming' 90, 130
Gross, E. 82–5
Gun Love (Folwell) 80–1

Hammond, D. 15
Happiness (Hindsgavl) 92
Harpham, G. G. 31
Hassanzadeh, K. 146, 148–50
Heritage Economy and National Treasure (Brownsword) 108–9
Hero (Dixon) 137–9
Highet, G. 19
Himid, L. 132–6
Hindsgavl, L. 91–3
Hockaday, M. 15
Hold my Hair (Wallace) 71
homosexuality 17–18, 73–4, 84
'honest pots' 67, 99
  see also studio potters
Hot Afternoon (Perry) 33–4

internet 123–4
Introduction to the Grotesque (Harpham) 31
istoriato native pottery painting 39–42
Italian Renaissance 38–42

Jardine, J. 38–9
Javadi, H. 28
Jellymould Pavilions (Himid) 134, 136
Johnson, P. 22

Kelly, L. 18
Kemske, B. 17–18
Kenaan-Kedar, N. 83, 85
Kettering, K. 57–9
Khan, I. 24, 26
kitchen environments 68–70
Kohle, H. 46
Kramer, H. 20
kulhar (honest pots) 99
kylikes (drinking cups) 36, 37

land and sea 104–7
Landscape Multiple (Slotte) 101, 102
LBGT groups 73–4
  see also gay movement
Le Charivari 48
Leach, B. 68
Leda and the Swan (de Vries) 115–16
Lewis, P. 143–5
Lezioni de Tromba (Barford) 118, 119
Liverpool Lou (Wallace) 71, 72
living room environments 70–2
Lost Childhood (Gamboa) 140, 142
Love Is... I & II 118–20
Love in Motion (Hindsgavl) 92
Love and Other Options (Cawsey) 32
Lovejoy, P. 53–4

McBride, K. 93–4
McNicholl, C. 99–100
Madonna and Child (Gamboa) 140, 142
magic 24–8
maiolica 38–42
Mannoni, E. 43, 45–6
Margolin, S. 52
marriage equality 74
Martin, S. 119–20
medallions 51
Memorial to Zong (Himid) 132–3
men
  masculinity 84, 118–20, 148–50
  redressing 33–4
  slavery 132–3
  transvestism 33–4
  see also feminism
Midgley, C. 51
mohareb (enemy of god) 27–8
Monster Aids Vase 125, 126
Morgan, M. 74–8
Muslim women 92–3

nakedness 29–31
Naming the Money (Himid) 133
Native American culture 78, 80–1, 95–6
Naughton Gallery, Queen's University 17
No Trespassing, Boys! (Radclyffe) 87–8
nostalgia 118–19, 138
Novak, J. 29–31
'Nu-shabtis' figurines 96–8

Oldfield, J. 52
Olive 1 (Lewis) 143–4
ornamentation 30
Ortiz, V. 81–2, 95–6
Palestinian water jars 83, 85
Pallisy, B. 43
Papet, E. 48
peace *see* war and peace
peasant's revolt 67–98
Perry, G. 18, 33–4
Philipon, C. 48–50
Photo-Op Jar (Folwell) 78, 80
Phrygian cap 44–5
Pipkin, J. 88–91, 120
political movements *see* social movements
Pollock, G. 67
pornography 92, 115–16, 118–20
postcolonial works 18
Power, Porcelain, Poetry (Hindsgavl) 91–2
Powolny, M. 61
Pretsell, P. 65–6, 68
Princess Hymen (Clare) 128–30
prostitution 124, 130
protest 35–64

racism 18, 60–2, 132–4
Radclyffe, C. 87–8
Rainbow Chess Set (McBride) 93–5
Ran Out (Bauman) 106–7
rape 88–90, 115–16, 128–32
'Realism to the Rescue' (Rueda) 21
Red Riding Hood (Pipkin) 88–9
Regan, L. 18
Reichardt, R. 46
religion 41–2, 43, 124
Remembering Atefeh 130, 132
Renaissance 38–42, 85–98
restoring of illusion 113–21
Revolution, France 42–7
Road Kill (Fayyazi) 26–7, 104
Rueda, M. 21–3
Rylander, K. 99–100

Sahaale, A. R. 130, 132
Sani, E. 38
satire 13–64
  American twentieth century 60–3
  anti-slavery ware 51–6
  Athens 35–7
  Daumier 48–50
  French Revolution 42–7
  introducing 19

Italian Renaissance 38–42
protest 35–64
Soviet porcelain 56–60
vice and folly 15–34
Schreckengost, V. 61–3
Scott, P. 17–18, 103–4, 146, 147
Sculpture on the Beach (Fayyazi) 104
seaworks 100–1, 104–7
Secrets and Lies (Radclyffe) 88
Self-Portrait (Gross) 83
Servitude II (Gamboa) 142–3
Seven Ages of Woman (Morgan) 74–8
sexual abuse 88–90, 115–16, 128–32
sexuality 118–20
see also feminism; gay movement; pornography
Shadrach Mesach and Abed-nego (Schreckengost) 62
Shattered (Clare) 128–32
Sheffer, A. 78
Shonibare, Y. 132
Slattery, C. 24–6
slavery 51–6, 124, 130, 132–4
Slee, R. 99–100
Slotte, C. 101–2
Smith, M. 73–4
Snakes and Ladders (Edge) 24–6
social movements 65–150
campaigning trails 123–50
emancipation 99–122
peasant's revolt 67–98
social networking 123–4
Soviet porcelain 56–60
State of Grace 31–2
Stories of Eve (Hindsgavl) 92
Street Ware (Rylander) 99, 100
studio potters 65–150
campaigning trails 123–50
emancipation 99–122
peasant's revolt 67–98
Study for a Fountain (Himid) 132
Suspended together (Dowayan) 126–7
Swallow Hard: The Lancaster Dinner Service (Himid) 133–5
Syrian ceramics 96–7
Tajeddin, Z. 96–8
Tatham Aids Vase 125, 126
teaware 51–2, 73–4
Tenderness (Hindsgavl) 92
The Awakening East (Danko) 57
'The Celebrities of the Juste Milieu' 48–50
The Chris Huhne Vase (Perry) 33
The Collection (Twomey) 110–12
The Dictator (Schreckengost) 62–3
The Dinner Party (Chicago) 19–20
The Foundation of Bakhchiserai (Danko) 57–9
The Jewel and the Frown (Edge) 24–6
The Lancaster Dinner Service (Himid) 133–5
The Reds and the Whites (Danko) 57
The Three Disgraces (Wallace) 86
The Three Graces (Wallace) 70–1
'The Tyrant's Foe, The People's Friend' plate design 53–4
The Vanity of Small Differences (Perry) 33
The World Service 15
Thing Tang Trash 99–100
'this is what a feminist looks like' campaign 123–4
Topographies of the Obsolete (Brownsword) 109
trafficking of women 124, 130
transgenderism 82–3
transvestism 33–4
'Tres in Uno' plate design 43–4, 46
Trois Ordres plate design 43–4, 46
trunKated (Fayyazi) 104, 105
Turkic Girl Reading (Danko) 57
Twomey, C. 110–12

Untitled, 103 terracotta sculptures (Wilke) 20, 21
Upstairs Downstairs (Shonibare) 132
Uzbeks Discussing the Stalin Constitution (Danko) 59, 60
vagina 19–20, 92–3, 128–32
Veiteberg, J. 17–18, 99–100
Venetian Maps, Ceramicists (Himid) 133
Vis Unita Fortior 108
'Vive La Montagne' plate design 44–5
voyeurism 118, 119
Vries, B. de 113–16, 120–1

Waal, E. de 67, 69
Wallace, R. 70–2, 86, 120
war and peace 93–6, 140–50
War and Pieces (de Vries) 113–15
War on Terror Waltz (Byrne) 116–17
Wedding (Gross) 84–5
Who do you think you are (Perry) 33
Wilke, H. 19–20, 21
willow pattern 100–4
Wilson, T. 38–9
Witness (Dickson) 112
WKD Women (Wallace) 70–2
women
beauty industry 90–1
FGM 92–3
nakedness 29–31
Shattered 128–32
slavery 132–3
trafficking 124, 130
working-class 70–2
see also feminism
working-classes *see* peasant's revolt
Wunderkammer (cabinet of curiosities) 85–98

You'll thank me later (I Hope) (Hindsgavl) 92–3

Zazzle (internet-based company) 123–4
'Zipora, if Eitan were a girl, I would wait for him' (Gross) 82–3
zurkhaneh (house of strength) 146, 148–50